WORDS ON FIRE

WORDS ON FIRE

One Woman's Journey
into the Sacred

Vanessa L. Ochs

A HARVEST/HBJ BOOK

HARCOURT BRACE JOVANOVICH, PUBLISHERS

San Diego   New York   London

Requests for permission to make copies of any part
of the work should be mailed to:
Permissions Department,
Harcourt Brace Jovanovich, Publishers, 8th Floor,
Orlando, Florida 32887.

Quote on pages 109–110 taken from
Four Hasidic Masters & Their Struggle Against Melancholy
by Elie Wiesel © 1978 by the University of Notre Dame Press.

Library of Congress Cataloging-in-Publication Data
Ochs, Vanessa L.
Words on fire: one woman's journey into the sacred/by Vanessa L. Ochs.
p. cm.
ISBN 0-15-198380-1
ISBN 0-15-698363-X (pbk.)
1. Ochs, Vanessa L. 2. Jews—Return to Orthodox Judaism.
3. Women, Jewish—Religious life. I. Title.
BM755.O24A3 1990
296′.082—dc20   89–29210

Printed in the United States of America

First Harvest/HBJ edition 1991
B C D E F

for Charles Weinstein, of blessed memory,
and Sally Weinstein

„ישרפו דברי תורה ואל ימסרו לנשים."

"THE WORDS OF THE TORAH SHOULD BE BURNT RATHER THAN BE
TAUGHT TO WOMEN."

Rabbi Eliezer ben Hyrcanus
Jerusalem Talmud, Sota 3:4

One

I went to Jerusalem to study Torah.

I had not believed I would ever go off on any sort of spiritual journey. I regarded seekers as yearners by nature, people who suffered tragedies and, overwhelmed by their pain, packed their bags, ventured to mountaintop retreats, and found illumination. They would return to the real world still practicing the mountaintop dietary regime and wearing queer fringed undergarments or headdresses, to friends who greeted this newfound serenity with skepticism: anything that worked this well and this fast had to be temporary; anything that curtailed free will was an affront to individualism.

To make your spiritual yearning public, I thought, was to announce that you were wounded. To turn deeply into religion was to admit that your own resources were so weak you had to resort to magic and miracle cures for healing. To acquire faith was to mobilize the powers of an overly active imagination.

If I held myself aloof from the sect of seekers, it was because I liked to believe I possessed sufficient resources to shield myself from private disasters. And should I nevertheless have to confront adversity, I liked to believe I would grit my teeth and bob back up again without the help of external palliatives: religion, psychiatry, drugs, or early morning jogging. In a word, I had faith in myself.

I was living in an upstate New York college town, in the little red house with a moss-covered roof that was originally Mrs. Sagal's chicken coop. The house was across the road from Mr. Wilcox's apple orchard and cider mill. Like everyone else, we never locked our doors. That way Mary Hess's granddaughters could always leave baskets of currants and cherry tomatoes in our kitchen or borrow the bicycle pump from our garage. This was real country, earthy and, until the Burger King and then Ames came, pristine. We didn't need little pseudo–folk art ducks or dotted "country lifestyle" wallpaper to summon a rural aura. In Hamilton, we dug our way out of snow drifts from November to May, and when the snow was too high, we could cross-country ski across the field and still make it to work. Summers we held our breath when tractors loaded with manure went by, swam with friends from the biology and Russian departments at the Lebanon reservoir, and picked raspberries and blackberries up on Spring Hill Road. If a sign said Cattle Crossing, we stopped the car and waited as cows slowly shifted from the pasture into their white barn.

In this Norman Rockwell setting, where time seemed to have stopped at the turn of the century and civic life revolved around a town green, I taught college and wrote. I was married and had two little girls. If mice invaded our cupboards, I toweled up the droppings I first mistook for tea leaves, trapped the mice live, and set them free in our woods. When children needed something to do, it was safe enough to dispatch them, with a dog as company, to the stream to dig up clay. When we got angry at ourselves or at each other, we went out for a walk and breathed in the lingering smell of the wood-burning stoves until we calmed down. While I did not want to spend the rest of my days in Hamilton lest I wilt from the dull peacefulness and from a lack of occasions to change from my scruffy farm clothes into something more stylish, I was grateful that during the time we lived there we had good jobs and good friends. And our relatives, who all lived out of town, flourished as well. We never had to attend a funeral.

The abundance of simple happinesses was contagious. When fast-talking New Yorkers, once addicted to Chinese food and the latest movies, joined the faculty, they eventually succumbed to the serenity and began planting radishes in neat rows or stripping and staining antique furniture picked up for a song at Depuy's auction off Route 20. I watched my own house fill up with herbs hanging upside down to dry and turn-of-the-century pine washstands.

I used to wonder if the faith I had in myself would stand up if put to the test. I feared that we and our bounty of blessings were a set of exceptionally fragile crystal vases on a low, vulnerable shelf: no precautions could be taken, and everything could be shattered in a moment. Each time my daydreams of disaster faded and I returned to my real life, so good and safe and comfortable, I was jabbed by a thought: sanctify this life, make it holy. I harbored a small panic. If put to the test, whether trivial or of Job-like proportions, would my powers suffice to make everything better?

Then I started getting sick regularly, and it was no longer necessary to conjure up hypothetical disasters. Nearly each winter there was another illness: pericarditis, hepatitis, thyroiditis, some other "itis" whose name I missed because I just didn't want to know anymore. The periods of acute sickness, though annoying, were nowhere as trying as the long recoveries that burdened my family. Wiped out for months, overwhelmed by the least thing, I dragged around, still skinny and frail, teaching and mothering with minimal effectiveness, until the healing warmth of late spring finally came to Hamilton and I'd be my old self again. Our family doctor couldn't connect the diseases. "A run of bad luck," "It could be worse" was all he could offer. Hematologists, neurologists, and endocrinologists in Syracuse and Rochester tried to trace some immunological deficiency, testing me for the most awful diseases. All came up blank. Certainly I was stressed by too much work and caring for small children, but all my women friends lived similarly. While they were always frayed at the edges and picked up every virus their kids brought back from the Chenango Nursery School, they managed to remain essentially robust. It wasn't fair.

My illnesses weren't deadly, but they were serious. Though I recovered thanks to accurate diagnoses and treatments, I became anxious with the approach of the new winter, fearful of another round. Understandably so, since I believed that the next inflammation would be the one to cause irreparable damage. Heart, liver, thyroid. Would my brain be next? I had no guarantees, no preventive measures at my disposal. I was too vulnerable, a sitting duck. I desperately needed to have some control over my health, some protection.

I blamed myself. There had to be something I was doing wrong. Surely if I were living right, I would not be such an easy target for sickness. This was the wisdom of my childhood, that sickness was a punishment from God that one brought upon oneself. I knew this explanation was a wicked lie conceived to engender guilt, but I had hit on no other rational or scientific explanation.

I had rapidly lost all confidence in my self-sufficiency. I came to see that initial faith I had in myself as nothing but an arrogant fantasy. I was scared.

From time to time I went to university church services at Colgate when freshman advisees invited me to hear their gospel chorus. But for the sermons of Coleman Brown, the University Chaplain, attending this generic Christian service might have been no more than a polite and easy ecumenical gesture. Each time I went I was jolted to tears by his words, which were never limited to a Christian's experience. I learned from him that there need be no shame in deriving personal strength from attending to the sacred. That experience forced me to recognize I was starving for some spiritual succor, something more than my doctor's platitudes. Though I doubted my capacity to be shored up with spiritual strength, I knew I needed to fortify myself somehow. And though I had little inclination to become more religious, there was that thought that kept returning: sanctify this life. I could hardly remember the last time I occupied myself with anything resembling spiritual concerns. I must have been a teenager, reading e.e. cummings and *The Little Prince*, with Simon and Garfunkel or 1967 Israeli victory songs playing in the background as I poured out my feelings into my tear-stained diary.

Good sense told me not to wait till it was too late before doing something for myself. I knew that I should heed that instinct to sanctify. But what should I sanctify? How? I knew what the sanctified life was not. Not a life filled with more rituals, more scrupulously observed. Not more praying. Not becoming a better person, being more charitable, more concerned with everyone else's pains. Sanctifying had something to do with a sense of constant wonder—feeling gratitude and finding significance everywhere, in every action, relationship, and object. The sanctified life was pure, calm, and full; it held no reproach, no disappointments.

The specifics of this sanctified life—how to go about the business of sanctifying as a Jew—eluded me. My own religious life had gone stale. Studying Torah never crossed my mind as a solution; it was more farfetched than joining a convent. (Truly more farfetched. Twice, I had accompanied a devout Catholic friend to the nearby Mount Savior monastery, where we listened to the monks chant psalms.)

When I finally came to immerse myself in Jewish learning, I believed the purpose of my study was to fill gaps in my knowledge. Tentatively, so privately I hardly admitted it to myself, I also hoped my study might amount to something more, that it might have curative powers. That I might know better how to live right. But I didn't count on it.

The idea of studying Torah came to me slowly, over the period of years when my husband, Peter, and I used to bring Colgate University students to Jerusalem during January for a four-week mini-course in ethnic and religious diversity. I looked forward to those trips. Going anywhere would have been energizing, simply to break Hamilton's winter regime, particularly during the winters I was ill. Jerusalem appealed to me, because dwelling on spiritual matters there was as matter of fact as talking about child care arrangements was in Hamilton. In Jerusalem, I could flirt with spirituality without declaring myself a bona fide seeker.

On our first visit to Jerusalem, made before I started to become ill, I had met a woman originally from Worcester, Massachusetts. I will call her Esther. She lived across the hall from us in our building on Michlin Street in Bayit Vegan, a hillside neighborhood in southwest Jerusalem. I doubt I would have spent time with Esther if we didn't both have toddlers of the same age who played together. Esther could have come from a different planet. Yet we found so much to talk about and eventually became intimate friends.

Esther was extremely observant. She wore a red wig, which, I gather, approximated her natural hair color; she dressed modestly, and she spent all week absorbed in elaborate preparations for the Sabbath. She devoted all her free time in winter to preparing for the Passover holiday in ways that were new to me, for example, by checking every pocket in the household for the bread and cookie crumbs that were prohibited on Passover. She made space in her tiny apartment for one red-headed baby after another, each named after two dead relatives: Yosef Menachem, Sarah Baila, Mendel Efraim. There were three children when I first met her, then four, then five. There are more now; there will be more later. Esther was always either pregnant or nursing, and I found it disconcerting that I had no idea what her normal figure was like.

In Hamilton, home to about a dozen Jewish families, I was considered to be as extreme in my observance as I knew Esther to be in hers. People thought of me, ethnically identifiable by my looks and language (a toned-down country version of Jewish New Yorkese), as an alien from a Jewish planet. Every time the college held a "women in religion" panel, I was tapped to play the Jewish woman. Once, when I placed some Hebrew National hot dogs (the only kosher food carried by our small Grand Union) on the checkout counter, the cashier asked: "Are you one of those Hasidics?" In Hamilton, I might as well have been. I could chant the prayers in Hebrew, I more or less observed the Sabbath and holidays, I drove to a kosher butcher in Syracuse once a month to buy meat.

But compared to Esther's religious observance, so strict and scrupulous, mine was consistent only in its always being low key and idiosyncratic. I observed the Sabbath by refraining from chores and professional work, but I did perform other activities prohibited on the Sabbath. I turned on lights, I used the phone, I drew pictures with my daughter. The practices I did observe were the same ones I had grown up with. Thus, if we had practiced a ritual in my childhood, I considered it normal; if we hadn't, I thought it bizarre and primitive. The rituals I retained from childhood had nothing to do with belief in God or a sense of obligation to fulfill commandments. I felt nostalgia for my family's traditions and was fond of those rituals that were particularly aesthetic, like lighting Sabbath candles or ushering the Sabbath out with a twisted candle, wine, and spices. Rarely did kindling lights, reciting blessings, or keeping kosher cause me to dwell on the presence of God. The rituals were ethnic activities Jews performed, family activities. Growing up, no one ever spoke of the rituals as opportunities to experience the sacred. The family practiced them partly to honor our ancestors, partly—we jested—to keep lightning from striking. For me as an adult, these rituals provided comfort and structure; they kept me from helter-skelter. Like beginning the day with coffee, like keeping

7

a diary. Practicing the ritual was sufficient to give some order to life. It required no belief.

Esther's piety was not simpleminded. Her husband said of her, "She can cook, but mostly she thinks. People think that a woman who covers her head is, in fact, covering her brains. They see a woman wearing a head covering and they assume she is either closed-minded or not a serious person." Esther was a sharp and constant thinker. So was her husband, Reuven (formerly Robert), who had raced through a doctorate in mathematics at the University of Chicago by the time he was twenty-two. His turning to Orthodox Judaism followed classic contours. Before beginning his first teaching job at Columbia University, he backpacked through Greece, India, and Israel on a lark. At the Western Wall in Jerusalem, he met a representative of a yeshiva who convinced him to spend a few days exploring his Jewish roots, which, until that summer, he had assiduously denied. He never left the world of the yeshiva. He immigrated to Israel, became a thoroughly devout Jew, and sat for hours and then years learning Torah. Not for a degree, not for ordination, although that would eventually be conferred upon him. Just to learn for its own sake.

Late at night, after returning from the yeshiva, Reuven, a robust and rotund man nearly bursting out of his black suit, would call on my husband, and together they'd drink whiskey at our kitchen table, lean back in their chairs, and work noisily through a few lines of a sacred text. Peter was delighted to have such an intense partner for Torah study, but he felt guilty about keeping Reuven from home. If Peter stayed out as long as Reuven did, I'd be desperate for his company and for help with the house and the kids. And I'd be angry. Why wasn't Esther exasperated with Reuven for leaving her with the kids day after day, all day long? Why wasn't she resentful when he abandoned her at night as well, to study with friends, just for the joy of it?

In the shady park in Bayit Vegan, where my daughter and Esther's three small children played, Esther told me that when her children napped and slept and when Reuven was out at night, she, too, studied Torah.

An Orthodox woman studying Torah? That took me by surprise. I couldn't even picture Esther surrounded by sacred texts. I told her I thought that the ideal Orthodox woman was a hausfrau. As a girl, she had learned enough of *halakhah* (literally "going" or "walking," figuratively the teachings that are followed, or the Jewish law) to run a home and observe the Sabbath and holy days. I assumed, as well, that before her wedding her mother had taught her how to comply with the laws of family purity, that is, when to abstain from sexual relations during and after menstruation, when to dip into the ritual bath. And that, I thought, was it.

"What made you think that?" Esther asked, as we guided our children home.

I replied that anyone who had read Isaac Bashevis Singer's story "Yentl" or had seen Barbara Streisand in the movie knew there was no place for a woman in the Jewish house of study. If a religious woman wanted to become learned in Torah, she, like Yentl, had to disguise herself as a man, literally or figuratively.

Esther asked if I believed everything I read and saw in the movies.

But I had more evidence. If I called to mind any Orthodox synagogue I had ever been to, the picture was essentially the same. The women sat in their section, half looking at their prayer books and Bibles, half tending their children and chatting. The men, whose attention wandered during the preliminary prayers, grew more alert for the Torah service. They waited to see who would be awarded Torah honors that morning. Those chosen took turns going up to the front of the synagogue. Some recited blessings over the Torah, others read from it, another blessed the one who made the blessings, another held the Torah up, and another covered it in its mantle. And all paraded with it until it was returned to the ark. Anyone watching

9

the men shaking each other's hands in congratulations after having received any of these Torah honors would have to conclude that the Torah belonged to men. Only men were invested with the power to reenact the ultimate man-God scenario, the giving of the Torah at Mount Sinai. The man who chanted the Torah was like God, the man who called up the men who would recite benedictions was like Moses, the men who recited the benedictions were like the Israelites assembled to receive the Torah.

In such a synagogue, a little girl could easily realize her Electra fantasies. While her mother sat cordoned off with the other women, she, being just a child, a neuter, and not a bona fide woman, could sit with her father in the men's section, near the Torah. Sitting in his lap, snuggling against his prayer shawl, she would finger its fringes. The rabbi would slam his book down and beg the women to quiet down. When the Torah was carried by in the procession, Daddy would hold her up to kiss it. But when she turned twelve, her gender all too visible, she would be sent back to the women, banished, no longer an honorary man.

Esther suggested that what I had observed was only in my head. Not likely, I told her. In my thirty-four years, I had prayed in many different Orthodox synagogues and I trusted I had seen correctly. "But you're wrong about observant women and Torah study," she said. She decided to set me straight. She had studied theoretical physics at Stanford after being educated in a women's religious high school in New York and at Stern College. Although she finished her dissertation these last years in between births, she had not yet been employed as a physicist. Her mother was a dentist. Her grandmother had been a principal of a girls' high school. All of them Orthodox women, professionals, mothers, wives. And all learned in Torah.

I didn't know what to think. Either I was profoundly ignorant about the status of women's learning in the observant community, or Esther didn't realize how atypical the women in her family were. The religious communities I knew did not recognize the intellectual presence of women. They acknowledged our expertise only on matters of procreation, housekeeping, and selfless acts of lovingkindness. Since motherhood was inevitable, all learning was wasted on us. (My upbringing instilled in me a sense that the most important thing I could do at college—and this was in the seventies—was to find a husband. Don't work so hard at Tufts that you miss out on a man headed for orthopedics or a dental subspecialty. If you're smart, you'll be realistic and take steps to secure your future.)

I knew that rabbis sermonizing from their pulpits about our Jewish sages were not referring to co-ed think tanks. Torah sages were the white-bearded wise men, God's fraternity brothers. When rabbis praised the sages' wisdom, they were praising the wisdom of men. That was truth, and there was no way it could be confused with homey maternal instruction. I could hardly believe there was an enlightened enclave in Worcester that produced women so learned in Torah as Esther.

The fact that I came of age as women were becoming business executives and astronauts did not make it any more likely that many women would become learned in Torah, even as foot soldiers, let alone as generals. Not in a thousand years. I knew there were quirky exceptions. In the second century there was a ninety-two-year-old maid in the household of Rabbi Judah who whispered correct scriptural interpretations into the ears of the scholar and his students while she swept, served, and tidied. Also in the second century was Bruria, the wife of Rabbi Meir. In all of the Talmud she is the only woman whose views on legal matters are considered. In the twelfth century, there was the nameless only daughter of Rabbi Samuel ben Ali ha-Levi of Baghdad, expert in Bible and Talmud, who taught Bible to men, but through a window so they could not see her. (According to Judith Baskin, a professor in the Department of Judaic Studies at SUNY Albany, this story, exhibiting the folkloric motif of the veiled woman teaching men, may be apocryphal.) In the nineteenth century in the Ukraine, there was another only daughter,

Hannah Rachel Werbemacher, known as the Maid of Ludomir. She observed men's religious duties, wore their prayer garb, learned mysticism, and built an apartment adjacent to a synagogue, so that on Sabbath afternoons she could open her door to the synagogue and deliver Torah lessons to the Hasidim who revered her. But these women who learned are like dancing bears: aberrations. Possible, yes, but unlikely and dangerous. One never forgets that the dancing bear is a bear, capable of bearish acts, and that is why it wears a muzzle.

Esther asked me, "Do you study Torah?"

She was surely kidding. In Hamilton, New York, I found keeping track of holidays and procuring Hanukkah candles and scouting the region for Passover foods to be challenge enough. It had never troubled me that my religious life lacked an intellectual component. Peter used to lead Sabbath services at the college and he would call on a student to read some of the weekly Torah portion aloud. I don't recall ever being inspired by hearing the biblical narratives or the laws concerning priestly behavior and the varieties of sacrifice. Peter seemed to be in cahoots with Esther. He sometimes nudged me on Sabbath afternoons to join him in study. "Don't you have any desire to study Torah?" he would ask. He asked more insistently after my illnesses started. He was convinced that I could draw strength from shoring up my religious life. I think what he had in mind was for me to believe in and worship God with more enthusiasm. I didn't see how that would work for me.

I would put him off, reaching for the *Times* or a novel, saying I didn't know how to go about studying Torah.

I thought it would be boring. Hebrew school had been horribly tedious. Along with history and language, Torah was just another subject that only minimally engaged me. Our teachers said we should love Torah. They said Torah preceded the creation of the world, that it was written in black fire upon white fire, that it served as God's blueprint for creation, that the world existed for the purpose of receiving its revelation. For me, these were no more than overblown metaphors: what it boiled down to was that we should revere the Jewish life outlined in Torah and be proud we were Jews. My teachers couldn't have meant we should love studying Torah. In my Hebrew school class, we were timed as we speed-read a page of Bible in Hebrew. The fastest, often me, was rewarded with an after-dinner mint or a handful of Raisinets. Peter, who had done serious Torah study at the Jewish Theological Seminary, offered to teach me Torah on an adult level: to read the Hebrew carefully, to compare the interpretations of the commentators, to recognize the various redactors and note textual emendations. I turned him down after some abortive efforts. I had already tried learning to drive a car from him, and divorce being as commonplace as it was among my friends and family, I believed only a fool would put a solid relationship to extreme tests. I resisted seeing Torah through Peter's eyes. If we ever studied Torah together, it would be when I could hold my own.

The Torah (the word means "teaching") is not just one important Jewish symbol among many. For Orthodox Jews, the Torah is quite literally the word of God as it was given to Moses on Mount Sinai. Each morning a Jew affirms this in prayer: "God gave his people the Torah of Truth, by means of his prophet, the most trusted of his household. God will never emend nor exchange his law for any other one, for all eternity." Jews of other denominations are likely to see the Torah as the testimony of holy men, divinely inspired.

Torah encompasses both the Written Torah and the Oral Torah. The former refers to the five books of the Hebrew Bible, which are written by hand on the parchment of the Torah scroll, as well as to the Prophets and Writings. The latter refers to the interpretations and dialogues of the rabbis that were eventually codified in writing. It is composed of the Mishnah (compiled in written form at the end of the second century and the beginning of the third century) and the Jerusalem and Babylonian Talmuds (compiled in the fifth and sixth centuries, respectively). The Oral Torah is considered the necessary human complement to the Written Torah; it is believed to be just as holy and just as divinely sanctioned as the Written Torah. Moreover, Oral Torah is a process that continues into the present. The teachings and interpretations of rabbis of each generation are also called Torah. Prolific Judaic scholar Professor Jacob Neusner, visiting member at The Institute for Advanced Study in Princeton, describes this process: "Whatever the most recent rabbi is destined to discover through proper exegesis of the tradition is as much a part of the way revealed to Moses as is a sentence of Scripture itself. It therefore is possible to participate even in the giving of the law by appropriate, logical inquiry into the law."*

A Jew's understanding of the nature of God, of how to fulfill God's will, of how to behave and worship, of the past and future history of the universe—all are contained in the Torah. For this reason, it is written in the *Ethics of the Fathers* (5:25): "Delve into it [the Torah] and continue to delve into it for everything is in it; look deeply into it, grow old and gray over it, and do not stir from it, for you can have no better portion than it." Even in death, a Jew retains Torah learning: "When a man departs from this world, neither silver, nor gold, nor precious stones nor pearls escort him, but only Torah study and good deeds" (*Ethics of the Fathers* 6:9). For good reason are Jews called the People of the Book.

Or at least the *Men* of the Book. For while Jewish men have always had opportunities to place the study of Torah at the center of their lives, women were given a back seat. "How do women earn merit?" asks the Babylonian Talmud (*Berakhot* 17a). "By making their children go to the synagogue to learn Scripture, and their husbands to the house of study to learn Mishnah, and by waiting for their husbands until they return from the house of study." I was not surprised to find this model of woman as enabler

---

The Way of Torah: An Introduction to Judaism Second Edition (Encino, California: Dickenson Publishing Company, 1974), 43.

in my daughter's Hebrew language primer: "There was a family in a small, nice house on the hill: a father, mother, and children. The father reads the Torah. The mother says, 'Children, learn the Torah!'"

The women in my family were always delighted to facilitate their children's (read "sons'") learning and to wait for their menfolk to return from synagogue. When one woman spied the sons and husbands walking up the street, she would holler back to the others like a colonial patriot: The men are coming, the men are coming! And all would race to finish preparing lunch as if hungry men forced to wait for their food could precipitate a nuclear disaster. What a relief to have the men back! The household regained its steadiness and they were no longer "just the women." The women thought it was a good deal that they could share the men's reward for Torah study in the world to come and serve as their footstools (*fusbenkele in gan eyden* is the traditional expression in Yiddish) without cracking the holy books themselves. How much better to stay home and cook and gossip than to walk all the way to synagogue in winter and summer, only to spend a good three hours, some of it standing, mumbling Hebrew prayers. When the women did go to synagogue, their tedium was relieved only by seeing who was there, commenting on the Carmen Miranda hats of the rabbi's wife, enjoying herring and sponge cake on the house after services, and catching up on the juicy news of Mrs. Zeitlin's daughter Pauline, who had twice dated gentiles and was obviously doomed. There was no feminism, and the ordination of women as rabbis was not even a thought. Even now, when I ask how they feel about women reading from the Torah in public, they state abruptly: That's going too far. We don't believe in it.

They never wavered in performing their religious roles. They were and still are the high priestesses of domestic spirituality, what a recent apologist for the traditional woman's role in Judaism, Rabbi Yisroel Miller, calls "the guardian angel of the domestic garden of

Eden.''★ Slapdash cooks all of them, women who made blintzes by squashing pieces of white bread with their fists and filling them with artificially sweetened cottage cheese, women who pureed canned string beans and called the results "mock chopped liver," they nonetheless cooked up an aura of holiness for their families from within their kitchens. My grandmother said she used to wake up tired on Friday morning after working all week alongside her husband in their liquor store, but with the Sabbath coming, she found a new energy for cleaning, polishing, and even cooking. She always burned her cakes (why bother with icing, she asked, when you can just brown the top?) and insisted that these cakes embodied the flavor of the Sabbath. And she was right. Through the burnt crust, an unearthly flavor emerged.

Of late, it has dawned on me that my grandmother found no more pleasure in being a domestic high priestess than I do. Thinking I would flatter her, I asked my grandmother if she would write out her recipe for rice pudding, a dish of hers we had been taught to eat with veneration, as though giving homage at an ancestral shrine. Many weeks later, she sent back the scratched out recipe with a note: "It took me all day to write this recipe down. It was the hardest job. You all think I like to cook. I don't. When I'm taking care of the business and doing the books, I'm in heaven. I love you very much, and from now on, if you want to know how to make something, copy a recipe from a regular cookbook." While we in the family would laugh when my grandmother would rest her stirring spoon and sigh, "I cook with a Hate!" it never occurred to any of us that she was telling us she wanted to be rescued from drudgery.

Meticulous though she was in her religious observances, I do not believe she ever consciously reflected upon the rituals she performed. She was always rushed and frantic: soaking and salting meat, lighting memorial candles, tucking incantations against the evil eye under the mattresses of the newborn, visiting those afflicted

---

★*In Search of the Jewish Woman* (Jerusalem/New York: Feldheim Publishers, 1984).

with real and imaginary ailments. I, by contrast, was annoyed by domestic Judaism. I couldn't chuck it though: my husband and daughters would be deprived of the sensory delights of Sabbaths and holidays that, courtesy of my women relatives, linger forever in my imagination. I know that women have the power, using food, to create not only joys, but civilization. Anthropologist Maurie Sacks, who has researched the food-centered rituals of Jewish women, explains: "In a patriarchal society in which distinct gender roles for men and women are carefully guarded, women, who construct and signify community and values, derive power to construct and signify community and values from their practice of food-related ritual."*

For the sake of my own family, for the sake of the Colgate students who came to our house looking for some authentic Jewishness, I have tried to be a domestic spiritualist, canceling appointments the day before a holiday, throwing carrots into pots, grouching around with a Brillo pad. I'm not a bad cook, but I am easily distracted because I try to keep working on articles or lecture notes in my head as I cook. I burn oil and set my pots aflame, and still I keep at it, whipping up egg whites for the Passover dishes, tossing balls of dough into a cauldron of honey for the New Year's *taiglach,* creating an environment for spiritual life that nurtures everyone but myself. After the last holiday guests leave, the children go to sleep, Peter does the dishes, and I sink, quite wrecked, onto the kitchen floor and grumble, "It wasn't worth it."

I once asked my grandmother if she had ever studied Torah. "That's for the men," she laughed. She said when she was a child of seven or eight living on the Lower East Side of New York, she was sent to a Hebrew school in the basement of a store. When she got there, it was dark and she fell down the stairs. "It so frightened me," she said, "I never went back again."

Each January when I returned to Jerusalem with the study group, Esther's questions were the same: What about this year? Did you

*"Computing Community at Purim," *Journal of American Folklore* (July–September, 1989).

study? Your daughters (by now there were two) are getting older. If you can't justify spending the time learning for your own sake, then do it for theirs.

But it had been drummed into me too deeply that Torah study was what men did. Men, it seemed to me, had cornered the market on Jewish intellectual activity.

Of course, I had seen no evidence of the superiority of the male mind, but that was the attitude I had grown up with. Take, for instance, the time my mother brought home a fruit that we had never seen before. She knew it was a pomegranate. She had looked it up in our dictionary and could spell and pronounce it. She did not, however, know how to eat it, so it stayed on the kitchen counter until the weekend, when my stepfather had some time to figure it out. We made his weekends busy. On Saturdays he was dispatched to the synagogue to pray for the women, and on Sundays he was expected to put together household gadgets that came with and without written instructions. My stepfather, putting on his glasses, said this pomegranate was simple. If we only used our heads as something more than hat racks, we too would have seen that it was a fruit and should be treated like a fruit. You scraped the peel, discarded the seeds, and ate what remained. We threw out the seeds and, with our red-stained fingers, ate the remaining white membranes. They tasted like chalk. He maintained my mother had chosen a bum pomegranate, but it was clear to me that my stepfather had bungled. My sister licked the red juice off her hands, and retrieved the trashed seeds. It was the only time we were permitted to eat food out of the garbage.

This was not the first time we witnessed my stepfather's fallibility. He bungled right and left like the rest of us, but he always had an excuse. "How was I supposed to know?" he would ask, suggesting the blame lay elsewhere. That we had waited until the weekend for him to deal with the pomegranate was pure pretense. We were sharp women who cut through surfaces like hot knives. We knew he was no more effective in penetrating mysteries than we three women, yet we couldn't admit this. My mother confessed she doubted if his prayers—if any prayers—would work for us; still she dispatched him to the synagogue to pray for us, for it made him feel useful. Even with ample evidence to the contrary, we could not let go of the myth that my mother was raised with, and that she in turn had passed on to her own daughters: that male intelligence was more rigorous, dependable, resourceful. That male intelligence would save us women from the disasters to which we were bound to succumb.

I did not conclude that women and Torah were incompatible only by observing my family. Abundant Jewish writings assert the supremacy of the male intellect. The important twelfth-century commentator Rabbi Moses ben Maimon, otherwise known as Maimonides or by the acronym Rambam, wrote: "The sages enjoined that a man should not teach his daughter Torah because most women's minds are not attuned to study, and they interpret the words of Torah irrationally, on account of the inadequacy of their minds" (*Hilkhot Talmud Torah* 1:13). An interpreter of history more forgiving than I might be able to look kindly at the Rambam's words by acknowledging that the women of the twelfth century whom he observed hardly resembled the women of today. But I lack this generosity of spirit.

Each January, as I came through Jerusalem with another crop of students, Esther persisted. Why was I turning my back on the most precious legacy of Torah, when it stood there open for me? She quoted from the Book of Ezekiel: God said, "Mortal, eat what is offered to you, eat this scroll." I told Esther it was no problem for Ezekiel to open his mouth and gobble down the Torah as a tasty treat; for him, the scroll tasted "sweet as honey." But for me, if the Torah is to be likened to a food, it is an uncrackable nut, a pomegranate without instructions. And that's just the Bible—forget the difficult commentaries. I confessed I had no relationship to these sacred texts. I didn't understand them. Nor did I understand how study of these texts could be a sacred act, a form of worship. I felt excluded from the Torah by virtue of my sex, my attention span, my nonanalytical intelligence, my wavering belief, and my distance in time from the people who stood at Mount Sinai and received the Torah.

Esther, who thought I only had an attitude problem, yearned to take me under her wing. During my last visit, my fourth to Jerusalem in six years, she told me,

> You're in Jerusalem now. It's only a short time, but you can make enormous strides. I have names for you of *talmidot hakhamot* [the feminine equivalent of wise students, or students of the wise]. I know women who teach in religious nursery schools who have more Torah learning in their little fingers than most American rabbis. You can learn with the women I'll introduce you to. You can learn from them. Not only texts—just be with them and you'll learn. Take my word.

First of all, I didn't have the free time for this kind of project. Shepherding the students around Jerusalem, supervising their research projects, and planning their adventures in Tiberias and Eilat was a full-time job for both Peter and me. Second, I didn't completely trust Esther's intentions. I wanted to believe that she wanted me to overcome my alienation from Torah. I feared, though, that her real intention was for me to become more devout in my religious observance. That was the last thing I wanted to do. I was not like her husband, Reuven, who could be jolted into an emphatic acceptance of Jewish observance. I had no appetite for religious hocus-pocus.

Third, how could Esther know what was good for me when she hardly knew me? Still, I tentatively agreed to meet one of her friends, because if it was true, as I assumed, that women who acquired a deep knowledge of Torah had done so against enormous odds, then this learned woman was, at the very least, a curious and memorable dancing bear, another Maid of Ludomir.

I had not expected that this one woman and then others would eventually be teaching me Torah. I did not anticipate how profoundly their drawing me into their lives, cross-stitched with sacred texts, would affect me.

I was sent to meet Aviva Gottlieb Zornberg. Monday nights she taught a class in English in *parashat hashavua,* the Torah portion of the week. Esther provided a bio: Aviva was in her forties, lovely, brilliant, a mother, once an English professor at the Hebrew University specializing in George Eliot. She was from Scotland, descended on her father's side from Polish Hasidim and on her mother's side, also, the descendant of rabbis and the niece of the chief rabbi of Rumania, her mother's brother. Aviva was known for motivating mature, adult women to forge spiritual connections to Torah. Esther arranged to have me picked up by her friend Judy, a psychologist who lived down the street, and taken to the class, which was meeting this week in an apartment in Rehavia.

I assumed I had to dress the part for an evening of Torah study with religious women. I had spent the day in jeans, prowling around the Old City with students. For the class, I changed into my long gray skirt and attempted to wind a scarf around my head as a Sarah Lawrence friend from Barbados had taught me in graduate school. My daughter Juliana sat on my bed watching me transform myself into a lady of a Caribbean shtetl. "Why are you doing this?" she asked.

I thought that my everyday dress would reveal that I believed it possible to be both a committed Jew and also at home in the secular world and that under those circumstances I would be unwelcome in the class. I was not comfortable about having to disguise myself. Was I so different from Yentl? We were both entering Torah study under false pretenses. Like Yentl, I believed if I wasn't prepared to learn Torah on the terms available, I would not learn at all. I checked myself in the mirror. I looked ready to audition for a chorus part in *Fiddler on the Roof.*

I called Esther. "Tell me this isn't really necessary."

"I once knew a woman," said Esther,

who lived in Mea Shearim. She had two dresses: one for week-days and one for the Sabbath. She shaved her head and covered her skull with a tight black cloth. If you asked her how she can dress that way, she'd say, "I'm going to let some *goy* in Paris dictate how I should dress?" What you wear every day, your jeans and your sleeveless ski jacket—isn't that a costume, too, what you wear to blend in with the university crowd you want to be accepted by? It's a social convention. Really it doesn't matter how you go to Aviva's class. It's a diverse group. They're very accepting.

I did think about it. If my clothes represented an image, that was an image I liked for myself. But Judy came to pick me up before I could change back into jeans.

In the car, I fiddled with my scarf. Make the best of this, look at this masquerade more positively, I urged myself. Imagine you were garbing yourself in special vestments for Torah study. I felt very silly and wished I were back home.

The apartment we went to was, by Israeli standards, splendid. There was lots of heat, three walls covered from floor to ceiling with sets of sacred books, a lighted display case holding silver spice boxes, candlesticks, silver wine goblets, Hanukkah candelabras. A bearded husband in a black suit and black hat gathered up some volumes of the Talmud and, without a word to anyone, went into his study and closed the door. In my mind, an aura of importance hovered over the study he was about to engage in. It would be serious, focused, bound in tradition. "Hush, children," his wife would say, seeing such a man surrounded by his holy books, "Papa is studying." By contrast, the casual women's coffee klatch I had joined felt trivial, something women did to fill their leisure time and improve them-selves. There were fifteen women sitting around a long, narrow dining room table, stirring artificial sweetener into their tea cups, dipping into plates of cookies, and sifting through piles of Bibles and commentaries for the one they preferred.

They were all in modest dress and were scarved or wigged. Several were pregnant. Religious women, religious women, I said to myself, I don't see the world as they do. I don't devote my life to scrupulous adherence to the law as they do. I don't see the hand of God everywhere. I don't see my every act as an opportunity to serve God. And I don't make babies with nearly their gusto. Just as well that I wore clothes that obscured me. No one would think: Ah, here's a neophyte who needs instruction and an invitation to come spend the Sabbath. It was more than enough to have Esther on my case.

Aviva arrived. Clearly it was she, for the women stopped chatting about their work in psychology or education or about their large families. Wearing a glamorous brunette wig, Aviva sat at the head of the table and received compliments. It seemed important for these women to begin the class by fussing a little over Aviva, to acknowledge that she was as attractive as she was learned and that that enhanced her status as a teacher. That she was still what they considered a normal, appealing woman. Had she not been a pretty, married mother, perhaps these women would have regarded her learning, not as an asset, but as a liability that kept her from attaining conventional happiness.

Aviva switched on her tape recorder. Judy whispered that Aviva would probably turn her lectures and the class discussions into a book someday. Aviva began to teach, her voice like a viola. She spoke an elegant, lilting English—a little Cambridge, a little Glasgow. The room took on a new life, and the display case and the cookies seemed to recede. It became a holy space and not someone's upper-middle-class apartment. What we were doing was dead serious. We were women in the holy zone. Aviva opened to the Book of Exodus and commented on the word *yetzei* (meaning "went out"), which in this context referred to the Israelites going out of Egypt.

She asked why the Israelites had to spend a generation in the desert before they were allowed to enter the land of Canaan. The women responded with strained articulateness, pressured by the running tape recorder to sift and prearrange their thoughts. Taking in all the responses, Aviva said that the word *yetzei* indeed meant more than just going out. It meant moving away from something familiar, taking on a new identity, leaving all convention behind. When the Israelites received the Torah, they were imbued with a new love and acquired a new understanding. It was the Torah that permitted that transformation. But it took time. They couldn't will it. And only when the transformation was complete could the Israelites come into full being, into glory, and into Canaan.

I felt as if Aviva were speaking only to me. I believed that as she looked into my face, she knew my present situation, my history, how my life would turn out. Chills flew up my spine.

I floated in her words: relinquish one's will . . . leave convention behind . . . the power of time. For that moment, I viscerally understood how the Israelites' wandering in Sinai could be both a historical occurrence and a state of mind that stood outside of time. How had this Orthodox woman become so learned? Was she a maverick, or were there many others like her? So Esther was right about there being learned women. How had Aviva acquired such a sense of familiarity with the Torah, of its power? What did her family make of her? How did she dare to come up with this wild mix of traditional Torah study methods and contemporary literary criticism? Would respected male Torah scholars take her teachings seriously? Would they even hear her out?

Then I felt the scarf tugging on my head. I become aware of the presence of the other women and dwelled on the oddness of my own study of Torah. I was pulled back into the physical reality of this apartment in Rehavia and got stuck there. In Aviva's terms, I was the Jew who was detained in the Sinai desert. I was open to new love and understanding, but I was as yet untransformed.

Back in Hamilton, I could not stop thinking about Aviva's class. Still, I didn't decide to give myself fully over to learning Torah. I feared I would remain forever on the outside. Three hurdles seemed most difficult. First, I had trouble accepting that women should even be studying Torah, for it seemed to me as though the very content and form of the texts conspired against us. Second, I doubted I would find some person or school that would teach me without expecting me to change my religious life to conform to their expectations. Certainly I knew I could take Jewish studies courses at just about any college, but dispassionate textual analysis and criticism were not what I was looking for. I wanted to know Torah study in the context of religious life (though I wasn't necessarily looking to become more religious myself). The third hurdle made me most anxious. I felt if I studied Torah as a sacred text, I would have to work through all my muddled thinking about God.

There was a fourth hurdle, more a practical consideration. How was I going to have the time and the funds to study Torah in Jerusalem with Esther's women friends? I suppose if I were convinced that my physical and spiritual well-being hung on taking a Torah-cure in the holy land, we would have scrambled to find the means to effect my salvation. But as I wasn't convinced that Torah study would be the life-giving solution, I couldn't ask Peter to drop everything, and go to Jerusalem with me.

Finally, a year later, the chance to spend a longer time in Jerusalem simply presented itself. Peter was offered a Fulbright to teach philosophy at Hebrew University, and I was invited to teach creative writing in the English department. But even then, I wasn't all that eager to go. We had taken a leave from Colgate and I was teaching writing at Yale. New Haven intoxicated me: the terribly clever students, the Yale Repertory Theater, ballet school for Juliana, the freelance writing assignments that finally fell into my lap. And I was healthy. I had been going to a naturopathic doctor who stuffed me with vitamins, homeopathic remedies, and an impossible diet free of everything but beans, grains, and vegetables. The doctor told me my immunological deficiencies were rooted in the way I saw myself, as a disembodied intelligence. She recommended therapeutic massage. Reason told me the treatment was probably hogwash, and so did friends who taught in the medical school. But it worked. Even when I quit the regimen, I remained well. My head was buzzing with the stimulating days and the good health I knew in New Haven. I could hardly recall how I used to hear the warnings to sanctify, to fortify myself in a lasting way, back in the quiet of Hamilton.

Esther was visiting her family in Worcester and phoned. When I told her we had the opportunity to come to Jerusalem for a stretch of many months, she said, "Don't pass this by. This is the right time for you to study. There is a creative energy among women studying Torah that is unbelievable."

I said I'd think about it.

An hour before sunset and the beginning of the Sabbath, my mother phoned. "Is Peter there? I have to know if in the Bible it says you must eat chicken on the Sabbath. It's snowing here. Wouldn't it be foolish to risk my life looking for a chicken? But if the Bible says it, I will. I have fresh salmon steak in the fridge. Daddy likes fish. Does it say in the Bible you can substitute fish? Put Peter on the phone, because I have to know."

She was dead serious. This is a woman who is a clear thinker in all secular matters, a regular Geiger counter when it comes to detecting absurdities and inconsistencies in any situation. Over issues of Jewish practice, though, her brain crumbles. Why had my mother suddenly become so scrupulous about correct religious observance? She must have made one of her deals with God: she would observe this Sabbath correctly and make a contribution to Hadassah, and God, in return, would give my sister the job at ABC she had interviewed for and wanted so badly.

I chose not to discuss the irrationality of my mother's religious life with her. I just gave her the facts. I told her it is not necessary to be a Torah scholar to know that serving chicken is custom and not law. "Believe me, Mom, fish is fine. So is lasagne, so is tortellini in brodo. Jews of different origins have their own traditional Sabbath specialties."

"Where is Peter?"

"At the library."

"I don't know what to do now. You're only telling me fish is OK because you don't want me to go out in the snow. It has to say chicken in the Bible. Why else would people serve chicken like their lives depended on it? I'll call the butcher and tell him to deliver an already cooked one."

At services that Sabbath, I was teaching my younger daughter, Elizabeth, whom we call Dede, to recognize the name of God in the prayer book. I told her it was easy. Whenever she saw two letter *yods* together like quotation marks, that was it, God's name. She started to scan the page with her finger. She stopped abruptly and ran over to Peter to double check. Returning, she reported, "Daddy really knows about God." At three, she was already onto it: Torah is not my turf, not mine to transmit to her. Then she asked me, "How come men wear prayer shawls?"

I said, "To remember the presence of God when they pray."

"How come women don't need to remember?"

I said, "Some people say women never forget."

"Do you forget?"

"I do."

"Then you should wear a prayer shawl."

Esther had been nudging me for years now. OK, I capitulated. I'll do it already. Off we all went to Jerusalem. The girls with Cabbage Patch dolls in their backpacks, Peter lugging books we both needed for teaching, and I embracing the computer we would try to share. We rented David and Frieda Macarov's apartment in a middle-class neighborhood called Nayot near the Hebrew University's new botanical gardens. The apartment came with a washing machine, a stereo, a TV, cloth place mats, a backyard with lemon, plum, peach, loquat, pomegranate, and pomelo trees, a lawn to mow, and a grill. During the period I studied Torah, I was never free of the clutter of familial dailiness—keeping house, dressing kids, fixing lunches, putting calamine lotion on their chicken pox. Not the setting Hermann Hesse or Somerset Maugham would have chosen for a spiritual experience.

But it was the setting for meeting the learned Jewish women of Jerusalem who became my role models. They provided compelling evidence that the world of traditional sacred learning was not absolutely and inherently masculine. They demonstrated that I could define my religiousness not just by the output of my kitchen or by my daily deeds, but by the activities of my critical intelligence. They stretched the boundaries of my learning and, consequently, the boundaries of my faith.

Two

As soon as I settled us in our Jerusalem apartment, enrolled my daughters in their schools, and squared away the details for my course at the university, I planned to enroll myself in a yeshiva.

The yeshiva, or academy for learning Torah, has existed since the destruction of the Second Temple in 70 C.E. The first yeshiva was created by Rabbi Johanan ben Zakkai in the city of Yavneh. In the absence of the Temple, the yeshiva and scholarship became the focal point for Jewish life and its source of sustenance. In the yeshiva, scholars studied, analyzed, and interpreted Torah. They ruled on the nature of Jewish communal life.

Wherever Jews have lived, no matter how trying the circumstances, they established yeshivot. Batya Gallant, a teacher of Jewish thought at Michlelet Bruria in Jerusalem, tells the story of her father, who had been learning in the Kamenetz yeshiva in Lithuania. During World War II, students of his yeshiva, along with students of the Mirrer yeshiva, escaped to Shanghai, where they learned for five years before reestablishing themselves in America. "In photos," Batya says, "the yeshiva boys look like they are still in Poland, but you can see Chinese people behind them, staring."

Yeshiva study is not only for those who wish to be ordained as rabbis. It is also for laymen who wish to become versed in sacred texts. In the yeshiva, one learns to venerate sacred knowledge. Batya describes her father:

> His supreme value in life was learning Torah. He had an enormous love of just knowing the material. He would say about a certain rabbi, "what he knew was unbelievable! What he knew!" The capacity for knowledge would overwhelm him to tears. Not how kind or how scrupulous, but what he knew. He didn't mean knowing in a dry, intellectual, scientific way: knowing was an emotional thing for him. At the Sabbath table, the main activity outside of eating was to ask questions in Jewish learning. I could see my father's excitement and sense of fun.

The word *yeshiva* comes from the Hebrew "to sit" and for good reason. People say that to be a good yeshiva student, you need to have *sitzfleish,* the patience and control necessary for endless hours and years of sitting with the texts. A pale face and a limp body are the yeshiva ideal. Walk around with bulging biceps and you reveal that you squandered your time at a Nautilus. Even the devoted students get antsy: my friend Hillel, an American professor of Judaica, recalls that in the yeshiva he attended in Jerusalem as a teenager, boys chewed paper to still themselves. I asked Hillel if yeshiva boys reflected in a self-conscious way on their yeshiva experience. Certainly, he said. They reflected on how they could get rid of their egos, how they could eat and sleep less so they could devote themselves more intensely to Torah.

I said that wasn't the kind of reflection I meant. I meant if they wondered what it all meant, whether they fitted in.

"Once you have thoughts like that," Hillel suggested, "you're halfway out the door already. The yeshiva is a world unto itself: you eat, sleep, study, and pray within it. It's compelling because it's your whole reality."

The activity that takes place in the yeshivot, and all study of Torah, is referred to by the Yiddish term *lernen*. To *lern* does not signify the activity of a teacher who possesses a body of knowledge transferring it to a student who soaks it up. To *lern* is to confront the familiar sacred texts together, the more experienced member of the pair or group guiding the less experienced. Those who *lern*, according to Samuel Heilman, author of *The Gate Behind the Wall*, "are people who come to the holy books not so much to exercise their intellect as to express their devotion and attachment to a God whose revealed word they believe the books contain."*

Until recent times, yeshivot—with the rarest of exceptions (apparently there was a women's yeshiva in Rome in the fifteenth century)—were male institutions. When Jewish women were educated, it was informally, within their families. They learned by observing and by imitation. The nineteenth-century Lithuanian work called the *Arukh ha-Shulchan* written by Yechiel Mikhal Epstein explains: "We have never taught women from a book, nor have we ever heard that people actually do so. Rather, every mother teaches her daughter or daughter-in-law those well-known rules women should know."

Women could not be totally ignorant. They needed to become familiar with a large and detailed body of material, because for the scrupulously observant, every aspect of life brings with it laws that must be followed to the letter. There are laws regulating the mixing of a baby's cereal and emptying its potty and its diapers on the Sabbath, responding to a child's fear of the dark, using breast pumps, and removing splinters. A modern pamphlet concerning the

---

The Gate Behind the Wall: A Pilgrimage to Jerusalem (New York: Penguin Books, 1984), p. 19.

laws pertaining to the care of children on the Sabbath and on holidays informs a mother as follows regarding the dressing of her child:

> A bow may be tied or untied (even if the bow is tied over a single knot). The two loops or ends of a bow may not be knotted, even with a single knot, nor may such a bow be undone; it is treated like a double knot. Even a bow may only be made with the intention to untie it within the following twenty-four hours. When a bow becomes a knot unintentionally, then it may be undone, or if this is impossible, it may be cut with a knife.*

A woman who was familiar with all these laws and scrupulous about observing them would be respected for her piety and would be a resource for practical advice for others. When the Talmudic sages considered certain issues within the domain of women, such as the laws concerning holiday candle lighting, dietary laws, and menstruation, they sometimes deferred to the authority of their wives, mothers, or daughters. In the Talmud we see an example in which Bruria, daughter of Rabbi ben Tradiyon and wife of Rabbi Meir, provides the correct legal decision:

> When does an oven [which had become defiled—that is, unfit for cooking dishes in accordance with the dietary laws] become clean? Rabbi Halafta of Kfar Hananiah said, "I asked this question of Shimon ben Hananiah, who asked it of the son of Rabbi ben Tradiyon, who said, "When it is removed from its place. But his daughter [her name is Bruria; here she is anonymous] says, 'When its coating is removed.' When this was reported to Rabbi Yehuda ben Bava, he said, "his daughter proffered a more accurate definition than his son." (*Tosefta Kelim, Bava Kamma* 4)†

---

*S. Wagschal, *Care of Children on the Sabbath and Yom Tov* (Jerusalem/New York: Feldheim Publishers, 1958), 17.
†Trans. Getsel Ellinson, in *Serving the Creator,* Volume one (Jerusalem: Torah Education Department of the World Zionist Organization, 1986), 245.

Why was the attitude toward women's learning so restrictive in almost all the classical sources? Why was the scope of what women were permitted to learn so limited? Three hypotheses come to mind. Men may have believed women had inferior brains; they may have believed women's menstrual blood would contaminate the holy sphere of Torah study; and they may have feared Torah knowledge would give women too much desire for a life of the mind, luring them away from making babies, keeping house, and running businesses.

Rabbi Zvi Wolff, a teacher of Jewish law at the Pardes Institute (and a father of five daughters and three sons, all of whom he teaches), has compiled and translated many of the classical sources concerning the legal status of women studying Torah in "Teaching Women Torah," which appeared in spring 1986 in the Pardes Institute magazine *Havruta*.

Rabbi Wolff explains that most restrictions on women's Torah learning are pinned on an interpretation of the verse in Deuteronomy: "Therefore impress these My words upon your very heart: bind them as a sign on your hand and let them serve as a symbol on your forehead, and teach them to your children." The problem is the word *children*. In Hebrew *banim* literally translated is the masculine plural form for "sons," but it can also refer to any mixed group of girls and boys. Girls in Hebrew schools are often surprised to learn that a teacher addressing a class of nineteen girls and one boy would, according to correct Hebrew grammar, address the students in the masculine plural as *talmidim*, literally boy students, corresponding, of course, to the way we have used *men* in English to refer to men or women. The fourth-century commentary on this line of Scripture in *Sifre Deuteronomy* (section 46) insists on a literal translation: "And teach them to your sons, and not to your daughters." Later commentators debated the implications of this interpretation. Clearly it meant that a father was obliged to teach his sons Torah. But was he forbidden to teach his daughters Torah or simply not obligated to teach them? If women were exempt from the commandment to study Torah, could they still study it if they chose to? If women were not obligated to study, could they look forward to any eternal reward?

The opinion of Rabbi Eliezer ben Hyrcanus (end of the first and beginning of the second century) in *Mishnah Sotah* 3:4 is adamantly against women's learning. He judged: "He who teaches his daughter, teaches her *tiflut.*" *Tiflut* has been translated in any number of ways: as trivial and irrelevant things, foolishness or frivolity, immorality, lewdness, licentiousness, or lechery. Rabbi Eliezer was adamant: "The words of the Torah should be burnt rather than taught to women."

In the twelfth century, Maimonides (in *Hilkhot Talmud Torah*) elaborated upon this point, indicating that not all women's learning was forbidden: He said *tiflut* referred only to teaching Oral Torah to a woman. While it was preferable not to teach Written Torah to a woman, it was not *tiflut.*

In the eighteenth century, Rabbi Hayyim Joseph David Azulai judged (in *Sefer Hasidim*): "One should teach his daughters practical law—not because there is a requirement for them to learn, but so that they should know the laws. Once they know the laws, there is no need for them to learn any more."

And in the twentieth century, Rabbi Baruch Epstein wrote (in *Torah Temimah*): "Girls do not have intellectual stability and are, therefore, unable to make profound inquiries with a sharp mind and appreciate the depth of Torah. It is possible that by using their own minds, they will transgress the will of Torah."

I am at a loss as to how to respond to the voices of these sages presented by Rabbi Wolff, which, with some variation, echo each other. They offend, humiliate, and demean me. If these sages have divine sanction, how poorly that divinity esteems me! It is a struggle for me to maintain a respectful attitude toward these sages. Should I pick and choose among their wisdom, taking only what seems pleasing to me? If I choose to disregard their opinions about women, should I feel free as well to dismiss the laws concerning honoring parents or adultery if, on a particular day, I find them offensive, inconvenient, or inconsiderate? If I accepted the Torah as the ultimate guide in my life, I could not dismiss attitudes within Torah that seemed unenlightened and unjust. In other words, is Torah an all or nothing proposition?

This is what it means for me to be estranged from the content of sacred texts. When those sacred texts say my mind is feeble, then I know in my gut that their sacredness is limited and they have no authority over me.

Amidst the prohibitors, there was the small voice of Ben Azzai, an unordained Talmudic sage (in *Mishnah Sotah*) who was led to reason: "A man is obliged to teach his daughter Torah." Until our times, his voice went essentially unheeded. Women who did learn were called "exceptional" or "unusual" women by the rabbis. Some rabbis judged that whereas the average woman should not be taught, an exceptional woman could study on her own. Imagine how few women scientists and mathematicians there would be in America if there was a ruling stating: Women cannot study physics and algebra in school. But if by some quirk they've picked up advanced scientific and mathematical skills by reading forbidden books or by spying on their brothers doing their lessons, they may continue to study on their own.

For a Jewish man, being clever or motivated has never been a prerequisite for receiving a religious education. He need only commit himself to years of study. And it is an ambitious program. Rabbi Judah ben Tema provides a curriculum for study in the *Ethics of the Fathers* (5:25): "A five-year-old begins Scripture; a ten-year-old begins Mishnah, a thirteen-year-old becomes obliged to observe the commandments, a fifteen-year-old begins the study of the Gemara." Even with ben Tema's rigid program, understanding doesn't come until forty and the ability to counsel, at fifty. Any young man has the opportunity to stick it out for enough years to acquire a respectable bundle of Torah learning. If he is particularly gifted, if he exhibits a potential genius, he is invited to continue even longer in the yeshiva. It is understood that he must not be distracted by having to earn a living. The honor of supporting him in this most sacred calling for as long as necessary falls upon his wife, his parents, his in-laws, and the community. In recent years, a new pattern in men's yeshiva studies has begun to emerge. Whereas continued yeshiva learning was once reserved for the elite, now *many* men (regardless of their intellectual promise, regardless of the ability of their wives and in-laws to support them) are encouraged to remain within the yeshiva, where, shielded from the temptations of the secular world, they maintain the strength of their Jewish commitment.

Formal Torah learning was never spoon-fed to women. A woman who wanted access to Torah study had to prove she was more capable than a man in order to be granted a man's rights and opportunities. She had to prove that all the female stereotypes did not hold true for her, that her intelligence and pure desire to learn made her the exception worthy of special treatment. In the sixteenth century, Rabbi Joshua Falk of Poland elucidates Rambam's description of women in his comment on the *Tur* (*Yoreh Deah* 246, 15): "Most women's minds are not geared toward being taught, but if she had begun to study properly herself, not making Torah into foolishness, she is no longer like 'most' women, and she is rewarded. A serious woman's serious study takes her out of the category of most women . . . and, it seems, frees her of the restrictions on study of Torah, both Oral and Written."

In terms of women's lives, it boils down to this: Women were generally taught what they needed to know in order to follow the laws and communicate them to their children. What many women did learn of the Torah in modern times came from the sixteenth-century "women's Torah," the *Tzena Urena,* written in the vernacular, Yiddish. The *Tzena Urena* is an interpretation of biblical stories presented as a folksy collage of vivid narratives, bits of textual exegesis, and instruction in upright living that is clear, inspirational, and moving. In memoirs of pious mothers, the *Tzena Urena* is the ever-present prop. Typically the mother knew the book well, and it easily brought her to tears. The unusual woman who did learn Torah from the primary sources in the original Hebrew was either exceptionally brilliant, curious, persistent, and self-motivated in finding ways to learn or blessed with a learned father of patience and pedagogic skills who disregarded convention to teach his daughter or provide her with a tutor.

A major revision in rabbinic attitudes toward women's learning has come about in the past century, when it became apparent that Jewish women, lacking access to Jewish learning, applied their intelligence and industry instead to secular subjects: languages, literature, commerce, science. Religious women were permitted to study these subjects, which were considered irrelevant and conferred no status on men. With secular knowledge, women could earn a living and free their husbands for full-time Torah study. Rabbi Abbahu, in the tractate *Sotah* of the Jerusalem Talmud, stated: "A man may teach his daughter Greek because it is an adornment for her." For a son, such study would be considered *bitul torah,* a transgression of idleness. This attitude continued into the nineteenth century, according to Deborah Weissman, who teaches Jewish Education at Hebrew University and specializes in women's education. In her 1984 paper "Bais Ya'akov," presented at the International Conference on Jewish Education held at the Hebrew University, Weissman stated: "The leaders of the Jewish community still often preferred that the girls study in alien environments rather than they be taught traditional Judaism in a school." In fact, Weissman noted, "In Galicia, Jewish girls would sometimes be sent to study in Catholic schools, run by nuns, so that sons and daughters within the same family might grow up living in two totally different worlds."

Women's familiarity with the secular world was eventually blamed by the religious community for causing any number of horrors, the worst being assimilation and intermarriage. To me, the exclusion of women from the intellectual life of the religious community was and is a major cause of the alienation from Judaism that so many contemporary Jewish women have experienced.

Radical innovation in women's education came about as a result of the Haskalah, the nineteenth-century Jewish enlightenment movement in Europe and Russia. Israel Meir ha-Kohen (called the Hafetz Hayyim), a leading rabbi in eastern Europe in the early twentieth century, wrote:

> Today, to our dismay, tradition is flagging . . . Especially those who have taught themselves to read and write secular languages must be taught all of the Bible and the moral teachings of the Rabbis so that our faith will be instilled in them. Otherwise, they may falter from the way of God and transgress the very fundamentals of our religion. (*Likutei Halakhot,* Sotah 21)

The Hafetz Hayyim endorsed the Bais Ya'akov movement, founded in Poland by the seamstress Sarah Schenirer in 1918. For the first time, there were institutions for women's Torah learning. Bais Ya'akov students studied Written Torah, one nonlegal tractate of Oral Torah, and philosophical and moral works. They did not study Talmud. Deborah Weissman wonders how Torah education for women is perceived by rabbis in our time, "whether women's Torah study is still seen as primarily of instrumental value, in coping with the alien influence of the outside world [or] . . . whether it can be seen as an act of intrinsic worth, a form of worship, even the fulfillment of a commandment."

It seems to me that Jewish education was not opened to women out of an enlightened revision of previous attitudes. Rather, it happened in response to a crisis (that is, the threat of assimilation) in the Jewish community, a crisis that persists in our own day. Without the threat of the crisis, rabbis might reason, women could be barred from study once again. Rabbi Wolff, too, reflects on this major change in attitude on the part of the rabbis: "The unusual circumstances modernity imposes on our generation mean that none of today's women belong to the general legal category which restricted their study. Today, perhaps, all women are in the category of the 'unusual' women of previous generations."

Esther said I might find a teacher for myself at the women's school called Michlelet Bruria, where the language of instruction is English. Some of the most learned women in Torah were teaching there; even Aviva gave a weekly lesson. I took this to mean Esther was advising me to enroll as a student.

She was convinced that if I wanted to take classes, I would do better going to an Orthodox women's school rather than to the schools of the Conservative or Reform movements or to a university. I didn't feel comfortable studying with the Orthodox, particularly because they separated the sexes for study. Nonetheless, like many non-Orthodox Jews, I did feel the Orthodox were "the real thing" and had a monopoly on authenticity. They were like tea essence, the concentrate from which others could prepare their drink. If I was finally to study Torah, I wanted to do it "right." I wanted to make sure I didn't end up in one of the yeshivot created in the last twenty years to educate newly religious young people who have minimal backgrounds in Jewish study and practice. I didn't want to study with people who wanted quickie soul transformations or easy proofs of God's existence. I wanted to learn, not be rehabilitated.

As far as she knew, Esther said, Michlelet Bruria had classes at all levels and for all types. There were college women who had never studied Jewish texts and were no longer willing to be ignorant in Torah. There were recent graduates of American religious high schools whose parents wanted them to have a full year of text study to strengthen their faith before they went off to secular colleges. Finally, and this was the group most familiar to Esther, as it constituted the original core of Bruria, there were adult women who were already learned and wanted to continue their studies. Recalling her own visits to Bruria in its earliest days in the mid-seventies, Esther remembered the excitement and commitment of women lawyers and psychiatrists who left their children in the Bruria nursery so they could study.

I was eager to begin my Torah studies, to experience the excitement of that third component of Bruria students—professional women learning Torah. Nevertheless, on the morning I was to make a preliminary visit to Bruria, I was overcome by nausea. I imagined the worst. Bruria would be ghoulish and dusty, with swarms of women in a smelly basement, swaying violently and jabbering over piles of books. I would be sucked into a nineteenth-century European shtetl, into the company of women swathed in piety and mumbling psalms and holy petitions. They would sneer at me as if I were pagan trash: Get out of our midst, you who run your dishwasher on the Sabbath, you who balk at our laws regulating sexual intimacy because you find them meddlesome. And at the same time, they'd dig their nails tightly into my clothes, restraining me as yet another soul they could count among themselves.

If I didn't get to Bruria quickly, I would lose my nerve. I consoled myself that it would be less humiliating if I disassociated my mind from my body. The approach had worked when I had to be examined by a gynecologist.

I took a bus from my corner to Kiryat Moshe, a religious neighborhood where mothers and fathers pushed baby carriages and were surrounded by swarms of toddlers and older children. The women were in religious dress, the men in what I thought of as diamond district uniform: the black baggy suits, the black felt hats. The children were miniature versions of the parents, with the exception of boys under three, who wore their long locks in ponytails. The children looked less robust than my daughters' classmates in Nayot. Something seemed lacking in their daily regimens, maybe sunshine, or exercise.

I found a plaque that read Michlelet Bruria on a narrow apartment building at 19 Ben Zion Street. On the first floor I found Bruria's nursery, smelling of babies and their diapers. Little ones crawled around, others slept in strollers. This boded well. A women's institution that provided child care recognized that without it, many of its students would be unable to study. "Cute babies," I said to one of the mothers. The mother responded *barukh hashem,* which literally means "praise God." Was I reading too much into her intonation? It seemed as if my comment had taken her aback, as if saying something nice about babies was tantamount to casting an evil eye.

Waiting to be noticed and directed to an office, I read the announcements on the wall: "Shiatsu massage by woman for women. Headache/menstrual tension relief in seconds. See Gittel or leave message here," "Free apartment offer. If you're a 'graduate,' you've learned all you have to know to keep a Torah home and raise mentshlach children. This is your chance to realize your studies. You can practice what you've learned on my 2½-year-old triplets and have fun doing it and get a free apartment. Call Devora." The massage interested me enough to jot down Gittel's number, but the apartment offer caused me some concern. Besides this Devora, who seemed so desperate for another pair of hands, did all Bruria students feel that the realization of their studies was to be a nanny or a mommy? Where were the lawyers and psychiatrists I'd heard so much about?

No one asked me who I was or what I was doing there. They were probably used to the sight of yearning Jewish souls wandering through their halls. I snooped around until I found an office on the third floor. It was a standard shabby Israeli office, cold and damp. Simple wooden chairs and tables, schedules on the wall, and the following poster: "Build people to build a new world. Rabbi Chaim Brovender. Rabbi Shlomo Riskin. Two dynamic leaders, two dynamic institutions, now they're one." I had heard of both men. Rabbi Brovender, a rabbi from New York's Yeshiva University, had made a name for himself as a leader in Israel in the education of *baalei teshuvah,* those who have returned or have come late to observant Judaism. His devotees were, for the most part, college-educated English speakers. Rabbi Riskin had been the charismatic leader of New York's modern Orthodox Lincoln Square Synagogue. He, along with a number of his former congregants, had moved to Israel, settled in Efrat (just outside Jerusalem), and established a number of institutions for Jewish learning.

I saw no women pictured on this poster, just men, learning alone or in groups.

A secretary told me to sit on the chair next to her desk until the administrator could meet with me. I watched the younger Bruria students, American girls recently out of high school, checking anxiously in the office for mail from home. Most were nineteen or so. Many had deep brown daughter of Israel eyes. They wore cute dangling earrings they had picked up from the nighttime vendors off Zion Square. They dressed in modest long skirts and sweaters brought from home. The rest of the students seemed to be married women—I could tell this by the scarves, laced with silvery threads, that they wore. Compared to the American students, the colors of their clothes were not as sharp, their shoes more scuffed. Many of these young married women—so young—were handing babies back and forth. I admired their ambitious effort to populate the State of Israel with Jews, to undo the Nazi killings literally and symbolically, but I couldn't help wondering about the extent of personal sacrifice they would make in order to raise and feed families that would grow to eight or ten. These fecund young women were worlds away from my usual crowd of professional women friends in their late thirties who made the rounds of the infertility clinics.

"Two children are challenge enough to me," I said to one Bruria student, whom I later met at our pediatrician's waiting room, where she sat with her sons, aged one, two, and four. She responded with a story. There was a religious woman who had three babies as closely together as was biologically possible. The woman was twenty-two.

She hated being a mother. She couldn't handle her children and was hospitalized for a nervous breakdown. Her husband brought the situation before the rabbi of their community. Would it be possible for them to use birth control? The rabbi consented. Birth control for three years, he decreed. At the end of the three years, the couple stopped using birth control. The woman conceived immediately. She gave birth to triplets.

"What's the moral of the story?" I asked the Bruria student.

"While our rabbis do their best to interpret the will of God in accordance with our personal situations," she replied, "God lets us know when an interpretation has gone against his will."

A woman wearing a beret, possibly the Bruria administrator, passed her baby off to a second secretary and told her, "You don't notice the crying as much when it's your fourth." She appeared to be in her late twenties. "Sweet baby," I said.

Barukh hashem, she said.

Still in my chair, I overheard the conversation the administrator was having on the other side of her partition, aware that if I was ever called over to the partition, whatever I revealed would become public knowledge. I speculated: Was the lack of privacy intentional, calculated to teach that the details of one's life, which seem so personally dramatic and revealing, are inconsequential in the great scheme of things? Was the only significant drama of one's life—my life—the movement of my soul and mind to Torah?

"What made you want to convert?" I heard the administrator ask her interlocutor. "Did you have a Jewish boyfriend?" The prospective student was German. She had already begun studying Hebrew, Torah, and prayer on a kibbutz study program. I was impressed by the commitment and preparation revealed by her answers. The administrator seemed not to be. She said study at Bruria didn't look likely. The program had already started, they didn't like part-time students, they took only one convert at a time, and that slot was already filled. For goodness' sake, I wanted to call over, admit her in the school! It's hard enough for me, an American Jew, to show up at a yeshiva. Imagine what it's like for a German Christian. Have some sympathy! The German was getting it from both sides—the traditional show of resistance to conversion plus the typical Israeli scenario (always say no first to show you're in charge, and only, only if they put up enough fuss, relent). The German said nothing. I imagined she was shocked to have been turned down. Then to her credit, the administrator relented, before the German woman even needed to plead for herself. She drew up a schedule for the woman: some Bible, law ("That will be especially important for you"), and Rambam. "You can start January 25, and we'll see how it goes."

Next, a woman who looked like a high school girl came into the office and found that her class was canceled. "I'll teach you something," said a second secretary. "What do you want to learn? Prayer?" They went off to learn. Then I was called in by the administrator and took a seat across from her desk.

"What is your background?"

I assumed she wasn't after my life story but a single word that would neatly define me.

"Conservative Judaism."

My answer was sufficient. Good. She didn't press for facts or nuances. Had she asked, I could have told her I grew up in two Jewish environments. There was the world of my grandparents' house, not a mythical world to me but a very real one, because my mother and I lived in her parents' home for a few years after her divorce from my father and before her second marriage. My mother, in her mid-twenties then, was restored to her old bedroom and childhood status; her family had considered her to be incompetent, and her divorce seemed to confirm this. I was made an honorary youngest sibling of my aunt and uncles, who were still living at home and going to school. It was an Orthodox home. Life revolved around my grandfather. Mornings he prayed quietly in the living room, wrapped in his tallit, a most calm and loving sight. He always interrupted his prayers to shower blessings on my head as I ran by, chased by my grandmother, who was bent on giving me a thorough washing after I had messily eaten her half-cooked eggs. At night, we rushed through dinner or ate late to accommodate my grandfather's going to synagogue to pray again.

Everything about the household had a Jewish focus. All special foods were for the Sabbath and holidays, all new clothes were for synagogue, company meant people from synagogue were coming over for a kiddush, wine and refreshments after services. Even though my uncles were sent to a religious high school and then to Yeshiva University, I never thought of my grandparents' house as a house of Jewish learning. My grandfather's piety was the piety of a simple man; Torah learning was the luxury he labored to provide for his sons.

My mother was miserable in this Orthodox world in which she had grown up and to which she had now returned. She found the strictness joyless and repressive, a religion of don'ts. She wanted to listen to the radio and paint on the Sabbath and not sit in the shadows reading the Jewish newspapers in New Jersey, waiting for sundown to liberate her from boredom and dreariness. She wanted to eat Moo Goo Gai Pan and veal marsala—anything but vegetable cutlets served by impudent waiters at the kosher dairy restaurants. Both times my mother married, it was pointedly to men who were not Orthodox. She must have thought that her parents wouldn't blame her for complying with her husband's more lax observance. A good wife followed her husband.

When my mother remarried, my extended family took pity on me, the child of the renegade, for having been dropped, once again, into my second world, the world of ersatz, watered-down Conservative Judaism. I don't believe my mother embraced Conservative Judaism because she preferred or even knew much about Conservative ideology. It was simply as far as she could go to escape from Orthodoxy without breaking her parents' hearts and without completely losing face in the family. Reform Judaism was out of the question. To her, that was a sham. It was the religion for Jews who yearned to have been born Protestant, the religion for Jews who were ignorant and were happier that way.

But I thought I had pulled a lucky straw. I was saved from the fate of yeshiva, from teachers who gave hours of homework in Hebrew after a day in second grade that didn't end until 4:30. I was sent to public school, where I learned to sing the harmony to "Jingle Bells." I got to go to an enormous Long Island synagogue where I sang in the choir and led the junior congregation. After Saturday services, we either drove to Sloan's Furniture Outlet to look at lamps or tried to peddle my mother's paintings at New York galleries. I had to wait only an hour between eating meat and milk, whereas my cousins had to wait six hours. If we went out for Chinese food, all the rules went out the window. In my heart, I knew our observances were cockeyed. Still, for a child, they were tons more fun than the strict stuff my cousins were stuck with. I was glad to be part of my mother's rebellion. It was freer, modern, American, and, with our outings to galleries and other artists' studios, as bohemian as possible in the suburbs. I had Christian friends, I acted in school plays on Friday nights. But the laxness whetted my appetite for more religious consistency as an adult.

The Bruria administrator now asked me, "How observant are you?"

"I don't observe all laws strictly." (I gathered this would not exclude me as a Bruria student, but rather offer hope that they could help me mend my ways.)

"Are you married?"

"Yes."

"How old are your children?"

"Eight and four." (Married and a mother. Excellent answers, both indicating I was the conventional good Jewish woman.)

"Where do the children go to school?"

"Secular Israeli schools." (Bad answer, possibly unforgivable.)

"What brought you here?"

"My friend Esther said that this was an intellectual school."

"Why did you decide Bruria was the right place?"

I didn't know that it was.

She filled me in. Rabbi Brovender had created Bruria so women could learn Torah. How each woman went about this depended upon her individual situation: "Every soul will find the most comfortable way to learn."

Later I nervously telephoned Rabbi Brovender. This was Esther's suggestion. She had said that if I wanted to know the soul of Bruria, I should speak to its founder. I was afraid he would dismiss me. "I know you're busy," I babbled, "I'll keep you only a minute." He said it would be a shame not to keep him for as long as necessary.

I asked Rabbi Brovender if it was true that he was the first to enable Orthodox women to study Talmud. He answered:

It was not early for me. It was just when I was able to do it. I didn't see a school for women as particularly revolutionary. I think you should teach women just as you teach men. You don't need a new curriculum. I had left Shappel's and was establishing another institution for men. When the women who had come to study with me at my previous school discovered I was no longer active, they asked me to open a women's school. I felt I couldn't do it, I had no economical base. But they kept annoying me. So we reached an arrangement which I thought would excuse me from setting up a school. I told them if they could find a place to learn and to live and make arrangements for food, I'd arrange the teaching. They found it. So Bruria was established by these seven women, college graduates, first in an apartment in Rehavia. Once the school existed, others joined them.

Why had they come to you?

They knew I would be willing to let them study, to open the books to wherever they wanted. They could study Talmud, whatever struck their interest. It was a very outrageous thing to do. There's been a swing to the right on all fronts, particularly to limit women's education. I'm not so interested in every fight, but certain issues have merited my taking a stand; enabling women to learn what they wish is one. Because I took this position on women's education, I was considered to be a little outside of the right-wing community.

I asked if Bruria was identical to Yeshivat Hamivtar, his men's school. I assumed he'd say it was, that equal opportunity had hit the world of Torah.

"It certainly doesn't compare," he answered, and continued:

Whether he likes it or not, a man is pushed by peer pressure to study Talmud. Many men suffer studying Talmud. Because they're not always capable. Talmud is not always the best way to educate oneself to be in a Jewish community. A man who doesn't like studying Talmud, nevertheless, understands that's what he has to do, in order to keep himself involved.

For women, there is no peer pressure. She can face her reactions. Does she like Talmud, does she want to learn it? [He added that women who feel under pressure to "get going"—by which he meant start a career, get married, and have babies— are not interested in sitting in a yeshiva for ten years to become well versed in Talmud.] Men don't have the opportunity to ask those questions. Men are constrained. Women can innovate. At Bruria, all opportunities are available.

In religious circles, women are not taken seriously. To be taken seriously, you need a certain kind of knowledge—Talmud—and connectedness to tradition. Most women have no framework to amass that knowledge. Finding ways to study with great rabbis of their generation is generally impossible. For instance, while Rabbi Soloveitchik in Boston taught his own daughters, no other women could study with him on an ongoing basis. Women could call him on the phone, but there was no framework for regular study.

But *because* women are not taken seriously, they can do creative things. I'd like women with backgrounds in music, art, and literature to establish an integrative position between their competence in these fields and Torah in order to create new Torah enterprises. It's an idea I'd like to develop, it's the next stage. Many *baalei teshuvah* [those who have turned to religious life] in yeshivot attempt to convince themselves that anything they knew before they came to the yeshiva was worthless. It's a position I find unfortunate and trivial. They try to imitate people in the religious community who do not have university backgrounds. They squash their own creative thinking. Women have an advantage, because they're not under pressure to think like seventeenth-century rabbis.

Will there be a coterie of women who will devote enough time to learning that their results will be perceived as serious? Some exceptional women have gone through Bruria, but they have had a hard time organizing structures to make an impact. Even though many women who've come recently have liberal backgrounds, they're conservative about their personal goals in Torah. They're not interested in new Torah goals; they come for a year and go.

The truth is, I do other things as well as Bruria. There's a limitation on my ability to carry out my thoughts in women's education. At Bruria, I'm like the old man who once started it. What's missing now is the next generation of leadership. I did what I did, and the truth is, it's not enough. Now there's the need for someone to come up with a new opportunity. Things are good, but not good enough. Whatever blessing can come from women's education has not come yet. There has got to be a greater contribution from women than has gone on for the last twenty years. Women's education has to do with creativity, sensitivity. Women aren't constrained by studying legalisms. If they want to be, that's fine, but they can study other things. The test is not if women can learn like men, but if men will say, "I wish we could learn like women."

I didn't think I would ever hear those words.

Three

The administrator showed me Bruria's spring schedule. For advanced students, a typical Wednesday could start at 8:00 A.M. with morning prayers. From 8:30 to 9:30 students studied the teachings of the Hasidic master Rabbi Nahman of Bratslav, with Rabbi Brovender. From 9:30 to 11:00 students went down to the *bet midrash*, the study hall, and prepared in pairs, called *hevruta*, for their Talmud class, which met from 11:00 to 12:30. She said the advanced students, mostly married women, were studying more Bible than Talmud this year. Since they had less time for studying than men did, and given the many hours and years Talmud study required, a great deal of Talmud study didn't make sense. Most women, she said, seemed to prefer Bible study, because it was immediately inspiring and directly connected to their lives. Nonetheless, some women felt their children provided enough immediate gratification so that they didn't need it from their studies: "That woman will learn

Talmud and law without budging. She wants the whole picture, the intellectual stimulation."

Lunch, then back for Jewish thought from 2:00 to 3:00, *hevruta* from 3:30 to 5:00 to prepare for later classes, a quick pause for *minhah,* the afternoon prayers, then law from 5:00 to 6:30. Dinner next, followed by a class from 8:00 to 10:00 called Women in the Bible. A grueling day, by any account. If I had any thoughts of full-time study, this schedule ended them. Women with children— wherever they got their gratification—obviously popped in just for part of the day.

I asked to audit a class in the Book of First Samuel and was pointed down the hall. The teacher was sitting at a little table in front of the room with her arms crossed across her chest. Four students spaced themselves around the desks that went along three walls. The teacher wore a fringed head scarf, a gray sweatshirt, a long skirt, stockings, and blue sneakers. On her table was a backpack, a bag of tissues, and a Bible. She didn't use notes. She read the Hebrew text aloud, and though the students had English translations, she provided her own translation. She dwelled on Samuel 1:15, in which Samuel tells Saul how God wants him to punish the Amalekites for their savage assaults against the Israelites. "Now go, attack Amalek, and utterly destroy all that belongs to them. Spare no one, but kill alike men and women, infants and sucklings, oxen and sheep, camels and asses." Saul doesn't carry this out quite right. He does kill the Amalekites, but he captures King Agag of Amalek alive and spares the best sheep, the oxen, the second-born, lambs, and all other valuables. This failure to heed God's instructions precisely angers God and costs Saul the kingship.

The teacher said:

"I'll explain in a minute what this means. For now, imagine the magnitude of the test God has given Saul. Yet Saul doesn't say to God, "I can't." This most merciful God is telling Saul to destroy babies. How can we resolve this? Imagine a baby in a cradle, a beautiful 1889 European-style cradle. And God tells you to destroy the baby because it will be Hitler. A human being standing over the cradle can't see that. We can only think of kindness and cruelty by its immediate effects. We can't see beyond our metaphysical present. Only God knows the baby will become Hitler.

How confident this teacher is that she knows God, how surely she knows what God knows. I thought to raise my hand and ask her if she could kill any baby if God told her to, and how would she do it. A knife, a gun, a pillow to smother it and muffle its cries? I want to ask how *she* could ever be so certain she had heard God right—that she had heard the word *kill,* that she was sure she was getting the right baby. And what if it were her own? I held my tongue. It is not for auditors to be pesky-mouthed. I kept thinking about how I didn't even trust my visual perceptions—that I could admire a coleus plant for its robustness for weeks before noticing that it was crawling with aphids. Could I speak with such authority about anything, let alone the will of God? What were students supposed to derive from this lesson? That we, too, were supposed to tune in to the voice of God and do what we heard?

Concluding, the teacher asked us to return to the text and look at the verse in which Saul counts his troops (310,000 strong) as they muster in Telaim before going out to destroy the Amalekites. She asked us why Saul didn't count the children of Israel by looking directly at them, but rather counted them indirectly, by counting some object that stood for each person, like his sheep. From my reading of the text, it seemed as if the troops were being counted in the regular fashion. But the teacher turned to commentary on the verse by Rabbi Shlomo Yitzhaki of the eleventh century, the foremost biblical commentator, known by the acronym Rashi, playing on the double meaning of the word *telaim,* which can signify both a place-name and the word *lambs.* Rashi comments: "Saul told his men to take a lamb from the flock of the king and then he counted the lambs, because it is forbidden to count Israelites, as it is said of them in Genesis, 'You shall not number them as a multitude.' "

The teacher made sense of this for us: "When you count a person directly, you take him out of the crowd and he loses his protection, the protective merit of being part of a community. How do we count people? By objects they donate, by how many chairs are used, how many pens on the desks. Or by using a verse you know to have ten words. You say it, keeping track of how many times you've repeated it." Curious to see how this was done, I counted the first ten people I saw on my way to the bus stop, using the ten-word blessing over bread, the *motzi*.

I continued to dwell on the lesson I had learned at Bruria about counting, sharing it with my friend the Israeli painter Rita Mendes-Flohr. We were sitting in my kitchen drinking cans of bubbling cider, as her children, Inbal and Itamar, chased my girls around our lemon tree. While I did not think I would fit in as a Bruria student, I had to tell Rita how taken I was by the prohibition I had learned there against counting people directly. Here was insightful psychology imbedded in Torah. Even though we're always saying that people like the limelight and to stand out from the crowd and be one of a kind, I think most people want desperately not to stick out. I know my daughter Juliana yearned to stop looking like "the new girl from America" at school and started wearing her ponytail up higher, thinking that might do the trick. For me, hearing my own name called out in grade school when I didn't expect it made me jump. It embarrassed me, making me feel as though I were caught in a wrongful act I was unaware of performing.

Rita, a secular Israeli, stared at me as if I had been put under a spell by yeshiva fundamentalists. She said the taboo against counting people directly reminded *her* of the folk superstitions to keep away the devil practiced in her native Curaçao, where on New Year's Eve,

Jews followed their servants as they carried about a shovel of seven kinds of burning incense to the corners of the household.

How I could even think of posing as a yeshiva girl? Rita, whom I often consulted when making major decisions, could not understand what I was up to. She would stand vigil lest I fall off the deep end. Going to yeshiva was not a normal path in my world, she reminded me. It was as though I had taken to wearing furs or walking on coals. Rita wanted to know how much "falsehood" this demanded of me. Did the yeshiva require me to live according to Jewish law, or believe there was a God, or believe that God gave the Torah to Moses? "When you're at the yeshiva," she asked, "don't you feel that it's a facade, a masquerade, that it's not really you who is there?"

Of course it was a masquerade, but that was the cost of my admission ticket. Just because Bruria was a holy place didn't mean I could enter without telling lies. I would have to accommodate. At Bruria I would keep my mouth clean and try not to let on that I thought there was nothing, nothing so sacred that I couldn't joke about it. I told Rita that *any* community I belonged to required some obscuring of all that I was. What place, what relationship would not burn up without lies?

Rita and I were part of a newly formed group of women academics, artists, and therapists that met each Monday night, essentially to share what was going on in our work and private lives and to offer friendly support. I welcomed the community of like-minded women but felt extremely uncomfortable with the rules this group had developed. I agreed we would benefit from some structure, but the structure the therapists came up with seemed so therapeutic. We were to spend the first minutes "checking in"; we were to spend the last half hour "summing up" or "processing"; we were to hold the contents of the meetings in confidentiality. And the husband of the host was not permitted to be home.

We were playing at group therapy, even though there were other, more natural ways we women could have spoken to each other and, over time, built relationships. I didn't want to be exposed to their emotional underwear. When I listened to stories of their professional insecurities, their cycles of ovulation, the deaths in their families that haunted them, their mothers who didn't understand them, I wanted to flee. Dignified people, I thought, shouldn't pollute the air with whining. These were smart, profound, accomplished women. I didn't want to spend Monday nights facilitating each other's healing. Learning about the aspects of their family lives and the careers they had worked out successfully would have been much more interesting to me. Rita, I reminded her, was the one who encouraged me to stick with the group, despite my inability to deal with this kind of public disclosure of emotion. "Instead of leaving the group," she advised me, "let us know what makes you uncomfortable." Despite the artificiality of our coming together, we in the group were becoming tied to each other, in trust and in friendship. And maybe that would never have happened spontaneously, in the way that relationships create themselves slowly, patch by patch. Despite the artificiality, I was beginning to feel myself at home with all aspects of the women in the group. I counted on them, I wanted to hear their private details, I opened up to them. But only because I had learned to stomach my initial squeamishness, my feeling of being an outsider.

I wondered if I could ever make enough adjustments and compromises to fit into Bruria.

I tried going to Bruria again a few days later. I had yet to see what was special about women studying Torah together. I had yet to see women's Torah creativity flourishing. But what can you know after one day? The secretaries were still giggling together in a single chair. The educational director welcomed me warmly into his office. I told him I was having a hard time. Life at the school felt diffuse to me, sinking almost. If there was intellectual electricity present, I was missing it in the hallway and in the classroom.

He said:

Most women's institutions had been teaching women selected verses, selected texts. Rabbi Brovender's innovation was to found a place to give a woman an opportunity to open all the books. Women are opening up all the books in every other world, and when one is catering to a Western woman, it is not logical that she should be exposed to everything in the Western world and be denied access to the secrets of the Jewish world. There are still highly cultivated Jewish communities that have deprived women; they've said it's taboo for a woman to study Talmud. The father is learned, the brother is learned, the husband is learned—but this woman, who went to the best universities, is an ignoramus on a Jewish level. At Bruria, the emphasis is on textual skills. That's why the Bruria day is broken up, as a traditional yeshiva day is, into research time and lesson time. In another institution, success might be defined by the development of the personality, of the student's ethical attributes. A successful Bruria student can *lern*.

This kind of institution appeals to me, but it didn't seem to describe the institution I was in. He assured me that I had perceived accurately. "Because of internal crisis in the institution [a matter of funding, I gathered], the student body isn't indicative of what it usually is."

I waited in the basement *bet midrash*, the study hall, before sitting in on a Talmud class taught by the educational director. There were sixteen little school tables with as many as four chairs around each table. There were two women studying; soon six others came. Nineteen still seemed the median age. I gathered these were the girls whose parents hoped a year at Bruria would serve as their daughter's amulet against intermarriage. I saw no lawyers or psychologists.

Students checked the shelves of reference books, eyed a bulletin board listing "What's happening at Bruria," and referred to a laminated chart that displayed the appropriate blessings for bread, wine, fruits, vegetables, cakes, cookies, soup, meat, milk, eggs, and cheese.

Between classes, more students came down to gab about where they would be for Sabbath (either up north to Safed for a mystical experience or in town as a guests of strictly observant families in the Har Nof neighborhood), or what they were going to cook if they stayed home (not schnitzel, a pain if you were having a crowd). One student invited another with the words "Why don't you come to me?" as if she were translating her English out of Yiddish. I had never seen a *bet midrash*. This one seemed more like a combination student union/library at a college on an austerity plan than a hall for sacred learning.

When the teacher came down finally for class, three young women filed into the classroom off the study hall. I followed them in. A girl watching them asked, "Are you doing actual Talmud?" She was told, "Yes, the real thing." I wondered if I was in the company of an elite.

The teacher read—really sang—the Talmud passages, his thumb zipping through the air, hand crashing onto the table. He was boyish, spunky. You could imagine him playing pranks as a yeshiva boy. He wanted the text to come alive for his students.

The classroom was ugly. I know that for pious Jews, this world is but a waiting room, a pause before the world to come. For them the accommodations in this world don't really matter. But for me, the world that counts is the one I see and touch. I stared at the storage room off our classroom, with its piles of plastic garbage cans and an institutional mixer. Give me Yale's Sterling Library, the green leather chairs, the stained glass, the gargoyles; even the sparsest seminar room that I had taught in was more conducive to learning.

It was so cold in this basement that I had to sit on my hands. The women looked like Siberians on a ski trip, their knit undershirts and leggings sticking out of their clothes. I know: Jews are supposed to yearn for the opportunity to sit in any house of study and learn sacred text. Jews are supposed to endure any discomfort—frostbite, starvation, imprisonment, torture—for morsels of Torah. When asked why he persisted in teaching Torah even when it was prohibited by Roman authorities, the Talmudic sage Rabbi Akiva is reported to have answered, "The Torah is our life and the length of our days. Though we are in great danger while studying the Torah, we would surely disappear and be no more if we were to give up its study." Concentrate, I said, think of the Russian Jews who would give everything to sit and learn Torah. Hopeless. The thought of starving children never motivated anyone to eat spinach. The cold made my nose run. I wanted to buy a roll of bread at the kiosk and go home to Nayot.

The teacher gave the students the key Aramaic words in the text and began to explicate it, bouncing between English and Hebrew. (I knew enough Hebrew to chat and buy groceries, but not enough to be sure of what they were talking about. Something about bringing out a table or sending it back to the kitchen, spreading and unspreading tablecloths in order to say the Sabbath blessing over wine. Whatever it was, it sounded tedious and picayune.) He then dispatched the women back to the *bet midrash* to work the text out for themselves. And though he had to leave (I believe, to save the school from some crisis), he promised that a rabbi would be around if they needed help. I joined the women at their little table, explaining that I was a prospective student, just listening in.

Two women were falling asleep over their text, either because of uninterest or exhaustion. It was contagious: I was becoming sleepy, too. They tried to get going. "Where do we start from? . . . Where did he go up to? . . . What's the issue? . . . One guy disagrees with another guy . . . So that's it without going into detail? . . . I understand words and sentences, but I don't get it. . . ."

And I was more lost than they.

The third student, more experienced, chided the others for missing earlier classes and then offered to go over the material they had missed.

During a lull in my group, I tuned in to the other women chatting between class. Someone called Hershel had become engaged. Ears perked up. The bearer of this news dropped chunks of bread into her coffee and moved to heavier issues: "Separation in education denotes inequality. Women still aren't taken seriously in a man's world. Women will always have to prove themselves." Then back to Hershel's engagement, a shocker.

My group came back to life, somewhat. The more experienced third woman said, "It's silly that we're studying Talmud at this point." (I think I knew what she meant. There was something about throwing the uninitiated into a Talmud class that was like registering open admissions students in an advanced physics seminar. Sure, they had a right to be there, but they would still find it impossible to catch up without the prerequisite skills.)

The others disagreed. They thought it was a brilliant idea. But they were so tired today, the page seemed to be swimming.

The third woman said, "We need to know more about how to learn it. We're probably focusing on all the wrong things. When you're learning something, you need to have an idea of how that knowledge works."

One of the sleepy women yawned, folded her arms over her books, and dropped her head. I was ready to join her.

After an hour of this preparation, having labored through a handful of verses, we went back into the classroom. The teacher kissed his chalk and held it like a cigarette. "What was the question? Explain the question!"

The students kept their eyes down and turned their pages.

"What's the question, what's the answer? Come on, ladies. Do you understand the process in Gemara or not? The Gemara is a like a *bet midrash*. One guy says this, one guy says that. This is fantastic!" The teacher exploded, throwing his chalk.

The basis of Judaism is people! What people accept becomes Judaism. I can stand up and say, "I'm making a law for all generations that men will wear hats." But if people don't accept it, it will have no bearing. It's the people who decide this will be a law for all generations. Are you with me? Go back to the text! You people are not reading the text! The text tells you. This is not good, people, not good, not good, not good.

The sleepiest student mumbled something right.

"Yes! Yes! I've got my job back! A disagreement between Rabbi Yehuda and Rabbi Yose. I want to know, according to whom does the law go?"

No one knew.

The educational director had said to me there were two Brurias, Bruria the ideal and Bruria the reality. From Esther's description and from Rabbi Brovender's, I'm sure the ideal and the reality were once coterminous. A gifted student in my writing class at Hebrew University who was about to study comparative literature at Princeton next year said that when she had studied at Bruria, learning in the highest level Talmud class, "I felt I was part of a new era, a pioneer, doing something important. However I rebel against Judaism, I never rebel against learning. It gives meaning to my life."

I wish I had been at this Bruria during its enchanted time. Now, Bruria struck me as in need of rescue. I had only a short time to learn; I couldn't wait for Bruria's rehabilitation.

Still, the very next week I was back on the bus to Kiryat Moshe, returning, if only to meet some of the other Bruria teachers whom Esther had so glowingly described. Why was I doing this? No one was even there. It must have been intersession. I hadn't thought to check. Yet I had an intuition that I had returned to Bruria for a reason, that it would be a mistake to turn around and go right back home. I stood at the front door. It began to rain, but I continued to stand there. Eventually I asked myself: Well, dear, what precisely are you waiting for? Do you really believe that God has plans for our lives and that they are revealed in curious ways? I wasn't sure

I did or did not, but since it was raining, I left. I could test out free will versus divine plan on a sunny day.

Just as I was walking out, a pretty American in her late forties who reminded me of Colleen Dewhurst drove up in a old black VW.

I motioned for her to roll down her window. "I think classes are canceled." (Was this the divine plan, for me to pass on this message and save her from getting wet? A sign on the door could have done the trick. Not much pizzazz in my prophetic debut. No burning bush, no whale's stomach, no lion's den.) I asked her for a lift to my bus—instant divine reward. Sitting next to her in the car, I saw that she wore an attractive long black puffy wig, wide movie star amber-tinted shades, and a blue down ski jacket. I assumed she was a *baalat teshuvah* who had become religious but was still partially stuck, by sentimental choice or by habit, in her old body. I told her I was a writer, about to study Torah. She said her name was Sara now—it had been Sherry. She had once been an engineer in Portland, Oregon, but now she invested her time planning communities based on Torah values. I didn't ask what that meant. I feared it was the project of someone who believed strict religious observance would answer not only all the problems in her life, but in everyone else's, too. She said maybe she could help me with my Torah study and I could help her write up her ideas about Torah communities. If I liked, she said, we could go around the corner to Angel's bakery, buy the newest food in Israel, American-style chocolate chip muffins, and spend the morning together. Supposing there was further divine purpose behind this encounter, I decided to stick it out to discover what it was. The rain stopped.

Our muffins bought, we drove past the industrial district of Givat Shaul and on to Har Nof (meaning mountain view), a new religious neighborhood, ledged between sky and stone and seemingly suspended on the edge of a mountain. I could see for miles from Sara's living room window. Through the gloom and mist I could still make out the hills and settlements and cemeteries around Jerusalem. It was impossible to pass this view without feeling wonder.

Sara apologized for the state of her apartment: it was already Thursday and not yet ready for the Sabbath. To me it was as spotless as a pharmacy. A tsimmis of carrots and sweet potatoes was simmering in a crock pot next to a cookbook, *The Spice and Spirit of Kosher-Jewish Cooking,* put out by the Junior Division of the Lubavich Women's Organization. The shelves in the living room held the basic beginner's library of sacred books, all in English translation, an indication of the newness of her switch to holiness. There was space for only a little frivolity in this apartment: an answering machine (the only equipment she said she needed for her fledgling real estate business in apartment sales to recent returnees to Judaism) and a vase of last Sabbath's flowers, more or less dead.

While Sara checked her messages, I heard someone coming in from the elevator. Her husband, she said. I expected a man in his fifties, awkward in his dark pants, a white shirt, some religious headgear—someone who had switched his life around as she had. I was right about the costume and the awkwardness, but the scraggly bearded man who came in was much younger than she. Like a ring bearer at a royal wedding, he carried an enormous blue velvet prayer shawl case edged in silver cord and a smaller case for his tefillin (phylacteries). I had heard that the religious community proposed curious matches.

He looked me over and then spoke to me, looking directly into my eyes. Now I was certain that his ultraobservance was new. Had he been ultraobservant from birth, he would have averted his glance out of habit. He was so thin and gentle, like a yogi. That I could not pin him or her down made me uncomfortable. I jabbered on about their extraordinary view: "I've read that people who feel physically oppressed by the lack of sunshine are physiologically incapable of mustering up good cheer on a bad day."

"The word sun stands for *hesed,* God's mercy," said the husband, in a reedy voice, "and the gloom represents *din,* the weight of God's law. That's why you feel heaviness on a gloomy day."

He asked Sara if he should fast or have breakfast. I couldn't understand why he was asking his wife for advice on this matter; she seemed hardly an expert on ritual. I said I hadn't known today was an optional fast day. He explained, "For a certain period, on Mondays and Thursdays, we fast, the purpose being *letaken,* to mend, the world." He pointed to the world outside his window and surveyed the brokenness. Brokenness for me meant today's news, the report of more stonings and tire burnings, more IDF soldiers shooting at Palestinians to squelch a riot. Surely we needed mending, and the government seemed to be making no progress toward that end. But what would his fasting do? For him, brokenness was a metaphysical state. He held that the uprising in the territories had come about as punishment for lax Sabbath observance. "Also because there are so many nonobservant people in the government," Sara added.

She pulled me away from the view and into her kitchen. I asked to wash. Why, she wanted to know? Didn't I know muffins were not made with yeast, making ritual washing unnecessary? I held up my dirty hands. But don't say the blessing, she said. Right.

We sat at a little brown card table. Between us, tacked on the wall, was a picture of a Hasidic rebbe, cut out of a flier. Sara told me:

> The highest level a man can attain to is the study of Torah. This is not the woman's role. A woman's job is to represent the force of balance. My personal goal is to bring people closer to God and to learn to master myself. When I feel anger, I know it is a test from God. If God loves you, he puts you through experiences to wake you up, to show you you're not who you think you are. If you can stay with the experience of your pain, you'll see the truth is that God energizes us and provides us with experiences.

I asked for an example of how Sara worked on her anger, knowing that I couldn't take her seriously until she stopped speaking like those Bible people who trap you at your front door. "What if my husband is angry with me because I forgot to do something?" she continued. "My natural inclination would be to scream back: I'm right and he's wrong. The humble thing to do is to think, maybe he's right. God is sending your husband to you as a messenger who gives you an opportunity to see that part of yourself needs to be changed."

I wondered if Sara preferred this approach because it allowed her to avoid working through her relationship with her husband. She simply assumes her husband is always right, giving him the upper hand. This could make for a harmonious marriage; it could also eventually hit her in the face.

"Don't you ever find yourself in the role of God's messenger?" I asked her. "Don't you get a turn to point out your husband's flaws to him?"

"I try not to be too critical. Never argue. Especially women. Always back up."

I pressed her. If there was any divine purpose in my being here, it was not going to be revealed if I continued to patronize her by nodding along. I saw two options: Either she had been planted to show me that the Jewish life she had chosen was true and right; or I had been planted to say: Wake up, sister, God didn't intend for you to live this way. What makes you so sure you know what God wants from you? Doesn't all the certainty rushing through your veins make you nervous?

I asked her: "What if you were convinced you were right and your husband was wrong? Say you had spent the day cooking for a sick friend with a large family—she had asked for your help—and your husband blows up because in all your cooking, you neglected to pick up his shirt at the dry cleaners?"

"He would have a point. Perhaps I was overdoing it. The goal is to live with God as a father. He wants to correct you as a parent would so you'll be perfect. It's hard! A person doesn't want to change."

Her engineering was a thing of the past. She gave it up, deciding "all careers for women were illusory." She hoped her new business venture would bring in money without taking up much time. She had more important things to do: "performing mitzvot (the commandments), engaging in "a very spiritually oriented study—learning the Torah portion of the week, but mostly studying books of ethics that tell what human beings should be. God plants opportunities for us to do good. You know that when someone asks you to do good out of the blue."

Like what?

"I was asked by a neighbor to drive a handicapped child to the hospital. The child came from a poor family. Her mother was a widow. Then the family happened to move into my neighborhood. I knew God had given them to me as my project. When we bought new bedroom furniture, we gave our dresser to the family. This was divine providence. God opened up an opportunity for me to help them."

She hinted to me that our meeting this morning also fell into the category of divine providence. "When you relinquish control, you give yourself up to divine coincidence, which is particularly prevalent in Jerusalem." I couldn't disagree with that.

Sara spun on: the world is full of veils, God constricts his light.

"I don't feel I know you at all," I said. Her wig bothered me: I needed to see her real hair, anything that revealed something of her private self. Especially a complaint, a misgiving, a hesitation that would convince me her kind of faith could coexist with reality. Perhaps she was exaggeratedly strident in her conviction because she still needed to convince herself and not because she wanted to convince me at all. "Can't you tell me about *you?*"

Only if I promised not to use her name if I wrote about her. I promised, and her voice changed. It was as if the missionary had walked out the door. This seemed dangerous to her, to speak in her former voice, to let who she was in the past, Sherry, leak out.

She came from St. Louis, her mother a lapsed Jew, her father a lapsed Methodist. No formal religion was taught or celebrated in the house. Their religion was science and community service from early on. As an adult, she set out on a spiritual quest: Buddhism, Hinduism, Zen, Yoga, TM. At one human-potential movement seminar in Portland she said to herself: This doesn't seem right. I wasn't in my body. My consciousness was in the mountains. The more I got into these things, the more I felt it wasn't right for a Jewish soul. At the seminar, she met the student from Santa Cruz who would one day be her husband. They would make their spiritual journey back into Judaism together. They taught themselves Jewish meditation. They read the stories of the Hasidic masters. She was living alone then, in a condo with a pool and health club. She began to light candles and keep the Sabbath. She traveled to Jerusalem, going through the various schools for new recruits, studying with a rebbetzen (a rabbi's wife), whom she called "a powerful high soul."

"I knew to be religious you needed to be married. So rather than meeting a man through going on *shiddukhim* (arranged meetings) I brought my former spiritual partner here."

She hoped the goal of my Torah study would be, like hers, to bring Jewish women back to a "Torah-true life."

"Who knows?" I said.

Sara saw me to the bus stop and I went down from the heights of Har Nof. The bus carried a load of holy folk, many with the Book of Psalms opened in their laps. Around each bend, someone performed another ethical act: shouting for the bus driver to wait until an old man took his seat, carrying a stroller down the exit stairs for a pregnant mother.

Back downtown, I found myself rushing to perform profane acts: handing in Juliana's school registration form, buying an umbrella, and picking up a barbecued chicken for lunch. Disengagement rituals to bring me back down to the world, to cleanse me of any toxic levels of holiness I might have absorbed during my captivity high above the world that needed repair. I needed to shake off Sara's world. Too self-effacing, too anti-feminist.

Nonetheless, there was something curiously seductive about it.

The cultural form her spirituality took may not have appealed to me, but there it was all the same. She worked nonstop at perfecting herself, developing her spirituality, and achieving sanctity in her every activity. It was admirable. For all her self-imposed shackling, Sara was not fully bound to this world. That it appealed at all to me was unnerving.

Four

When I lived in Hamilton, I befriended a man who had just emi-
grated from Russia, a talented translator, linguist, and science fiction
writer. He and his family were staying with friends until they could
get their lives in order. On the day I came to take his wife to buy
oatmeal at our health food store, I found the man building a cabinet.
"You do cabinetry, too?" I said. "Were you trained to do this in the
Soviet Union, did you study woodworking?"

He said, "You Americans. You want to learn something and you
think you have to take a course. There are other ways of learning.
You watch others. You figure things out for yourself. I've been
looking at cabinets my whole life, and now I'm making one."

Esther had been telling me that some of my most important Torah
learning would come to me through individuals. I heard her, but
didn't catch her point, for the kind of soul-to-soul transfusion of
knowledge she had in mind was not a model of learning with which
I was familiar. The Russian was right. I wanted to learn Torah, so

I thought I needed to find a class. Having decided that Bruria, in its present state, was not the right school for me, I forged ahead, trying out another school that catered to English-speaking students. This was the Pardes Institute of Jewish Studies, which I had heard about from a former Colgate student of mine who had studied there. (The word *pardes* means orchard and is also a name for paradise. As an exegetical term, it is a mnemonic for the levels of interpretation of scripture: *peshat* [literal meaning], *remez* [symbolic or hinted meaning], *derash* [allegorical meaning], and *sod* [mystical or esoteric meaning.]) My student had billed Pardes as a serious place, hard to get into, populated mostly by recent college graduates from America, who were genuine, nice, smart, sincere in their religious search, and emotionally stable. Pardes welcomed older students as well: educators, doctors, lawyers, college professors on sabbatical, journalists. One student, whose impulse for coming to Pardes seemed typical, told me, "I came to Pardes feeling spiritually and intellectually torn, realizing I had to approach Jewish texts in a rationalistic frame of reference, but they had to be meaningful to me spiritually."

Learning at Pardes, being educated spiritually and intellectually, took time. Students put in long hours, from eight in the morning until nine at night. In addition, they were required to volunteer for community service projects, such as tutoring new immigrants or caring for the elderly. Many students also worked studiously and self-consciously at becoming more traditionally observant, modeling themselves on their observant teachers or their teachers' wives. But no coercion here. Being observant was just more in the spirit of the place. A student explained, "At Pardes you're not forced to pray, but you wouldn't feel comfortable going through the whole year without asking yourself: What does it mean to pray? What does it mean that I can't do it when Jews have done it all these years?"

When Pardes students prayed, a low white ribbon of cloth painted with a rainbow emerging out of the Old City was drawn exactly midway down their *bet midrash*. Half for men, half for women. Men led the praying, but women sang along wholeheartedly. That was the only visible separation of the sexes at Pardes: Otherwise it was co-ed.

My former student had since switched to a more strictly observant, unisex yeshiva. "Co-ed learning is terrible," he said.

> There's all this tension, people trying to be tough and serious, and at the same time, suave and pretty and sexy. I think some girls at Pardes tried to make themselves ugly so as not to be thought of as flirty girls. We would joke, "You shouldn't look up when you study Torah." Did we look up! There was a lot of flirting going on; a lot of marriages, too. At first I thought single-sex learning was so abnormal. But I prefer the men's yeshiva now. It's like going to the office. It's relaxed, you know what you're there to do, and you do it. You have to have the desire to commit yourself to a monastic community.

Being coeducational made Pardes most untraditional as a yeshiva, "unkosher" in the eyes of some. Esther never mentioned Pardes to me, although I believe she knew I would gravitate toward Pardes on my own and, in important ways, fit in.

Physical separation of the sexes, in study, in prayer and in large chunks of life, is legislated in several Jewish sources. Semimonastic lives are thereby possible for Jews without having to build monasteries or cut back on baby production. One law referred to as *kol ishah* (a woman's voice), means a man is forbidden to listen to a woman sing (unless it's his wife), for her voice may excite him erotically. Women, in turn, are not supposed to sing in the presence of men, in order to prevent them from transgressing. Ideally the silence should be continuous, but it's particularly important to hush when men are directing their attention to holiness, through prayer or Torah study. The rabbis elaborate on the law. A man can listen to his own wife's singing provided he's not trying to pray and provided it isn't during the time of her menstruation or her approximately seven additional "clean" days, that is, days in which there is no bloody discharge. Girls who are over eleven should not sing too loudly in school, lest men walking by hear them. Women can listen to men sing, not just their husbands, and can do so while praying or studying Torah.

I first saw *kol ishah* in action some years ago when I visited ultraobservant relatives on a festival and went with an uncle to synagogue. As always, all the other women in the family had stayed home to fix lunch or mind babies. My uncle deposited me and my daughters in the women's section. I heard the worshipers singing a beautiful prayer whose rousing melody I knew well. Eager to teach my daughters this prayer and moved to add my own voice to the powerful communal petition, I sang a little more robustly than my normal whisper. I wondered why the young girls sitting near by were all staring at me. Because I was from out of town? Because the collar on my dress wasn't high enough? Perhaps these girls thought the sound of my voice or the way I pronounced the Hebrew words was strange.

Several verses along, I noticed how very clearly I could hear my own voice, as though I were the only woman in the entire synagogue singing. I looked around me. I was. All the other women were moving their lips, but no sounds came out. Like actresses in a silent movie. I had never seen anything like this. In other Orthodox synagogues I had been in, women did not lead the prayers, but they certainly prayed aloud, often with enthusiasm. Unlike the women of generations past, women now are trained to pray in Hebrew, the sacred language. I thought the days when women had to limit their prayers to empathetic weeping were over.

I did know that women who chose to pray silently or to offer private, heartfelt supplications that are unbounded by the standard liturgy followed a long, respected tradition. Some consider the prayer of Hannah, mother of Samuel in First Samuel 1:10–13 to be the ideal model for a Jewish woman's prayer. Hannah, whose childlessness caused her immense suffering, went to the Temple and uttered an extraordinary prayer. Weeping, she vowed that if given a son, she would dedicate him to serve God in the Temple. The text tells us that she prayed in her heart; only her lips moved. The priest Eli saw Hannah and took her for a drunk, accusing her of making a spectacle of herself and admonishing her, "Sober up!" Hannah corrected Eli, he echoed her prayer, and within a year, Samuel was born.

But a tradition of woman's public, vocal prayer exists, too, and that is the tradition I feel more comfortable with. There is the prayer of Miriam, sister of Moses and Aaron, which she sang to the accompaniment of dance and timbrels, after the Israelites escaped from the Egyptians through the parted sea (Exodus 15:20–21). There is Deborah the judge, who uttered a long and eloquent prayer for deliverance along with Barak, her fellow warrior (Judges 4,5).

I stopped singing midword, embarrassed and angry. As a guest, I wanted to respect the rules of this place, but there were limits. I could comply with separate seating. I could comply with wearing a hat and long sleeves on this hot day. But I could not comply with stifling my praying voice for the sake of the men on the other side. Was it so impossible for them to contain their erotic impulses? Let them pray with earmuffs on; let them take tranquilizers; let them rush out to the bathroom between prayers to douse themselves with cold water. But let me pray aloud.

No one asked me to stop praying aloud. No one asked me to leave. But those disdainful looks . . . I couldn't stay a minute longer. I took my girls back to the house, changed all of us into pants, and hiked down to the nearby state park. There, in the quiet spot I found, I finished singing the prayers: *one* solitary voice in a state park. The joggers who ran by me must have thought I was a drunken woman talking to herself.

There is a second law enforcing the separation of men and women. Called *yihud,* it refers to the prohibition against a man or woman being alone with anyone of the opposite sex other than a spouse, grandparent, parent, child, grandchild, or sibling.

The main purpose of this law is to prevent sexuality outside of marriage. It's not enough just to say "Thou shalt not." The law takes auxiliary preventative measures. Marital fidelity and premarital chastity are protected by preventing the unchaste behavior and forbidden impulses that could be aroused when men and women are together. Even schoolchildren—boys over thirteen and girls over twelve—cannot be alone together. Co-ed learning, it goes without saying, is forbidden.

Then there are laws of modesty. *Kol guf haishah ervah,* says the Rambam: every exposed part of the woman's body is seductive. No kissing, no hugging, no touching anyone of the opposite sex over nine years old other than a spouse, parent, grandparent, child, or grandchild. Some say shaking hands between siblings won't do either. Some say fathers shouldn't kiss daughters over three years old. Some say fathers shouldn't kiss their married daughters. No dancing together at weddings: no cha-cha, no tango, not even a hora. And don't sit next to someone of the opposite sex on a bus.

Many women have experienced rude behavior that followed from these laws. A man on a bus leaps away from you. A nephew ducks away from your kiss at a wedding. You extend your hand to a man in greeting and he recoils. While rabbis say the correct response for men in such situations is to explain the law politely and provide assurances that nothing personal was intended, I have yet to observe this courtesy extended.

Knowing these laws, I can navigate among strictly observant Jews. I keep away from the men. On one level, it's a simple cultural courtesy, like remembering to take your shoes off when visiting in Japan. Any woman who has been annoyed by catcalls can see some positive aspects in these laws. Nothing wrong with protecting the privacy of an individual's physical space. Nothing wrong with the impulse to curb lewd, lascivious behavior. Nothing wrong with providing strict social structures for teenagers so they don't feel pushed into sexual relationships too early. A community abiding by these laws does not need to provide its teenagers with birth control.

But the flip side troubles me. Young people on a steady diet of sexual separation would probably be inept in sexually challenging encounters as adults, unable to respond to sexual impulses other than to squelch them. And how would a young woman who studied and socialized only with other women have an effective career, say, as a lawyer? What would prepare her for meeting privately with male clients or colleagues and for bargaining in judges' chambers? She would have none of the skills of restraint we develop for getting along with and enjoying friends and co-workers of the opposite sex.

I asked several observant Jewish men, graduates of American yeshivot, why they thought the sexes sat separately in prayer. Their responses indicated to me that separation of the sexes is enforced not only by law, but also by superstitions so dearly held as to have acquired the force of law. Most of the men said the main reason for separation was *niddah* (the menstruant), the set of laws concerning the period of uncleanness of a menstruating woman. By law, a woman who is a *niddah* must refrain from intimate contact only with her husband. Her "impurity" cannot be communicated to anyone else. Moreover, according to Rachel Biale, author of *Women and Jewish Law,* though in certain communities women refrained from going to synagogue during their period of *niddut,* "the laws of *niddah* proper do not exclude a woman from attending synagogue since it is of no consequence if others come into contact with her . . . and since the Torah scroll, *the* 'holy object' in a synagogue, is immune to impurity."* But these yeshiva graduates I questioned— and their wives as well—said they assumed that all menstruating women communicated some kind of defilement, some pollution of sacredness, and since you didn't know who was menstruating, and you didn't want to know, you had to assume all women potentially leaked defilement.

Odd customs concerning menstruation arose, and even though they lacked legal foundation, they were practiced. A menstruating woman in sixteenth-century eastern Europe was kept out of

Women and Jewish Law (New York: Schocken Books, 1984), p. 167.

synagogue. In various communities she was prevented from lighting the Sabbath candles. She was said to pollute the air by her presence. If she walked between two men at the beginning of her period, it was said one would be killed. If it was at the end of her period, she would cause strife. If she cooked food for a sage, he would forget his learning. Menstruation was surely not seen as natural bodily function: it was synonymous with blood, guilt, and death. Why was the precept of menstruation was given to woman? asks the Midrash (a compilation of biblical exegesis and homily). Because a woman brought about the death of Adam. And how is she cursed? asks the Talmud. During her periods "she is wrapped up like a mourner, shut up as in a prison, and banished from the company of all men."

The director of Pardes, Rabbi Levi Lauer, told me to come to our meeting early so I could look over the Pardes brochures. I found Pardes in Bakka, essentially the SoHo of Jerusalem, an address now chic *and* bohemian. To get there, you have literally to cross over to what was once the wrong side of the tracks and pass through a mix of old Arab houses, some gentrified, some tumbledown, and the classy new town houses of freshly hewn Jerusalem stone and orange clay tile that are going up all over.

In front of Pardes's narrow three-story building on Gad Street was a picnic table. A bearded young man, wearing a golden *Hai* in one ear and a daypack on his shoulder, read the *Jerusalem Post;* next to him, a young woman, wearing a sleeveless ski jacket and a large crocheted *kippah* over frizzy blond hair, looked through a text on biblical grammar. In Pardes's sunny little waiting room, I looked through the brochures. They said all the right things: "Pardes . . . is a school which teaches adults how to learn Torah. . . . At Pardes, respect for free inquiry, the culture of the university is combined with the warmth and spiritual vitality of the yeshiva. . . . Pardes is unaffiliated with any denomination or political group. . . . At Pardes, men and women learn together. Pardes is . . . sensitive to the problems posed by the Halachic delineation of men's and women's responsibilities." If Pardes came close to resembling its PR material, I had found myself a school.

Rabbi Lauer called me into his office—part American academia, with books and large, meaningful black-and-white photos of women and children, and part Middle Eastern, with oriental rugs and ceramic tiles. Lauer was thin, delicate, bald, serene. He seemed more like a college professor than a pulpit rabbi. He drank mango juice for his cold, he wore wire-rimmed glasses and a sweater with an alligator appliqué. Trained by the Reform movement, he had gone on to become more traditionally observant in his practice. He had immigrated to Israel, and when the Israeli army called him, he served in a crew that operated self-propelled 155 millimeter guns in the artillery corps. I was familiar with his world, knew his kind. I believed I could be straight with him.

"What would you like to learn?" he asked.

Texts, I said, Bible definitely, perhaps Talmud.

I had studied a little Talmud when I was fifteen years old and enrolled in the high school program of the Jewish Theological Seminary. My teacher was Judith Hauptman, now a professor of Talmud at JTS. She is probably the first woman teaching Talmud since Bruria and certainly the first woman in the world to earn a Ph.D. in Talmud. This unique opportunity was lost on me. My notebooks for Professor Hauptman's class are stuffed with notes to and from my girlfriends about collecting money for Biafra, campaigning for McGovern, and, much more frequently, speculating on what romances might be kindled or extinguished during recess in front of the hot chocolate dispenser. I remember that when I did pay attention to the Talmudic arguments, my brain fizzled. Talmud was harder for me than eleventh-grade chemistry. We girls thought it neat that Professor Hauptman had the freedom to pursue a career in Talmud at the Seminary, and while we admired her learning, we were certainly not interested in following in her footsteps, trudging around with those big dusty books, thinking about issues as dreary as who is responsible for paying damages when one ox gores another ox. Who cared about gored oxen, tithes, sacrifice, and Nazirite vows? There was no way we girls would study Talmud as adults. Give us a life of the mind, but give us the glamorous secular subjects: art history, psychology, literary theory, history of ideas. (This was not a dull group of girls. Most in the class are now tenured, killer-competitive professors in these secular fields. Only the boys became rabbis and Jewish educators.) We didn't envy boys we knew in Orthodox schools who got stuck studying Talmud for hours each week. As for the honor of receiving Talmud for our generation, they could have it. It seemed to us that we girls had been spared and were free to learn the really interesting subjects. It never occurred to us that the boys had been chosen or specially honored.

Now, after only a few days in Jerusalem, I had become wildly ambitious, like Donald Trump, who buys the Plaza Hotel one month, and instead of spending the rest of his days inspecting the fronds in the Palm Court for aphids, bids on an airline shuttle the next month. At first I had thought I would study some Bible. Now I was contemplating becoming an expert in Talmud. In this elaborate fantasy, I would be able to read the sacred texts and reinterpret them in the light of a new understanding of women's lives. I would redefine women's role in Judaism, finding a place for myself and all other disenfranchised women. I would be respected by my community for my learning. I would be in touch with its needs, and it would bestow upon me the authority to interpret texts, make judgments, and change laws. I would be one of the voices actively engaged in the continuation of Torah in my generation.

How could a woman become a participant in the process of handing down of the law?

If a woman wants her voice heard, Talmud is the way to go. Those who are well versed in the traditional study of Talmud are considered among the elite of the Jewish religious community. No other role brings quite the same status: not being the rabbi of a large congregation, the president of the Jewish Federation or its key contributor, or a professor of Bible at the university. If you know Talmud, you are, as Rabbi Brovender said, taken seriously. You are linked in conversation to all the previous rabbis, to Moses, and to God. The respect due Talmudists goes beyond admiration for their absolute recall of over five thousand pages of Talmud or their ability to weave lucidly through debates. The Talmudist is revered for being pure of spirit, a master of right and virtuous living. Only the expert in Talmud is in a position to interpret the texts for the current generation and legislate issues such as surrogate motherhood, gene splicing, and euthanasia.

You do not reach adulthood and then start thinking about preparing to be a Talmudist, let alone a major decisor. The making of a Talmudist, like the making of classical ballerina, begins in childhood. Take Professor David Weiss Halivni of Columbia University, acknowledged by some as the greatest contemporary Talmudist. He began to learn and memorize Talmud at five and was ordained as a rabbi at fifteen. The late Rabbi Moshe Feinstein, who had been America's leading decisor, was mastering tractates at seven and issuing learned opinions at nineteen.

To have an equal, authoritative share in Judaism, a woman needs to know Talmud. But if she hadn't begun learning Talmud as a child, it was essentially too late for her to ever amass sufficient expertise. It would be crazy even to try. Or that's what everyone says.

Linda Gradstein, an advanced part-time Pardes student who worked as a stringer for the *Washington Post,* was just crazy enough. Fluent in both Hebrew and Arabic, she shuttled between studying at Pardes and holding interviews: "One day," she said, "I can be in a Palestinian refugee camp and the next day be in Rabin's office talking about the government's policy in handling the disturbances."

I visited her in her little Bakka apartment, decorated with souvenirs from her graduate studies at the American University in Cairo, and heard her story:

> I come from a traditional feminist background, where there are no differences between men and women, and anything men could learn, I could learn. My goal was to learn Gemara [the Aramaic word for the commentary on the Mishnah, but also used to refer to all of Talmud]. That to me was the symbol of Jewish learning. The Gemara is man's response to the destruction of the Temple. How do you understand what God said thousands of years ago? What does it mean for today? The Gemara is the way people have tried to interpret the Torah. I almost dropped it three or four times: it was so difficult and I was so frustrated. I find it's fascinating but very male. The method of thinking is male: it seems to me that one of the problems in Torah is that there are really very few women who are learned enough but who are also feminine, who have a woman's approach to Torah, not a copy of the male approach. There's a competitiveness among men which certainly exists in studying Gemara.
>
> My *hevruta* (study partner), Susan, is incredibly bright—she's the one who's pregnant and wears a head covering. We'll sometimes argue but there's not that edge of hostility. To learn Gemara you have to have an opinion and follow it through. But I think you can have intellectual strength and power without being competitive. I can argue a point with Susan, and if she proves to me that I'm wrong, I'll say, "You're right." We complement each other, we're each better at different things. I sense that when men learn, there's more competition: Who can learn more? Who can be right eight times out of ten? The Gemara is called the *milhamta*, a struggle. There is an intellectual struggle going on, but I don't think it has to be a battle. It can be a building together. I remember hearing Leah

Shakdiel [a member of the Yeruham Religious Services Council who took her seat only after the Supreme Court decided a woman could not be denied membership] say that when her husband studied Gemara with her, he would scream at her. And when she asked why, he said that you have to scream when you study Gemara. She said that when women start really learning Gemara, women will find it is not necessary to scream. They will teach men they don't have to scream either.

Batya Miller was also a late starter at Talmud and singleminded in her determination to know the sacred texts and give herself to them. After graduating from college as a philosophy and Jewish thought major, she studied for three years at Pardes and was now continuing to study Talmud at Hebrew University. She recalled her own first frustrating days at Pardes: "We were learning the *Mishnah Masekhet Taanit,* about fasting." She sang in mock Talmud study style,

> I came here to understand about God, what is my relationship to God, and is there a God, and if there is, what does God have to do with these picayune details about whether or not a person remembers to include this prayer: "He makes the wind blow and He makes the rain descend" during the winter months? I was very frustrated. Then my teacher told us to look up all these sources on shofars and bugles, to read in Numbers, to fly over to the Mishnah and read that Rabbi Eliezar says that the rain should be mentioned on the first day of a festival. And I was saying to myself, What is this baloney? Why did I come here?

Given where she is now, Batya clearly succeeded in overcoming her blocks. "It happened slowly," she explained.

> When you first come to Pardes, your questions are more important than the text. And they should be. If you have any respect

for yourself, then you believe that what you've thought about your whole life is worthwhile. You reach a point, then, where you have as much respect for the text as for yourself. Then you get to a point where you begin to sense: What is this text? It's not a piece of paper with black ink on it. It's all of your ancestors, it's your grandparents, it's the quickest, brightest, most intelligent committed minds of the Jewish people sitting in front of you. And you're going to think every time you have a problem with the text that you're right? Maybe you are. And you should feel strong enough to fight for your opinion. But there comes a point of balance for me: the text takes precedence, it becomes more important than my questions. I don't deny my questions, but I will place them on the side until I understand the text. At the end of a year at Pardes, students realize they had a great year learning about themselves and about the text, but they didn't learn the text. They realize there's not only one tractate of Mishnah, but sixty-three to go, and they didn't even learn a whole one, only three or four sections. They realize how awesome this literature is and how little they know. In Torah learning, people come to a tremendous sense of humility, not to the point of paralysis, because that's unhealthy. But a humility that brings about self-respect, respect for others, a deep respect for the tradition.

Convinced as I was that Talmud study was important for women, beyond my fantasy, I couldn't see myself studying Talmud. What I knew of Talmud seemed dreary, irrelevant, and often impenetrable. That it was written in terse, elliptical Hebrew and Aramaic did not help. It demanded a facility for rigorous and convoluted logic, and if you're going to study Talmud as a sacred text, and not as an example of the literature of late antiquity, it helps if you accept the divine origin and authority of the text. I prefer reading novels attributed without question to mortals, authors capable of both soaring inventiveness and complete bombs, and unless I have to teach from them, I read them dreamily, making intuitive sense of them. The Talmud, which does contain sections on ethical comportment and tells wonderful legends, sounds to me, by and large, like a boring legal transcript.

Look at this section of Talmud, from the tractate *Hullin:*

Mishnah: No meat may be boiled with milk, save meat of fish and locusts. It is also forbidden to bring it to table together with cheese, save meat of fish and locusts. He who vows to abstain from meat is still free to partake of fish and locusts. Gemara: Meat of fowl, cooked with milk, is thus forbidden biblically. Not so according to Rabbi Akiva. For he says, "He who vows to abstain from meat is still free to partake of fish and locusts."

This section is not atypical. Reading it, I'm not sure I see the point to knowing that it's acceptable to boil locusts in milk if I don't generally cook with locusts. It seems irrelevant. What's more, if every rabbi quoted in the text has a different opinion and there's often no indication that one opinion is more valid than the next, then what's the point of the debate? How can it be that the opinions of rabbis whom we traditionally do not follow are considered to be as authentically "Torah" as the opinions of rabbis whom we do follow? If the text demands our interpretation, aren't we sullying it as we yank it out of its sacred zone and pull it down into our lives? I don't know in what spirit I'm supposed to take the text. Certainly, face value won't work. I needed a key, a reader's guide.

In the second century Rabbi Ishmael formulated thirteen hermeneutical principles by which we interpret the words of Torah that are cited in the Talmud. The first rule is *kal vehomer,* translated into the language of logic as inference a minori ad maius and vice versa. Inference is drawn from a minor premise to a major one, or from a major premise to a minor one. The second rule is *gezerah shavah,* inference by analogy; that is, if the same word or phrase occurs in two different places, it is assumed that the meaning in the first case is the same as in the second.

These rules, plus eleven more, give me no clue as to what I am supposed to take from my study. If anything, they convince me that to learn Talmud, I would have learn to think differently, a project I feel unable to undertake with any hope of success at my age. And if Talmud study is supposed to be a form of worship as well, I am missing it altogether.

I was relieved, then, when Rabbi Lauer presented the Pardes policy on Talmud study for both men and women: "Everyone rushes to study Talmud because it's considered the pinnacle of Judaism. But it's premature, like studying Shakespeare before you've learned the ABCs."

I would happily comply with Rabbi Lauer's policy and postpone becoming a Talmudist. I needed to know the Bible better before I went on.

He wanted to know if I brought any biases to studying text, which would help him determine the best teacher for me. I saw no harm in telling the truth. Eager as I was to get inside Jewish texts, they seemed dusty, alien, and boring to me. I wasn't sure I could penetrate that fence that was keeping me out. While I wanted to know what it meant for the study of Torah to be a sacred act, I wasn't interested in becoming wildly observant, if that was required. I added, "How are women treated at Pardes? What were 'the problems' of gender difference the brochure alluded to? Whose problems were they?"

Rabbi Lauer had read Carol Gilligan's book *In a Different Voice.** Gilligan demonstrates that not only do men and women follow different paths in their moral development, but they also differ in their definitions of what is morally correct. The whole faculty (all

---

**In a Different Voice: Psychological Theory and Women's Development* (Cambridge: Harvard University Press, 1982).

male when I was there, but previously there had been a few female teachers) had been asked to read the book. Rabbi Lauer considered the implications of Gilligan's book for Torah study: "Women tend to bring human relational priorities to the text. Men bring a search for universal absolutes." Carefully, he added:

There are exceptions. . . . If there is a place in the Jewish tradition for hard justice—male—and mercy—female—then the outlook of the two genders can temper each other. The informing of the text by this dialectic brings a texture to the learning not there in single-sex learning. That is a prime justification for men and women learning together. Women have been denied access to learning. The only way women will be taken seriously is if men give them the keys to the kingdom of learning. But now that women have access to equal study, who stays home with the kids? The stability of traditional Jewish living depends on women who are willing to stay home with large families, especially in Israel. Even men who voice an interest in women being learned say they won't stay home with the kids. It's a tension that isn't resolvable. Any man who says he'll be 50 percent responsible for his kids is bluffing. Who am I kidding? When I'm home, I help. I understood my wife would stay home with the children, and I'm happy she made that decision.

He said two-thirds of the students at Pardes were women. Why the disproportion? For one thing, men had other places to study, hundreds. There are not many choices for adult women if you eliminated certain schools that see all secular learning as a threat and teach women only the laws they'll need to keep Jewish homes. "At Pardes, women are treated with dignity for their spiritual depth; they are respected for their ability to think clearly and keep on the agenda. Unlike at some other yeshivot, at Pardes, women are measured by their intellect, not by the length of their sleeves. Our priority is not to get them married, although I hope they will."

I trusted that Rabbi Lauer respected the women who came to Pardes and valued the learning they could accomplish. We agreed I would get in touch with Jonathan Cohen, a Pardes Torah teacher finishing his doctorate in Jewish education at Hebrew University. Rabbi Laurer thought I'd find Jonny's approach to Bible sympathetic. He synthesized Torah, literary theory, and modern Jewish thought.

Fine with Jonny. I could squeeze into his class on Exodus. Jonny, his wiry hair and beard streaked with gray, looked like college teachers used to in the sixties, wearing jeans, rolled-up shirtsleeves, a tooled leather belt. He introduced me to the other students as a writing teacher from Yale and they introduced themselves by name. There were young graduates of Oberlin, Brandeis, the University of Chicago, and several more mature students, among them Pinhas, a charming retired gentleman in a dapper suit. If I was ever going to learn some Torah, I believed I could do it here, with Jonny Cohen illustrating how "the Torah conveys its message artfully. The story is a piece of art, deliberately structured to bring across a certain message." Jonny's eyebrows lifted each time he checked to be sure his point was clear, and as he paced around our rectangular table, he showered us with compliments, "*yafeh,* nice; *meod yafeh,* very nice," for any accurate or original interpretations on our part. They were studying Exodus and were just getting their feet wet in the plagues. Jonny sent us to the *bet midrash* for two hours with these tasks: Look at the first three plagues again, read Rashi's commentary. Is there an escalation from plague to plague? Is there an accretion of motifs that are deployed? Is there any system in Pharaoh's reaction to the plagues? And what does it say about his character?

If this was Bible study—thinking about language, theorizing about narrative structure—then I could do it. Not much different from performing literary criticism upon Flaubert and Nabokov. I knew my shaky Hebrew would be a problem at first, but I would progress. I liked everything about Pardes—the blue calico curtains, the kerosene heaters in the classrooms, the announcement of social action programs ("We need to raise $300 for dental work for a Russian Jew"; a sign-up for visiting a student who was "physically uncomfortable, but still welcomed company"; requests for old clothes, for volunteers to help mop the floor for the elderly on Fridays, for friends to bring soda or dairy desserts to a Saturday night singing party). Pardes felt vibrant, kind, innocent. It reminded me of a dorm at Colgate University called Ecology House, which housed the idealistic students who wished they had gone to college in the sixties.

After Jonny's introductory remarks, I was invited to join Jeff and Phyllis, Jewish educators studying at Pardes as part of a sabbatical program, in their *hevruta*. They relieved me of imposing myself upon a study pair, and I was grateful. Because they found the *bet midrash* too noisy, they remained in the classroom and studied there. That, too, was fine with me. I didn't think I could concentrate amidst so much noise either. We went through the texts, line by line, first in Hebrew and then in English. It took us nearly all the preparation time simply to get the meaning of the words right. They made sure I took a turn reading from the text, encouraged me to take a stab at the questions Jonny had posed. Phyllis wrote down our answers to Jonny's questions in different colored pencils, then underlined possible thematic links. Jeff and Phyllis were mature, easygoing, smart, thorough. They included me on their walk during recess to the nearby minimarket, where we bought newspapers, yogurts, and pretzels. We were a fine trio.

I was disappointed, nonetheless, because I wanted to see what it was like to study Torah with a woman partner. Now I wasn't at a women's institution. My teacher, clever and compassionate, was a man, and all I had left in the female sensibility department was Phyllis. Maybe Jeff would be absent on occasion.

I recalled a conversation I had had with Deborah Weissman, the specialist in Jewish women's education, about the influence of a female sensibility upon Torah study. She told me that when she studied Talmud at the Hartman Institute (essentially the same type of place as Pardes, but on a more advanced level), her study partner was a woman. Whereas the male students usually sat across from each other—a confrontational pose—she and her partner decided to sit next to each other. They would go off on tangents, and even chat, but their conversations remained related to the text. The rabbis believe you can study Oral and Written Torah with a genuine friend, she said, someone with whom you can eat, drink, sleep, reveal life and Torah secrets. "You do reveal a lot about yourself to your study partner. You challenge each other, keep each other on the right track. You learn how each other's mind works. You anticipate what the other will say. You become like married people." She called paired learning "learning mediated by relationship." She wondered if mixed *hevruta* was possible.

My next day at Pardes I, too, wondered.

I was ready to go off with Jeff and Phyllis to tackle Jonny's next assignment, when a good-looking American man, I thought in his late twenties (dark hair, athletic, a backpack slung over his shoulder—the antithesis of the pale yeshiva type) greeted me with a handshake that was both strong and gentle. He said his name was Raphael. I noticed he was not wearing a *kippah*. His partner had left Pardes and how did I feel about becoming his *hevruta?*

He phrased his offer considerately enough so that I had the option of saying no thanks. But I didn't see how I could I get out of studying with him without being unbearably rude. I tried though. I said I would have to miss classes sometimes because I was also teaching at the university. If he was looking for continuity in his study partner, I was a bad choice. To my dismay, he said no matter, when he went on reserve army duty, he would miss classes, too. Again I tried to wriggle my way out. I said I had already begun studying with Jeff and Phyllis, and it seemed to be working out. He said Pardes frowned on three people studying together.

I was stuck with this man, probably a recent college graduate trying to find himself. I wondered if Sara, of Har Nof, would say: See what happens when you step outside the law and study with men and women? Or maybe: Your desire to study with a woman has been thwarted for some reason which you must discover. This is a test.

When I knew Rabbi Lauer better, he told me that at Pardes "sexual energies are carefully contained and appropriately expressed. There have been few days of excess." I assumed he meant couples walking arm in arm, what we used to call "public display of affection" in summer camp. Rabbi Lauer said, "What we consider immodest behavior here, my friends in New York would laugh at. I think the healthy thing about Pardes is its sense of humor about halakhic rigidity concerning sex and its acceptance of healthy sexual impulses. Sexuality is understood here, there's no denying it. You wouldn't come to a yeshiva in Jerusalem to screw around."

I told Rabbi Lauer that while I never saw women students at Pardes discriminated against in any way, I feared that the women came away with the message that the greatest achievement was to marry a future Pardes instructor and bear and educate his many children—and not to become deeply learned. I had no concrete grounds for this fear, yet I couldn't shake it. Maybe it was the longing looks the Pardes women gave the wives and children of Pardes instructors when they came to visit. So many Pardes students came from homes where parents were divorced—to them, the tight bonds of the large traditional families must have looked enticing.

Rabbi Lauer, who has two daughters and whose wife, Chaya, is a psychiatric social worker, took up my concern.

Despite the equality of opportunity here, teachers admit they go easier on the women, don't push them as aggressively, and are kinder to them. It's not good for education. It's good the faculty can admit this. In a secular environment, you take sexual equality for granted. But I don't trust it. Is there a natural equality of opportunity? Men don't take to sexual equality naturally. If we pretended it's as natural as breathing, then we're lying, and lying to the women we live with. We all come from environments where equality is not a natural state of affairs. Some of the teachers at Pardes have never learned in a class with women. I appreciate when they push the women students as hard as the men and when they try to look them in the eye.

Rabbi Lauer said that a teacher leading a seminar once raised the issue of sexual energies between teachers and student. The students giggled. The teacher said that if he had the courage to deal with this issue, then there should be no laughing.

I followed Raphael, my new study partner, into the *bet midrash*. More calico curtains; books everywhere; even a shelf of books on women in Judaism donated by a former student in memory of her mother. Adults of all ages were studying animatedly at little tables, some women wearing *kippot* or scarves, some bareheaded. There were even some men studying the sacred texts bareheaded. Clearly Pardes tolerated a range of observance and nonobservance. Raphael and I took chairs across from each other at the only little table left in the room, and I got out my English Bible. "Why are you using English?" he asked. I said it was senseless for me to use the Hebrew if I didn't understand it perfectly. If I didn't start using the Hebrew, he said, I'd never understand it. Fluency came only when you had no choice but to use a foreign language. He took a Hebrew Bible down from the shelves and put it next to my English one. I recalled less biblical Hebrew than I thought I would. It was hard just to find my place and not lose it. I would reach for the English, and Raphael would say, "Wait. Let me try to explain."

We were still on the plagues (I was at Pardes for months, and we never left the plagues). Raphael said he hoped I had written down Jonny's questions for this morning because he hadn't. *Why* hadn't he? Did he assume I would be the good girl who took down every-thing the teacher said in my best penmanship? Had the woman who was his first study partner been all too happy to handle the tedious tasks? In any other setting, I would have said to him I had written down the assignment this time, but buddy, don't count on it again. But I was so tense about getting our relationship off right, so determined to keep our study free of gender stereotypes, that I lied to prove I was his match in classroom negligence. "I didn't get it either," I said. "We'll have to ask Phyllis." (Later I learned that diligent Phyllis was the one in class *everyone* turned to for assignments.)

At each point, Raphael and I refuted each other's interpretations. I made assumptions about the text; he said they had no basis in the text. "Just because God told Moses to do something," he argued, "why are you assuming he did it?" We did not raise our voices: this was civilized strife, like a fencing match. He was sharp, eloquent, funny, even wise. He was no college boy. The creases around his eyes had at first been hidden by his glasses. He was probably my age, but I couldn't be sure. He had a Peter Pan quality. I wondered what he was thinking about me. God, what distracting thoughts to be having while I was supposed to be studying Torah.

I remembered my aunt advising me in 1970 to go to a women's college as she had, because there I wouldn't have to worry about setting my hair, since there were no men in the classes. I would only have to set my hair for the weekend mixers when the men from Yale came. Maybe because I was born into a generation untutored in curlers and inept in rites of formal dating, the presence of men in my classes when I was a student, and certainly now that I was a teacher, never seemed to make a difference. I could acknowledge the attractions I felt and then impose the appropriate restraints.

Today at Pardes, I felt my nails digging into my palms. It was hard getting the male-female dynamics just right. He is a man; I am a woman—I couldn't push this gender business out of my mind. Just because I was a beginner at talking about Torah and he was far more conversant with Hebrew and more experienced reading the texts, I didn't want Raphael to think I would happily listen to him instruct me over the next few months. He was no pro at Torah either—I picked that up right away. He couldn't have been at Pardes for more than three months. I would prove my intellectual toughness. I would show him I was a heavyweight just as soon as I could read the words on the page.

Flipping from plague to plague, our fingers crashed. It meant nothing to me; nonetheless, it registered. With a woman, I wondered, would I have paid any attention at all to an accidental touch?

Everything about studying aloud with a partner was difficult. I couldn't concentrate in public. I was used to working at my own pace, in the privacy of my own brain. And studying with this man unnerved me, although I still felt sure that if we had been working on some project together at the university, I wouldn't have given gender a minute's thought. But today in this yeshiva I felt like Yentl, trying to keep her mind on her studies and off the distracting presence of her male partner, Anshel. Who is this Raphael who learns Torah all day but does not cover his head? What was he after at Pardes?

I would be studying Torah with Raphael for many months. I hoped that after that first awkward day, we might establish a routine of study in which we could speak deeply and easily. In fact, after studying together over the next days, I found our partnership more comfortable, both intellectually and socially. When I became annoyed by the slow pace of our class, it was Raphael who helped me improve my attitude. He urged me to compare Torah study to studying a play in order to produce it. First you read the play to see what's going on and who's who; then you read to figure out what the characters want and feel; then you read to see what was meant but left unsaid; then you memorized your part to know it inside out; then you performed it each night. And each night the play changed, because you were different and because the audience was different.

Initially, I restrained myself from asking Raphael for the details of his life. There was a lovely European-like formality to our relationship that I was reluctant to disturb. Not that I wasn't dying for information. When I found out that we had mutual friends in Jerusalem, Naamah Kelman, a rabbinical student at Hebrew Union College, and her brother Levi Weiman-Kelman, rabbi of Congregation Kol Haneshamah, I begged them to tell me what they knew about Raphael. Both adored him. Levi said Raphael had been his teacher in a massage class. Naamah listed a few women she knew who had crushes on him and said, "I wish he'd get married."

I eventually succumbed to my curiosity, and asked Raphael to tell me his life story. He let me look at his résumé, which he had been using to find a job teaching English as a second language. These were the high points: born in Glens Falls, New York; graduated Exeter in '68; volunteered in Chicago in the civil rights movement; was a student radical, a farm worker coordinator; graduated New College in Sarasota, Florida, then went to the Ringling Brothers and Barnum & Bailey Circus Clown College; trained at Esalen as an encounter group leader; was the boss clown in the George Matthews Great London Circus; played piano at Legal Seafood in Boston; went to Israel to fulfill his Zionist destiny after the American countercultural movement disappeared on him; served as a sniper in the Israel Defense Forces; taught massage; lived for six years on a kibbutz, gardening and working as a vegetarian cook; did a masters in teaching English as a second language. Then Pardes.

When I reported to Esther on my studies at Pardes, I told her my study partner was a man. She said it would be impossible, of course, for her to consider a male study partner. On the grounds of modesty. But not physical modesty. "Studying together, you develop a profound personal intimacy. You open up spiritually to each other. If you're learning Torah seriously, you bring your whole being into it, share your deepest inner experiences. What are the limits of appropriateness if every day a man and a woman come together for hours and become close personal friends? The problem isn't sexual tension, but modesty on a more profound level." I understood what she meant.

During my first weeks at Pardes, it rained continually. Finally the rain stopped, and the sun came out. Jonny's early morning class in the *bet midrash* on the laws regulating interpersonal relations (called literally "between man and his friend") was just ending, and I slipped in to listen before his class in Exodus started. He was discussing Bruria, one of the few women mentioned by name in the Talmud. It was said in the Talmud that Bruria distinguished herself by learning three hundred laws from three hundred teachers in one day, and carried out this regimen over three years. A thousand years later, Rashi commented on a curious phrase in the text, a reference to "the incident about Bruria." Rashi completely discredited Bruria's reputation. He wrote that she was punished for daring to believe she was exempt from the feminine liability of light-mindedness. According to Rashi, Bruria's husband arranged to have his student seduce her. She succumbed, then strangled herself, and her husband ran off in shame from Palestine to Babylon. Rashi's coda to the life of our most exemplary woman sage is so bizarre as to be unbelievable.

Jonny translated a legend about Bruria from the tractate of Talmud called *Berakhot:*

There were toughs in the neighborhood of Rabbi Meir, and they would cause him a great deal of anguish. Rabbi Meir was praying that they would die. Bruria, his wife, said to him: "What is your rationale for this action?" Rabbi Meir said, "Because it says in Psalms, 'And sinners shall perish.'" Bruria said, "But doesn't it say 'sins,' not sinners? And further, read on to the end of the passage: 'And the wicked shall be no more.' Because sins will end, so sinners will be no more. Rather, pray for them that they should repent, and then the sinner will be no more." He prayed for them, and they did repent. (*Berakhot* 10a)

Jonny analyzed the psychology that typified Bruria's interpretation of Scripture. She avoided head-on confrontation with Rabbi Meir and spoke to him calmly and rationally instead of emotionally. She did not reproach him for his lack of compassion for the sinners, but rather redirected his actions by showing him a more appropriate way to understand Scripture. "Bruria always knows in advance what will happen in the end," said Jonny. "My wife does too. She sees days, weeks in advance. She can tell you what will happen. I see only the day."

I had never heard the cerebral virtues of a woman in Jewish texts extolled in public and held up as a model. This deserved cheering. Like the matriarchs, Bruria was a loving wife and mother, unwavering in faith. But she was also an intellectual who was taken seriously by her learned husband and by the rabbis of her day.

It was getting even sunnier out. Students were flinging their ski jackets and sweatshirts to the side of the room. It would be difficult to concentrate on such a day.

Raphael came in time for Exodus class, wearing a bright yellow bicycle helmet, announcing that he had gotten his bike fixed: "No buses, no waiting, so free to ride." As always, we moved from our class into the *bet midrash* to study. The din no longer distracted me. In fact, I was inspired by the rumbling of so many voices working to make sense of Torah. Now Raphael and I were trying to decipher the commentaries by Rashi that Jonny had assigned, and we were getting nowhere. Rashi is written in a different script than Torah. We were struggling through the letters, then looking up half the words in Jastrow's dictionary; then trying to figure out which words are omitted from the text because it was assumed one could fill them in; then trying to penetrate the meaning, which can sometimes be obscure.

We were looking at the plague of frogs. Exodus 8:2 says, "Aaron held out his arm over the waters of Egypt and the frogs came up and covered the land of Egypt." That's the English translation. Raphael showed me that the Hebrew doesn't say "frogs came up" but rather "frog came up." If I saw that in an English book, either I'd assume it was a typo, or—more likely—I wouldn't catch it. But taking the traditional Jewish attitude that every word and every letter in the Bible is meant intentionally and has a meaning that must be discovered, I am forced to ponder why "frog" is in the singular here. (At Pardes, one wouldn't—as a biblical scholar might—suggest that a scribal error had crept into the text.) Clearly one frog, even an enormous one, wouldn't be much of a plague; besides, elsewhere in the text, the word "frogs" is used. Rashi looks for what is problematic in the text and then makes sense out of it. So, in fairly legible conventional Hebrew in the Rashi column, it says: *And the frog came up.* Then in the impossible Rashi script, it says (literally): "There was one frog but when they hit it, and it split into swarms-swarms, this is a midrashic explanation from *Sanhedrin* 67b [the next phrase is omitted here, but a seasoned Rashi reader knows to complete the sentence with] of the usage of the singular noun here."

We struggled to pin down the language. The point? "Frog" meant "a swarm of frogs." We had spent nearly our entire morning's preparation figuring out Rashi's solution to the problem in the text. I could not bear the pace of this yeshiva. Life is too short to worry about frog or frogs. I couldn't keep dwelling on these inane issues. One frog, many frogs. I didn't care. This stuff was endless. No wonder it kept yeshiva boys off the streets well into adulthood and implanted masks of dullness on their faces. The *bet midrash* was filling up with sunlight; there was an epidemic of spring fever. "I think I'll cut out early," Raphael said.

The Talmud, which touches all subjects, does not lack for things to say about the beauty of nature disrupting Torah studies. Jacob Neusner, in his book *Invitation to the Talmud,* explains well: "As the Talmudic warning about not interrupting one's study even to admire a tree—that is, nature—makes clear, man cannot afford for one instant to break off from consciousness, to open ourselves to what appears then to be 'natural'; to be mindless is to lose touch with revealed order and revealed law, the luminous disciplines of the sacred."★

I was having as much trouble concentrating as anyone else in this room, which surprised me, because when I'm teaching a class, I'm so focused that I've ignored fire drills. Perhaps now I was standing too far outside the pages of the Bible to be drawn into it—only through enormous will and energy could I keep my focus. Perhaps becoming a student again had made me regress into the spitball and doodling mentality. We were not getting very far. We were as lethargic as the sleepy young women who had yawned over their volumes of Talmud at Bruria.

Raphael called the tutor who monitors the *bet midrash* over for help. "What if we can't concentrate on a day like today?"

"If you look up from your Torah study to look at a tree, you will go to *gehinnom.*" (Gehenna is where sinners face eternal punishment in the hereafter.)

Even said in jest, this was not the answer we deserved. Concentration is a spiritual skill. We needed real guidance to focus on the text, not chiding. Raphael said to me, "Isn't the tree part of God's creation?"

"You're not thinking about the tree or its reflection of God," I said. "You're thinking about going off on your bike."

He said, "Raleigh was inspired by God."

Just as we tired of goofing around and gritted our teeth to hit the text again, Rabbi Lauer came up to our table and said he had heard I was studying at Pardes without a formal application. I felt as if I were a trespasser and he were a police officer demanding to see some license I had failed to acquire. I didn't know there was an application waiting in the office for me. I just thought I had been admitted to

★*Invitation to the Talmud* (New York: Harper & Row, 1973), 225.

Pardes on the basis of my interview and credentials. Three weeks
ago I had met with the assistant director and made arrangements for
paying tuition. I didn't want to put myself up for inspection: Was
I religious enough, were my motives pure enough? . . . I just wanted
the chance to study Torah. When Rabbi Lauer left, Raphael whispered, "I noticed you were taken aback. We all had to fill out
applications. Don't worry about it, just do it. It gives power to the
institution." He teased, "Wait till you see the initiation rites."

I tried to keep my mind on the letters in *Mikraot Gedolot,* a volume
of Exodus annotated with commentaries. The page was looking less
like a Chinese phone book to me than it had the classes before. I
could find my place, keep it, and recognize words. I should have felt
some satisfaction about my progress. But I was holding back tears,
and mumbling to myself what I wanted to say to Rabbi Lauer: Do
you know how hard it was for me to decide to interrupt my life and
try to study Torah? You have to encourage women to study Torah,
not put stumbling blocks before us. I remembered what an observant
uncle had said to me, half jokingly, when he heard I was off to Israel
to learn Torah: "There's no role for women in Judaism anyway. You
know that, so why waste your time? Men sit in the yeshivot, women
are going to stay at home, so why waste learning on women? That's
the way we believe God intended it. Men don't want women to be
learned." My uncle loves me dearly and is proud of me. He brags
that I teach college; he photocopies my articles for his friends. So
I know he meant to be helpful, to say, why are you hurting yourself
by going where you're not wanted?

Peter and the girls were picking lemons from our tree when I got
home from Pardes.

"Look at the yeshiva girl," he said. "Your body is wilting away
from so much sitting; you're pale and don't have a muscle left."
While I told him what had happened at Pardes, I ran in place with
the rocks he had put in my hands. "You should have checked to see
if there was an application. But if filling it out seems so humiliating

to you—and I can't see what the big deal is—then don't do it. Maybe you're looking for an excuse to drop out."

The phone rang. Rabbi Lauer was calling to apologize in case he had embarrassed me in public, a major no-no in Jewish interpersonal ethics. He had, but I denied it. He hadn't meant to. The application was protocol, he assured me. This was what I needed to hear from him. Some approval, some encouragement. I would stick with Pardes. I'd fill out the application. I'd write whatever I thought they wanted to hear. Then I looked at the application. It was a killer. What nosy, snooping questions! "Write in full about the nature of your current commitment to observing the commandments, if any." Did they want me to make lists of the laws I did and didn't follow? Was it their business to know how scrupulous I was in observing menstrual discharges, to know if I had ever tossed milk and meat silverware into the same sink? And then: "What is your earliest Jewish memory? What are some of your happiest Jewish memories? Most painful? Please describe one of the most difficult situations you have encountered and how you dealt with it." Why was baring my soul the prerequisite for study at Pardes? I tried to keep a sane perspective on the application—Pardes did need some screening device to keep out crazies and deviants.

Several days later, Rabbi Lauer called me into his office before Jonny's class began. I feared I would be out the door for having failed to demonstrate the proper motivation for Torah study in my application. He did not find my fudged, marginally revelatory answers problematic. Apparently healthy reticence from adult applicants was a point in their favor, a sign of their well-being. He said only American applicants spilled their beans; Europeans tended to write that their most trying moment was being in a foreign train station and not knowing the language. Rabbi Lauer was, however, concerned that I had written, "I feel immensely estranged from Torah." He had underlined this sentence in red. If I were truly estranged, if it was not just rhetorical hyperbole on my part, wouldn't it be impossible for me to study?

Maybe it was, I said. But I wanted the chance to find out for myself.

Rabbi Lauer dismissed me from his office as an official Pardes student. "Learn well," he blessed me, and I returned to the buzzing *bet midrash* to tell Raphael the good news.

Raphael had not come yet. Standing in the doorway of the *bet midrash,* I overheard two women wearing scarves look up from their Talmuds and conclude: "At Pardes, the Talmudic opinion that women are light-headed [*nashim datan kalot hen*] does not hold."

I walked over to the balcony off the *bet midrash* to contemplate that statement. Today's winter *hamsin* was so peculiar. Golden sand from the desert was blowing across the city, covering the cars on Gad Street in gold dust. It was impossible for me to breathe outside, yet I couldn't tear myself away. The air looked like the orange cellophane that delicatessens use to wrap fancy platters. Then it suddenly began hailing, and all the gold washed away.

I returned indoors, having stayed out overly long.

I hovered over the little table of the scarved women as the tutor would. "Maybe we're in a dream here," I whispered to them. "Maybe Pardes is an unrealistic island."

About Pardes, I had one tremendous concern that I couldn't ignore. Pardes was an institution that welcomed women. It was sensitive to women. In the *bet midrash* of Pardes you could overhear a pregnant student and her female study partner taking a break to speculate on the effects on a child of its mother's studying Talmud during pregnancy. But Pardes was kind men opening up their doors to women. We were guests on male turf.

Five

Esther could never see me. Each time we planned to meet, she had to cancel. Strep and the flu ran through her children. Then she caught some of what they had. Then there was chicken pox for each child, followed by someone with lice and someone else with bronchitis. Her house sounded like a plague zone. She was sick as often as I had been in Hamilton. Ironic, I thought, that her thick spiritual life provided her with no immunity. Proverbs (3:7,8) says: "Fear the Lord and shun evil. It will be a cure for your body, a tonic for your bones." Today Esther couldn't see me because her pulse was racing. Even though she was eating more than usual, she kept losing weight.

Though she got proper medical help for the children, she didn't take care of herself. I begged her to see a doctor. But even with medical care, how could she expect to get well? She had no oases of calm, no indulgences, no professional ego boosts. If her religious life was nourishing to her, it didn't nourish her health. More than medicines and a germ-free environment, more than more prayers and Torah learning, I thought she needed to be set out on a Sunfish all by herself on a placid lake. Or better yet, to sit alone in a quiet institute for advanced scientific studies where she was known as Esther the theoretical physicist and not as anyone's wife or mother. So many children, such little money from her husband's yeshiva stipend to spend on physical comfort.

She didn't complain. She seemed content to chug along, postponing her career to mother full-time and serve God, oblivious to chaos. The recurrent sicknesses, she claimed, indicated blemishes on the soul she needed to inspect. "Lovely, inspect your soul," I said, "but get the right medicine. And get some help at home, OK?"

Esther called me frequently to allay my concerns about her health and to monitor my Torah progress. I was glad I could share some of my experience of my sick years with her and quote from my *Merck Manual of Diagnosis and Therapy;* that way, our relationship was less one-sided. She always called at hectic times—in the morning when I was rushing to get the girls off, or when I was trying to fry chicken and read my students' papers without getting oil on them. Esther, having no sense of conventional time, would say she, too, had only a second to talk, and from the children's shrieking in the background, I knew she meant it. But she could talk through the noise breathlessly for an hour, supplying more names of the learned women I should get to know.

I would motion to my family that I really would be off the phone in a moment. But realizing it was Esther, they fended for themselves. I recorded the names Esther gave me in a notebook and took down the thumbnail sketches she provided. One, a daughter of Holocaust survivors, once a follower of the charismatic singing rabbi Shlomo Carlebach; one an exceptionally bright convert with a degree in history from Harvard; one expecting her eighth child, teaching Hasidic insights to women. Most of the women, plucked from Esther and Reuven's large circle of friends, were originally from English-speaking countries. Nearly all were university educated. So this was no random sampling of Israelis, but rather a group of what Israelis called "Anglo-Saxim." My notebook of learned women was getting thick, and Esther told me to begin by meeting the English speakers, and when my Hebrew improved, to meet the women who spoke only Hebrew. She asked if I had begun to meet any of these people. I would, I promised.

Studying was going OK at Pardes, I told Esther. Each day I became a little less ignorant. We studied so slowly, I whined, we didn't miss a detail. It drove me crazy sometimes. There is a saying, "Torah study should lead to love of God, and love of God should lead to Torah study." I was learning material and it was leading me nowhere. Moreover, I would have to rush out of class at 12:30 to pick up my girls at school, turning my thoughts from Torah to tuna fish sandwiches. If I were studying around the clock like the younger, single Pardes students, perhaps the intensity of the study, the relentless day and night efforts, might have propelled me toward some kind of breakthrough. My effort and my expectation were disproportionate. It was as though I was taking an adult education class in ballet once a week and considered dropping out because Baryshnikov hadn't yet tapped me to be his partner.

Esther detected that I wasn't forging any emotional connection to the text; she feared I would abandon my studies. She asked if I had heard that Aviva Gottlieb Zornberg was now teaching over two hundred people each week in different classes held at Bruria and the Jerusalem College for Adults. And she still taught the evening class in private homes. Keep up the studies up at Pardes, she advised me, keep acquiring textual skills. But go back to Aviva. "Torah cannot be taught as a written text. The text is not a hieroglyph on the Rosetta stone. It must be transmitted orally by a teacher, and the teaching communicates the teacher's understanding of the text. Without a teacher—one who is working spiritually—the text is partially silent."

On the day I was to go back to Aviva, I got my girls off to school, taught at the university and met with students, raced back to give the girls lunch, hung out with them as they played at the playground and did homework. I did laundry, marked papers, prepared for the next class, braved the lines at the supermarket, made dinner, got the girls bathed and ready for bed. At eight o'clock, Peter came home from his class for the changing of the guard. There didn't seem to be space or awakeness left in me to go to the movies, let alone listen to a Torah lecture, no matter how inspirational. I would wake up tomorrow grouchy and bark at the kids.

When I was with the girls at the playground, I had met a daughter of a Canadian rabbi, the very young mother of two sons, who clung to both sides of her waist and yanked on the ends of her wig. We got to chatting. I said I was going to a Torah class. She told me learning Torah was her greatest love, and yet she felt torn. She could justify taking the time to learn only if it meant learning the laws that would lead her to perform deeds more correctly and with more conviction. "But how can I justify studying Torah for its own sake?" she asked. "How can I justify my own intellectual pleasure if there are so many acts of *hesed,* lovingkindness, that are left undone in the world? If I don't bake chickens and bring them to the sick or to families sitting *shiva,* who will? That's why men are commanded to study Torah day and night, but women are exempt."

She looked to me on the verge of tears. I believe she wanted to tell me that it wasn't fair. But she had been, as we say, too well brought up.

While I wouldn't have owned up to it as frankly as this young woman had, I too felt that I had to justify the way I spent my time—to prove that my choices benefited, or at least didn't take away from, my family. I couldn't recall the last time I had thought: I need this, I want this for myself. Let everyone else accommodate to me. Attempting some self-assertion, I drank two cups of real coffee, quickly tied a scarf over my hair, and took a cab to an apartment in an old Arab house in the German Colony, off Emek Refaim, where Esther had told me Aviva's class was meeting that week. There was a handwritten sign pointing into a muddy court-yard: Aviva's *shiur.*

Aviva's private class had undergone liberalization since I had last attended it. The hostess, a young Australian woman, her hair uncovered, was bouncing around a graduate student–like kitchen fixing cups of coffee. Her husband wasn't disappearing with a volume of Talmud under his arm into some back room. Rather, he was arranging bakery cookies and Israeli snacks in baskets. He took coats and served apple juice to the women who sat, not around an austere table, but on chairs, couches, and pillows on the floor of this modest living room. I squeezed onto a couch next to an older woman who was knitting a pink and gray sweater. Aviva floated in at 8:30 carrying a man's briefcase. The adoration of Aviva's physical presence hadn't changed. The knitter, for one, said, "Oh, Aviva, what a pretty sweater, look at that black and white design." Aviva, her hair ruffled, her smile beatific, looked as lovely as before, and a little tired. The hostess's husband closed the kitchen door and joined the twenty women in the living room. Some of the women wore pants. Many adorned themselves in jewelry and chic eyeglasses. There were perennial graduate students, middle-class grandmothers, and a cluster of women who covered their heads. There was another man, in a corner, hugging his knees. This was a group I could disappear into. Slowly I worked my scarf off my hair and onto my shoulders, as though I had meant it there in the first place. Aviva caught my eye and nodded. I waved back, as if to my mother from the stage at a school play.

I couldn't contain my enthusiasm. She was there! She noticed me! What she would say would matter.

Aviva took a seat at a small table in front of us, arranged her spiral notebook and the old volume of Midrash, pages marked with many bits of paper. Before she could begin to discuss the portion of the coming week called Vaera (Exodus 6:2–9:35), women switched on the miniature tape recorders they had stacked on her table. Were they afraid of missing a word? Were they bringing the tapes back to husbands and bedridden friends? It looked like a press conference with Margaret Thatcher.

Vaera means "I appeared." The subdivisions of the Torah are usually titled either by the first word of the section or by the first significant word. Just before this section, Moses had asked Pharaoh to let the Israelites leave Egypt. Pharaoh responded by making the Israelites' lives more wretched, and the Israelites complained to Moses that his interference only made their lives worse. Moses agreed with them and mentioned this to God. So in Vaera, God assures Moses that he knows what's going on. He has not forgotten his covenant, and everything will eventually work out: he will free the Israelites from bondage and bring them into the land of Canaan. Then the sequence of plagues that seem to have no effect gets into full swing. Quickly, we gather that no plague, no matter how impressive, will change Pharaoh's mind. For God has hardened Pharaoh's heart, making it impossible for Pharaoh to be moved by the plague. So why all the plagues? Surely God could have brought the Israelites out of Egypt, snap, just like that. If the plagues had a purpose, if they were to affect Pharaoh in some way, what was it?

We began with the first plague: the Nile turns to blood. Moses is told: "Go to Pharaoh in the morning, as he is coming out to the water, and station yourself before him at the edge of the Nile, taking with you the rod that turned into a snake."

Aviva taught: "Pharaoh must have his need for God demonstrated. For him, God is redundant. Pharaoh sees himself as a person without needs." Nonetheless, she pointed out, when Moses encounters Pharaoh, Pharaoh is down at the Nile doing what any man does first thing in the morning, relieving himself. She offered Rashi's comments on the text: Because Pharaoh claimed to be a god (and clearly a proper god would have no need to relieve himself), he used to rise early and go to the Nile to relieve himself secretly.

Aviva said, "The emblem of human need is bodily evacuation." As an aside, feigning modesty, she added, "I'll say this only once to make it clear and spare my maidenly blushes. 'Tis mixed company."

We were reminded of the prayer said after going to the bathroom: "Blessed are you *Adonai,* our God, King of the universe, who fashioned man with wisdom and created him with many openings and cavities. .... If but one of them were to be ruptured or but one of them to be blocked, it would be impossible to survive and stand before you."

Making the connection between Pharaoh and the bathroom prayer, Aviva said:

Without openings, the existential standing of man is impossible ... the balance between openings and closings. A person cannot stand before God if he denies his existential nature, his openness and his closedness. Pharaoh goes to the Nile to evade attention. Moses stands before him so he can't evade his real being at the time he is demonstrably needy. Pharaoh is exposed in what Milan Kundera calls his "unbearable lightness of being." What does Kundera mean by this? Heaviness is necessity: I am, I was, I will be. God is the ultimate necessary being. Pharaoh is not a necessary being. He will die. Since Freud, we're aware of anal anxiety as the fear of mortality.

Before the night concluded, Aviva wove into the lecture the voices of medieval biblical commentators, Lady Macbeth, the testimonies in the Demjanjuk trial. She used all the scholarly tools—literature, linguistics, psychology, law—to crack the text open, to let multiple levels of meaning escape. Aviva concluded: "Praising God shouldn't be a matter of peak experience. A frog's being constantly affirms God. A human being can't achieve that. A frog is impervious to highs and lows because he is what God intended him to be. People aren't always alert."

From phrase to phrase, breathing seemed to stop in the room as each of us marked those particular moments when the learning touched us, almost with unbearable depth. What Aviva had to say never seemed abstract; she never performed intellectual waltzes for their own sake. It seemed to me that she made discoveries even as she taught. All stemmed from the lives we live and dwell on. Aviva's teachings resounded with relevance, her words were life-enhancing. Even when my attention lapsed for a moment, my heart stayed wide awake.

At ten o'clock, Aviva smiled, touched her mouth, and took a sip of juice. We hung there in silence; no one wanted to shatter these holy moments Aviva had carved out. Then a child cried out from in a bedroom. The husband went off to check, and the class broke for coffee. The husband returned to pass out cookies. "Aren't you being a good host," his wife teased.

"Didn't you tell me this is what all the other husbands did?"

I got a ride home with a woman who was a molecular biologist at Hadassah Hospital. She said next week her husband would come to Aviva's class, and she would stay home with their newborn baby. Aviva, who doesn't drive, was a passenger, too.

I asked her if she remembered me. She said I was unforgettable, and to her, everyone is. I asked if I might traipse after her, listen to all her classes, if I might eventually write about her. She said, "In all modesty, my students are the interesting ones, at each place they're so different. There's a real hunger for learning."

I told her I had kept the notes from her class four years ago and referred to them. I knew they were important but didn't know to what use I could put them. "I think what you're teaching might resonate in me now."

"Perhaps the factor is maturity?"

"Maybe. I think I'm willing to be moved. I'm saying, I'm not afraid to be."

We drove through the city, past balconies with laundry hanging, past new construction sites, past the new craze—baguette shops— past bus stops with posters of sexy women dressed as strawberries and pineapples advertising yogurt, past Mercedes cabs with pine tree–shaped air fresheners hanging from rearview mirrors. Torah is called the blueprint for the whole world. I found it hard to imagine that this earthly Jerusalem, neither simple, stark, nor sandy, was a world God once had in mind. Had God intended in the blueprint the sewage and hospital strikes, the explosive anger in the territories? But if God's presence was so clear to Aviva, in Torah and in the world, then it was potentially there for me. When she looked at Torah, she harvested dazzling, moving flashes of lightning.

I joined the ranks of Aviva's followers, women who caught her lectures and spent the rest of the week quoting them, teaching them to children at the Sabbath table, sharing them with friends at work, with husbands in bed. For busy women, Aviva's lectures had a great advantage: even if you had no time to prepare the material, the lectures were still accessible. The only commitment you had to make was to show up each week. And the large crowd made the class no less intimate. I adored the way Aviva looked at us all when she taught, the way she made us all think her remarks were directed specifically to us at this moment in our lives, the way she gave us the impression that she could see the content and potential depths of our souls. Her presence reminded me of a Hasidic legend told by Elie Wiesel. In it, a disciple, overwhelmed by distress and doubt, turns to Rebbe Pinchas of Koretz for advice. His master says, "Go and study. It's the only remedy I know. Torah contains all the answers. Torah *is* the answer." This is not acceptable to the disciple. "I am unable even to study. So shaky are my foundations, so all-pervasive my uncertainties, that my mind finds no anchor, no safety. . . . I open the Talmud and contemplate it endlessly, aimlessly." The rebbe responds that the very same thing once happened to him. That study, prayer, and meditation did nothing to alleviate his doubts.

Then one day I learned that Rebbe Israel Baal Shem Tov would be coming to our town. Curiosity led me to the *shtibel,* where he was receiving his followers. . . . He turned around and saw me, and I was convinced that he was seeing me, me and no one else—but so was everyone else in the room. The intensity of his gaze overwhelmed me, and I felt less alone. And strangely, I was able to go home, open the Talmud, and plunge into my studies once more. "You see," said Rebbe Pinchas of

Koretz, "the questions remained questions. But I was able to go on."*

Lying in bed, I looked over my notes from this class, interesting in itself, but also interesting because it described Aviva's technique. She said the Hebrew women in Egypt were central in the story of redemption, not as leaders, but as biological forces, as midwives and women giving birth. Even though Pharaoh commanded the Hebrew midwives to put all newborn to death, the midwives spared them, saying to Pharaoh, "Because the Hebrew women are not like the Egyptian women: they are vigorous. Before the midwife can come to them, they have given birth." Rashi comments that the Hebrew women can be compared to animals who give birth in the fields. Aviva said, "The image of a bloody animal is the image God adopts for himself. The Israelites can bring one thing out of another thing without aid. This is an intellectual faculty associated with women. One thing, *barukh hashem,* women are given credit for is *binah,* the capacity to pull out of a situation its implications that will lead further, to draw from a given something that will move onwards."

Aviva's words, copied onto my page, were insightful here, obscure or disjointed there, highly creative, pushing the boundaries of traditional exegesis without being sacrilegious. They were lyrics without melody. They didn't begin to convey Aviva's power as a teacher. Her presence was the necessary element. She took us in with her eyes; she strained to listen to the questions we asked so she could hear our intentions. Necessary, also, was the presence of the other women, simultaneously nourished by the Torah refracted by Aviva's vision.

I met a poet who had been studying with Aviva. She was American-born and had been living in the German Colony neighborhood of Jerusalem for a number of years with her husband and their children. I had read a manuscript of her poems. The subject matter—ritual baths, prayer, repentance—indicated she was a religious

---

*Four Hasidic Masters (Notre Dame: University of Notre Dame Press, 1978), 1–3.

woman. Yet her tone suggested a strained intimacy with Torah and Jewish law.

When I first met the poet, a fragile and reticent woman wearing a flowing black skirt and floppy hat, she said Aviva had had a striking influence on her poetry.

The poet had met Aviva's husband, Eric Zornberg, first. I had heard that Eric was a physicist from Canada, and had become an *instalator* in Israel. I didn't know how that translated: It sounded top secret, as though he installed nuclear reactors. The poet said an *instalator*, or plumber, installed and repaired washing machines. Eric Zornberg was a wiz, everyone said so. He had been fixing the poet's washing machine when he invited her to see his house.

"So," said the poet,

I went to see his house. I saw that woman in the other room, and he said that she was a George Eliot scholar, teaching at the Hebrew University. That picture of the woman who went into her room and was preparing something stayed with me. Much later, I was encouraged by a friend to go to her class in *parashat hashavua*. She said, "Oh, it's the thing to do to go to Aviva's class." I didn't really want to go. But I had the image in my head of Aviva going into her room—obviously, she had work to do—and I connected to that. I also go into a room and close the door and have work to do. I was curious, but I didn't know of Aviva's reputation then. It was a nighttime class in someone's house, and hard to get to. I was tired. It was just after my fourth child was born. I had read the Torah portion for the week. It wasn't something I had been doing regularly—it was just a preparation I did for the class. I had no expectation of the class other than being able to understand the text in some way. I was compelled and continue to go. Little by little, it became much larger than a class I went to. Aviva began to frame my life in a very freeing way. What Aviva does is brilliantly choose one moment and crystallize it, shine it. I don't know exactly how she does it. Maybe because her way of speaking is so close to literature: she's a human being with multidimensions, a spiritual-looking woman. As I was looking at her, I realized how beautiful she becomes. There's something like Mona Lisa about her. All of her together is an extremely beautiful, wonderful experience.

When I look at the notebooks that I have on my desk, I see how many of them are of my poems and how many of them are from Aviva's class and how many of them are combinations, because I sometimes grab the wrong notebook. Her notes and my notes: I need them both. Aviva's classes touch on whatever I'm thinking about. I'm very curious about the desert landscape now. Aviva can drop a line as simple as "God would have given the Israelites a shorter way to Canaan, but they didn't have enough desert." Desert is an inner wilderness to which one takes oneself. To find quiet, to be able to face oneself, to make changes. It is disorganized space to begin with, but one can focus in the desert. Aviva can make a provocative statement, then she can go on and give me layers upon layers that will fill out that statement. Aviva helps me think. She helps me live. She makes me think better about my own ability to live in the world, which therefore helps me write. She's my mentor, my muse. She gets that mechanism going, that feeling in my nose or ears that a poem is going to be written. Aviva remains within the law and is endlessly creative with it. It's such an unusual phenomenon that someone both teaches and lives the things she's speaking of. It's a tremendous challenge to have encountered Aviva. A constant challenge. I don't fulfill it.

I told the poet that an Israeli philosopher I had met was taken aback when I told him I was studying Torah and tried to share some of my enthusiasm about studying with Aviva. "How can a woman who is smart and modern and deeply creative connect herself to a religion that reflects a medieval, oppressive, archaic attitude toward women? How can you ally yourself with a patriarchal system that systematically demeans you?" How would you answer that? I asked the poet, as I had been unable come up with a satisfactory response.

"It's the religion Aviva teaches that I'm connected to. The religion as we know it, as practiced in the synagogue, is the religion I feel outside of." The poet did not identify with the virtuous, loyal, nurturant, obedient matriarchs but with seductive, deceitful ones.

The women in the Bible I focus on are Esther, Tamar, and Yael, ones who come out in the man's world to prove a point. They are the forces that confuse and compel me in the poems and in my life. Because these women had a basic drive to be *in* the world, deceit became necessary for them. I align myself with these *other* women who are very active, very strong, and have a constant place at the crossroads where a man is in confusion and they have a way of straightening his vision out.

Take Tamar, whose story is in Genesis 38. Tamar is Judah's daughter-in-law. Her first husband dies before she can conceive. Then, according to the custom of levirate marriage, she marries his brother Onan. Onan, who knows their offspring will not count as his own but rather as his brother's, keeps Tamar from conceiving. Then he dies. Judah, blaming Tamar for these deaths, banishes her from his house. Because she desperately wants a child, she dresses like a harlot and waits for Judah at the crossroads. Judah, recently widowed, comes by and takes her as a prostitute. She asks for payment and takes his ring. She becomes pregnant and he takes her to court. In public, he starts to chastise her. She reveals his ring and says, make your choice. You can chastise me in public, take me to the limits of punishment—or you can see in yourself a need similar to mine, a need to be honest with oneself. Because of her insight she is rewarded. She gives birth to twin boys. Her son Perez is in the line of King David; he brings on the future. The deceit of this woman would not be OK according to strict law; her strength is her flexibility in understanding law. Human lives are weighed down by a future sense of history. That's why I'm drawn to Tamar. She leads me to a place in myself I work on, where deceit and disclosure are at odds and are trying to work out a place in Judaism.

The two kinds of legends about Bruria in the Talmud came to the poet's mind.

Some legends about Bruria point up her high standards, her brilliance, her sensitivity, her belief. And other legends, by virtue of who is creating the legends and who has to live with her as a presence in the world, have to demean Bruria by saying she seduced a student and committed suicide. The legends say: Look what a brilliant woman Bruria is. But she can't be brilliant only. She's a woman in the end. A woman in the midst of Talmudic scholars must have been a terrible threat.

To some, I suppose, Aviva Gottlieb Zornberg must pose a similar threat.

I visited Aviva in her house in the Katamon neighborhood of Jerusalem. Her square Arab house was across from a small grocer and a tiny clothes and fabric store. A neighbor's child sat on the swing suspended in the small courtyard in front of the Zornberg house. I had brought Aviva a bouquet of cut flowers wrapped in cellophane from the corner florist on Palmach Street. Immediately after bringing me through her door, she filled a vase for the flowers, "It's a mitzvah [a commandment] to attend first to the needs of animals, although your needs for a drink are probably more consequential." Books were piled up on the living room coffee table: *The Brothers Karamazov,* Italo Calvino's *Mr. Palomar,* Arthur Green's book on Rabbi Nahman of Bratslav. On the shelves were stacks of literature and philosophy books, many sacred texts, and children's board games. Over the dining room table was a colorful frieze of two lions holding the Ten Comandments, and on the piano was a miniature Torah ark covered with lace, like a little shrine. Photographs on posterboard recording the family's life were everywhere. She then brought me a drink and cakes and ushered me to the couch in her comfortable and modestly elegant parlor as though I were someone of note. I was sure all guests were treated this way.

I asked how it happened that she began to learn Torah.

It was pure pleasure, and probably the reason that things continue is because it was pure pleasure. The story began almost in infancy, three, something like that. And it was always with my father, Rabbi Doctor Zeev Gottlieb. He took my learning on himself. We were first of all in London, and at the age of four, we were in Glasgow. My father was the *av bet din,* the head of Glasgow's rabbinical court. We lived in a rather severe and grand apartment building; the synagogue paid the rent on this house. We had two large lounges which we never went into. There were little electric bells in every room you could press for the servants. There was a maid's room. No maid! We lived the most austere life, with a minimum income. Absolutely no luxuries. Everything bare and lofty, gaunt and gothic.

Very few people in Glasgow were observant. Few people thought it was a value to teach children to study Torah at a high level. So my father had an adversarial relationship with the community. He was seen as rather exotic: he didn't look like a Scottish Jew. So we grew up somewhat differently from people around us. There weren't any Jewish schools in Glasgow, except for *heder,* an hour after school three or four times a week. It wasn't for us. The standard was low and dull, a delinquent atmosphere. No one liked it. There wasn't an opportunity for good Jewish education anywhere else but at home.

I went to public school, a non-Jewish school. We couldn't go to the houses of non-Jews beyond a very young age. Socially it was certainly restricted. Which perhaps put even more passion into learning and the things of the mind and spirit. There was a sense that this was what it was all about. Deemphasizing the social. My mother, Bracha Rosen Gottleib, probably worried about the fact that my social side was not very much developed. But she and my father had great faith in God. They had gone through so many things themselves, they were Holocaust survivors. They just assumed that one day things would take their right course. That I would go away from Glasgow to somewhere, and things would move in a more whole direction.

Rabbi Gottlieb didn't have sons. There were two daughters: Aviva, the elder, and Freema.*

What there would have been had there been sons, I don't know. My father, of blessed memory, was a very liberal person, so I'm sure in any case we would have gotten a good education. But because there were no sons, he really put everything into us. From a very young age we had daily sessions with him, and that was really our only Jewish education, because we didn't go to any outside formal Jewish school until much later. What we had with my father was something absolutely unique which I can never be grateful enough for. First of all, by working our way through the text. By the time I was eight, I had finished the whole Torah. Just sitting and learning, reading, translating, talking about issues that arose. He got a doctorate in Judaica along the way, so he was interested in scholarly questions too: grammar and syntax and the roots of Hebrew words, how words work and how they alter. So from childhood, I was very aware of words, of the power of Hebrew words, the way words work in the Torah. Things opened up quickly as we started doing commentaries, Mishnah, and philosophy. Any text that

---

*Freema Gottlieb is the author of *The Lamp of God: A Jewish Book of Light* (Northvale: Jason Aronson Inc., 1989), a study exploring how the metaphor of light is used in Jewish ritual and thought.

came up, that occurred to him, we would open up and start working on. We had this every day after school, often in his study. I have memories of his lying in bed, resting, and me sitting beside the bed and working with him, or at the seashore when we went away on holiday, we'd always take books with us.

This seemed idyllic enough, Papa and daughters soaking in the salt air and sacred texts. I tried to translate this into the way I lived. Periodically, I'll feel delinquent about expecting schools to do all the educating of our daughters, and I'll remember that it's ultimately a parent's responsibility to instill in children the material we believe they should know. Before we had children, we talked about stuffing our progeny with Latin and Greek, languages we didn't even know. Peter has had some success teaching them Bible informally, but as soon as they get wind of the fact that an adult is teaching and they are supposed to be focused and learning, their attention flags and they want to break away. Didn't Aviva, the child, wish to run off and play? No resentment that other children weren't spending their free time studying Torah?

A minimum of resentment. There must have been some, at certain times, but it's not what I remember. I remember it was interesting. I felt good. I felt he was proud of me, and that was very important. I was very quick with language as a child; I remembered words very easily. I have memories of how astonished he'd be that I'd remembered a word that we had once, weeks and weeks before. That sort of childish level of accomplishment. But it made a basis for a sense that the sky's the limit, there's no reason not to go and do whatever you want to. We didn't learn Gemara, although every now and then we would just do a little bit. He'd open the Gemara up and say, "I want you to know what goes on in here." If I had said I wanted to learn Gemara, I'm sure he would have taught me. That was somehow his natural border; for Gemara he didn't see any need. I didn't have a sense of taboo about it.

He had a capacity for projecting enormous love, both for the material and for me. Which is everything you could want from a teacher. We continued learning until I went away to university, and thereafter, more occasionally. The aim was not to produce a scholar. I think he wanted to convey to me a love of tradition, the love of everything he loved. He certainly didn't see me as a teacher of Jewish subjects. I wasn't being groomed for any particular role. This was just basic equipment for life.

The next stage, when I was seventeen, I went to Gateshead, a little town in the North of England, the setting of *Jane Eyre*: a little coal-mining town, a coal-engrimed environment, an impoverished working community. Gateshead was a *makom torah,* a place where there were several institutions of Torah learning. And a women's seminary. I wasn't sent there. My parents weren't at all interested in this brand of Judaism, which I will describe as sort of *haredi* [the term used in Israel for right-wing, superscrupulous observance]. Gateshead was to the right of where we were. I had paid a visit to Gateshead and fell in love with it. I wanted to go because of a kind of religious idealism, something about the purity of the spirituality that went on there. With some misgivings, my parents agreed I could go. But with this condition: that I prepared at Gateshead for the entrance exams for Cambridge. For a couple of hours in the afternoons, in a cold "shilling in the meter" bedroom, I would get on with the work for Cambridge, preparing Donne and Herbert and other poets for the entrance exams. I wrote my essays with gloves on because it was so cold. What I was doing was quite, quite foreign to the atmosphere around me. I got into Cambridge, and the truth is, though it's not in keeping with my image at this moment, I wanted to stay on at Gateshead.

I wanted to become a Gateshead girl. I liked what I was experiencing at Gateshead, even though it really excluded, ideologically, not just practically, things like going to Cambridge and secular studies, and the possibility of woman's self-development. It's a different view altogether, the *haredi* view of self-fulfillment, which to a great extent I bought. I found things that touched me quite deeply in that view. It provided a very emotional sense of integrity, that life was going to be lived for a single purpose, with great emotional satisfaction, a feeling that life hung together. I really did buy the ideal of marrying a *talmid hakham* [a Torah scholar] as the purpose of my life.

I had minimal ideas about what I would be doing. My mother was disturbed by this. My parents insisted I take up the option of going to Cambridge. They thought: Here is this talented girl. They thought I was finishing my life at an early age. I didn't have any sense that I had talents or that I might be doing something in the world. To this day, who knows? One never knows about decisions that took place in the past, what alternatives might have been. I'm sure that—I also believe in God—I'm sure that whatever path I would have chosen, God and I together, would have worked out. I wouldn't have ended up just washing the nappies. But my mother had a kind of horror that I would end up frustrated, just slaving in the kitchen, producing baby after baby, and that I didn't have a clue to what this *haredi* life entailed. Bear in mind that I'm not at all practical. My mother knew better than I did at the time. I'm bad at washing dishes and all that, and to this day I do the minimum, and I can get away with it because, *barukh hashem,* I have other things that make up for my failings in this area. If that had been my whole life, it wouldn't have been easy. So my mother was probably right.

Ahavat torah [love of Torah] was something I got from many sides. From my father, from Gateshead. It was a gut sense that

"Turn it [Torah] over and turn it over, because everything is in it" is true. You could take the texts and it didn't matter how opaque they might seem as first, if you kept going at them, you would find enormous treasures. Everything is there.

I did my B.A. in English literature. Then I took a year off, went to London, worked at various jobs. I wasn't sure I wanted to do a doctorate, so I was trying out the work world. I realized you couldn't do very much with a first degree, and I went running back to Cambridge to do a doctorate in George Eliot. At Cambridge, there was a Jewish student society: I sometimes gave *shiurim* [Torah classes], but mostly I learned by myself. It was an absolute for me to learn in order to maintain myself. It was a matter of developing a certain way of looking at the world which I had begun to develop and didn't want to lose. In a place like Cambridge, it's very easy to go awash completely. I wanted to experience everything I could experience in Cambridge, that is, that was permitted according to Jewish law. Culturally, to take part in everything. There were all kinds of limits on what I could do. Social relations with non-Jews were very limited. There were incredible ratios of women to men, like one woman to nine men. So it meant that women were the focus of unnatural interest. Quite unfair. You got grandiose ideas about yourself there; you thought you were the world's gift to masculinity. As a religious woman, there was no way I could encourage anything of this kind. So it somewhat limited me in what I could do, where I could go.

Did it never enter her mind that her classmates at Cambridge must have thought she was a stick-in-the-mud?

Of course it entered my mind. I suffered a great deal about it. More even among Jews. Among non-Jews, it didn't bother me. They respected me. I found good women friends among non-Jews because there was an understanding that I stood for a certain idea and wanted to maintain the integrity of that idea. Among Jews it was more difficult, because I was *so* extremely religious that there were very few people who had a common language with me. It was difficult and I did suffer. Though I felt I had a strong inner life and didn't feel like I was suffering. I didn't want to lead the kind of life—sexually—the people around me were leading. It didn't attract me at all. I didn't like the feeling of being different: but on the whole, I didn't feel an oddball in the negative sense. It wasn't easy, but I felt I was gaining things at Cambridge I wouldn't have gained if I hadn't been in this environment. I value what I got at Cambridge. It will always be with me. I never thought of a profession or a vocation. Just studying for studying's sake, and we'll see what happens. I was extremely flighty. My mother had a more practical bent. She wanted me to be an international lawyer.

After Cambridge, Aviva came to Jerusalem and was hired to teach literature in the English department at the Hebrew University. Her former colleagues, now my colleagues, spoke of her with enormous respect. They said she was a superb teacher, very well received by both students and faculty. They said she was let go because she didn't have enough publications.

Aviva's leaving the university was an enormous blessing for all of us who studied with her. I asked Aviva how her new career as an itinerant teacher of Torah began.

A woman in the neighborhood rang me up one Friday afternoon just as I was leaving town for the Sabbath and asked, very low key, "Would you like to give a class to women in *parashat hashavua?*" She knew me as an academic, she knew my university side, and she just assumed that having been a rabbi's daughter and a student at Gateshead, I would have enough knowledge to do a little *shiur* [class]. *Parashat hashavua* hasn't got a very high status. This was 1981, I think. I wasn't working at the time. I had left the university and must have had all three kids by that time. So I started teaching this group of women from the neighborhood. They were English teachers, librarians, many with five or six children, modern Orthodox, intelligent. Some had backgrounds, some didn't. It was at people's houses. I did it with a great hesitation. I wasn't sure I was qualified to do this. And as I tend to do things, I took it terribly seriously, completely disproportionate to what it was. It was the kind of *shiur* that you're supposed to look at the book for an hour and go and give it. That's the way anyone gives a *shiur* like that. And I would spend the whole week preparing for the one class. I didn't even think that maybe I could be out earning goodness knows what. I didn't feel I could. I had small children, I didn't want to take on a high-powered job. So the *shiur* would be a kind of pretext to get me into learning again in a serious way.

Didn't Eric mention to you that you were overpreparing?

I'm lucky that Eric is very loose. He was earning a sufficient living to keep us going. It's just quixotism. I didn't make any long-range plans. There's an expression I always apply to myself, that "God guards the fools . . . the unwary." And I was very unwary. I did this for several years. I didn't take any money for it, and at a certain point, academic American friends who knew me and appreciated me said, "This is crazy. You should at least be getting paid for this." I felt that it was disproportionate that I should spend the whole week preparing for something and not earn any money. So I had a certain restless feeling at the time.

Then I was hired to teach for Rabbi Gold at the Jerusalem College for Adults, a Monday evening and Wednesday morning class. It's largely women, but it's open to both sexes. When it started off I would have a few students in class and my heart would sink. I'd think, what am I going to do? Over the years it just snowballed. I learned to respect many of these rather unprepossessing-looking middle-aged ladies who come. There's much more to them than meets the eye. They are frustrated in many ways. They are frustrated learners, people with enormous thirst and capacity to take in whatever you give them. It really moves me that they're so excited. Now the class has become huge—all kinds of people, very varied. And I meet people I have to make no effort at all to like and admire and find interesting. There's a very interesting relation with the men, I don't know if you've sensed it.

I told Aviva that I had been paying some attention to the men the time I went to her morning class held downtown in the library at the Jerusalem branch of Touro College. Women had come early to unstack the chairs and pick choice spots for themselves, and by nine, there were one hundred and fifty women and two men accompanying their wives. The man behind me said to his wife's friends, "This is the best class I ever took. But where is the other gentleman? Don't tell me he's not coming and he tricked me."

There was lots of hubbub in this room, as though an important ceremony were to take place. Esther was right about women's Torah learning exploding. The man behind me, who could not help noticing the energy in the room, told his wife in a voice of some authority, "Ninety percent of this is socializing, 10 percent is learning."

The second man came up to Aviva's table after class. He held a Bible in his hand and was wagging his finger at her. He was trying to tell her that he agreed that her points were important, not that he hadn't thought of them himself, and not that he didn't have other insights into the texts that she neglected to mention. He opened his Bible and continued to shake his finger at Aviva as though she were a naughty but dear girl. Aviva smiled at him, and as he turned away from her, he tucked his thumbs under his belt, and with no small amount of force, yanked his pants up high, satisfied. He believed he had made his point: Aviva had important things to say, but he still knew more. Aviva said to me:

I'm sure I'm partly to blame. If I had less of a sweet feminine attitude, then it would decrease. Nehama Leibowitz [Israel's grande dame of Bible studies] doesn't get that kind of reaction, I'm sure. She terrifies them out of their seats. So my personality has something to do with it. What I find interesting is the relation between the wives and their husbands. I sense a woman will turn up with the man in tow, obviously to show the man "This is the woman I've been learning from who I think is so ai-ai-ai." You can just feel the husbands' skepticism. They sit there looking "Hmmm." And the wives are a little anxious on many scores. Their self-esteem is at stake. If the husbands go away afterwards and say something derogatory, then that will really put an end to the wives' sense of "Aha, you see! We can do it!," their sense that it is possible for women to do really interesting things. And with all due modesty, I know what I do in this field is more interesting than almost anything that's going on. So I should have a certain amount of confidence. I view whimsically, a little bit, the reaction of these men who come and lecture me afterwards. Some men do have a very nice attitude. There's one Conservative rabbi on the verge of retirement—he would stand up when I came into the room. It's right, according to Jewish law, if a teacher comes in, you get up, it's *kavod letorah,* honor to the Torah, it's not personal."

I told Aviva that there was a little titter of excitement in the circle that surrounded the men. As if in the absence of some divine sanction for women's learning coming down from the heavens, the presence of men meant that this must be the "real thing."

There are good reasons for it, what can I say? To be fair, it's men—men who learn Torah, not just any man, just because he's got trousers on doesn't mean that he knows anything—a man who's been in a yeshiva has a certain state-of-the-art sense of the norms. These men have a certain basis for judgment of the way you learn that women really don't have. And since what I'm doing is slightly eccentric—it's not exactly the way you are taught in any conventional environment—there's a need to have it approved by someone who has a good technical sense. If an approach is firmly rooted in the central tradition, you can say, Ah yes, that's interesting. Otherwise you'd say, Ah no, that's beyond the pale. So it's true, the men have that sense and the women don't. The women who are very well educated are not the ones who bring their husbands along.

I shared a disturbing commentary on Leviticus that I had come across. What it had to say about the lengths one should go to to keep peace in a family was a touching ethic; what it suggested about attitudes held about a woman's learning troubled me. The commentary, in the form of a legend, goes like this:

> Rabbi Meir used to deliver discourses on Sabbath evenings. There was a woman there in the habit of listening to him. Once the discourse lasted a long time, and she waited until the exposition was concluded. She went home and found that the candle had gone out. Her husband asked her, "Where have you been?" She answered, "I was sitting listening to the voice of the preacher." (*Midrash Rabbah* to Leviticus 9:9)

Were I rewriting Jewish tradition, or had I been in the group that wove these commentaries, I would have had the husband then conclude:

> You are some woman. You readied the house and prepared the food for the Sabbath, you served us, you got the kids off to bed, and then, because you are a pious woman and an intellect, too, you spent half the night studying with Rabbi Meir. Even

though that meant postponing until your return the intimate time we spend on Friday night. And you knew you still had to get up with the kids in the morning. Given your commitment to study, no sacrifices that I make for you so that you can further your studies would be too great.

My ending would hardly be original, for this is essentially the spirit of self-sacrifice (though with a twist) behind the legend of Rabbi Akiva's wife, Rachel, who forfeited her father's approval and her dowry, who lived like a poor widow for twenty-four years, selling even her hair, so that Akiva might go off and study in a yeshiva to become the greatest Torah scholar. There is even a legal provision for Akiva's protracted study: a man can go off to study Torah for two or three years without asking for his wife's approval.

But this is how the commentary of *Midrash Rabbah* continues:

Said he to her, "I swear I will not let you enter here until you go spit in the face of the preacher." She stayed away one week, a second, and a third. Said her neighbors to her, "Are you still angry with one another? Let us come with you to the discourse." As soon as Rabbi Meir saw them, he saw by means of the Holy Spirit [what had happened]."

Were I continuing, I'd have Rabbi Meir, husband of the learned Bruria, give this complaining husband a piece of his mind, telling him that for the sake of his wife's Torah learning, he would have to bend a little, break his rigid self-absorption.

But the commentary pays no mind to the inappropriateness of the husband's behavior. No one asks: Isn't it appropriate for men to make sacrifices for their wife's Torah study? The questions that draw the attention of the legend makers are How can the husband be released from his vow? and How will Rabbi Meir save the marriage? Rabbi Meir asked if any woman in the room knew an incantation that would release the husband from the vow he had taken so his wife could return home. A woman who knew charms said that if the wife spits in Rabbi Meir's eye, the husband will be released from his vow. The wife, understandably, could not bring herself to spit in the eye of this sage, whom she obviously revered. Rabbi Meir told her to spit not once, but seven times and then to go home and tell her husband what she had done. She did this because Rabbi Meir insisted, and then she went home.

The text doesn't worry about the horror the wife must have felt at being forced to humiliate her rabbi, and through him, herself. Didn't her gesture mean, "I admit it is foolishness for women to place their learning above the whims of their husbands?" Didn't it suggest a sage should chase married women out of his classes and send them home to their husbands, where they belong? Not concerned with exploring the wife's state of mind, the legend turns to the disciples who could not understand how Rabbi Meir could have encouraged the wife to act so disrespectfully toward him and, consequently, toward Torah. Rabbi Meir responded by quoting Rabbi Ishmael's teaching: "Great is peace, since even of the Great Name, written though it be in sanctity, the Holy One, blessed be He, has said, 'Let it be blotted out in water for the purpose of making peace between husband and wife.' " That is, if God will allow his name to be blotted out by water for the sake of marital peace, then Rabbi Meir could do the same.

In the absence of any traditional lore to sustain her, I asked Aviva if she was able to justify the sacrifices made by her husband and children for her Torah learning.

It's the same with any career that a woman decides is important to her. She will try to arrange her family life so that, as best as possible, she can accommodate both spheres. The whole family has to feel that it is an important value for Mummy to carry on with what she's doing and to do it well. The whole family accommodates; everyone just moves in their elbows a little bit closer and shifts around and understands me. In our family everyone knows that on Sunday and Monday, Mummy is in a pretty bad mood. And it's too bad. I wish it weren't that way.

I'm very fraught on Sunday and Monday when I'm coming to full boil in my preparation. Those days I'm working full steam and wondering if I'm ever going to come to a head. I spread my net very wide and learn as much as I can within a short period of time. I learn as much as I can about the *parashah,* as many of the commentaries and midrashim as I can. I take a lot of notes and gradually what happens, as with any creative work of this kind, structures begin to emerge and I realize there's a connection here and there, and things begin to stretch tentacles toward each other. It's very hard to do it without anxiety, but meantime, everyone knows they come home for lunch and I'm still in the study and they sort of rustle up something to eat. Not what you'd set up as an example of your happy Jewish household. I'm quite anxious and can't pay much attention to what's going on around. It's like any profession, except to me, this is like having a creative profession. There are times of great tension, times when I feel almost attacked by subconscious forces, and I don't sleep well at night. All kinds of things are cooking. It's not just a matter of sitting down and doing a job in a professional, cool, rather distanced way. I'm extremely involved on many levels, and this must take a toll beyond an office job.

Still, rationally, I know it's not so terrible. It's one day, at most two days a week. And the days I'm high, I'm very good with the family. When a class goes well, it spills over into the family and I can do much more with what goes on at home. *If the children acquire their own love of Torah, I hope they will learn to love Torah enough to understand what I'm doing.* And Eric accepts it. In any case, he sees it as more or less successful, *barukh hashem.* But even if it weren't, if it were something important to me, he would accept it. I think a family where the husband is seriously learning—which is the case in our family—would certainly appreciate the wife's seriousness in learning.

A family senses whether it's working or not. For me person-ally—and I imagine this is so for most women—the family is of primary value. To see one's family not flourishing while one's learning is flourishing would not be acceptable. I take off in the summer, partly out of the sense that I want a certain amount of time when I'm not tense, when I'm not constantly coming to this boil each week. I want time when I can be on a fairly even keel emotionally and take whatever is coming to me from the family and deal with it without putting up my own needs as a screen sometimes. Brachi is almost twelve. The boys are ten and almost eight. Not babies. I don't feel my learning is at the cost of the family. Sometimes they groan, "You're going out at night again!" Moshie has this exaggerated sense that it's every night. It's two nights, but it seems a lot to him.

I don't think my children have a clue about what I do. They know Mummy's a teacher. Sometime, even though it goes against the grain, I'd like to have Brachi come to class. Just so she knows. I have a ghoulish sense, What if I died tomorrow? God forbid. Brachi wouldn't have a clue at all about what Mummy was doing those years. I just want her to know. I don't want to impose it on her. Maybe when she gets older. I don't want to share my intolerance with the way her school teaches Torah: they don't try to break out of the bubble of familiar terms and concepts, and I'm constantly asking questions that break the bubble, that dive in there and say, Yes, but how does this relate to things outside?

Do you know Thomas Kuhn's book *The Structure of Scientific Revolutions?* A friend who's a linguist lent it to me. Kuhn has the idea that in every age, every stage of scientific development, there are certain questions that everyone is dealing with and these are the only important questions at the time. And then there's the innovator, who pushes the questions onwards, who thinks of the question no one else is dealing with. Ninety-nine times out of a hundred, that question gets shunted aside because it's not where the thrust is. But if the innovator is lucky, or a forceful enough personality, he can change the face of science, moving things on to a different age. In Torah learning, there's a certain sense of tact, decorum: that one doesn't ask certain questions. Nevertheless, I continue to do it, because they are questions that arise very sincerely out of my life experience, my way of thinking and feeling. These questions seem to appeal to a number of women, who you could argue, by virtue of being women, are marginal to where the "real" questions are.

I wondered how Aviva's father felt about her teaching Torah, to know his daughter was, certainly in the religious community, a little bit of a maverick. Perhaps he would have regretted having ever taught her.

On the contrary, said Aviva,

I often wish he could see what it is now. He was always terribly proud when he heard me teach. It was one of the real *nachas*-[joy] giving experiences. Sometimes, after people have died, the spirits meet in a certain way, and I think now I can imagine him enjoying very much what happens in class, not just pleasure for his daughter, but the ideas. I think he would be excited by it.

Eric Zornberg walked in with many groceries in plastic market bags and began to wash the fruits and vegetables in the kitchen. He wore dark blue work clothes and a dark cloth *kippah*. "Hi, hello," said Aviva, "I could hear you coming." Aviva's kids and mine would be returning from school. I needed to get home, we both needed to get ready for lunch, the day's main meal. The external rhythms of family life were urging us to tune in. I gathered my things together to leave. At the door, Aviva, who must have been uncomfortable spending so much time focusing on herself, asked how my Torah studies were going. I was stumbling around the idea of the sacredness of Torah, I said. If I believed the Torah, Oral and Written, was God's word, then how could I not want to take the text literally and follow all the laws? If I felt uncertain about God's presence, then the Torah had no different a status than any other text. Given her background, I said to Aviva, I'm sure none of this is an issue for her. She probably never even has these kinds of thoughts.

She said that regardless of one's background, belief in the existence of God doesn't just come with one's genes. That aside, the sacredness of the text shouldn't be a problem I concerned myself with. "Just keep going back to the text to find out what it has to say to you, by yourself, with teachers."

She compared a relationship to Torah to a love relationship. You don't ask every moment what a marriage means. You live together, you have a physical relationship. Maybe after five years, you might begin to dwell on the nature of your love. Love of Torah, she said, was real. You lived it. "Study the text, and worry about the sacredness later."

Six

Sitting across the aisle from me on my Pan Am flight to France en route to Israel had been an elderly man wearing a prayer shawl underneath his black vest, a *kippah* over his nest of white hair, and then a black hat. He waved the stewardess on when she offered him headphones and the tray holding his preordered, supremely kosher meal that was certified fit by the pickiest of rabbis. His wife, a gray-green wig perched on her head, called the stewardess back: "Give me the tray, sweetheart. Later he'll eat." The entire flight, except for when he went over to the curtain separating first class from economy and leaned into it to pray as though it were the Western Wall, he held a minuscule Talmud inches from his eyes and studied it through a magnifying glass. While he absorbed himself in the sayings of the wise, I passed the time leafing through airline copies of the magazine *Working Woman,* and while the girls slept, I began the Amanda Cross mystery in my satchel. I blended right in with most other passengers on this flight, cosmopolitan-looking gentiles and secular Jews who carried Wash n' Dries, who freshened up their hairdos from time to time, who obeyed the pilot when he said to sit down, who saw a flight as a few hours of life that didn't count. If this plane were to tumble onto an island and I were to spend the rest of my days with this group, I trusted I would have enough in common with them to live harmoniously.

I could not keep my eyes off this big religious man. Even as we waited to switch planes in a lounge at Charles de Gaulle, he continued studying his Talmud. Travelers, Jews and non-Jews, must have thought him an eccentric, a fossil, like the Amish riding a horse-drawn carriage on an interstate highway. Yet it struck me, superficial differences of style aside, I had a great deal in common with him. Both our hearts break when we hear about Jewish misfortunes. We mourn and bury in the same way. We greet births and marriages uttering the same incantations, dancing the same dance. We share the same destiny as Jews. We call God by the same name. The significant difference between us? His God seemed so much nearer to him, more accessible, more certain, reachable through Torah, prayer, and the unfolding of history. His God, I believed, existed.

I kept up my learning at Pardes, going back to the text each day, trying, as Aviva suggested, not to worry so much about how what I was learning was going to fit into my life. It was a leap of faith to invest so much time in the texts and to push aside my doubts. My Bible with Rashi's commentary became my constant accessory. I was like a person obsessed, like an old lady who carries around her Book of Psalms on subways, like the elderly man on the plane. I worked through verses while waiting for buses, as well as during the breaks between students during my office hours, when it would otherwise have been tempting simply to stare from my office window on Mount Scopus at the view of the clouds and golden haze lifting and lowering over the turrets, towers, and domes of the Old City.

It was my hope that if I learned enough, if it started to come more easily, then maybe something would click. I clung to a saying: Just as water is tasteless to the person who isn't thirsty, so Torah is tasteless to the person who doesn't labor at acquiring it, bit by bit.

I was meeting the women Esther described to me daily, but rarely by plan. Women occupied with Torah kept crossing my path. While searching for a Jerusalem synagogue I could comfortably pray in, I met a woman I shall call Yehudis, a friend of Esther's, a daughter of Hasidim who had become a scholar of Jewish subjects.

My search for a place to pray had originated in a beautiful synagogue on the hill that was just above my apartment in Nayot and just below the sculpture garden of the Israel Museum. Here was the perfect house of worship. It was a tiny stone building roofed in red tile, smaller than a one-room schoolhouse. Too small even to hold a bathroom. If you needed one, you returned home or took your child behind a tree. When the *kohanim,* descendants of the high priests of the Temple, needed to rinse their hands before administering the priestly blessing, they washed in a wall-mounted portable sink that drained into a bucket. While American seminarians studying right down the road affectionately dubbed the synagogue "the little shul on the prairie," its proper name was Ohel Leah, the tent of Leah. My Hebrew name is Leah, so I saw the name hung on the synagogue as a personal welcome sign. None of the worshipers chatted; no one even whispered inside. The stone walls magnified every sound, and prayers resonated as if in an echo chamber. From the window, I saw that clouds enveloped us, as if we were in an airplane. And straining through clumps of rocks on the hill, I could see red anemones and purple cyclamen. If God dwells in buildings, God dwells here, I thought. This was the ultimate antidote to glitzy synagogues with ballrooms and bridal suites. If prayers were heard, they were heard from here.

I had a single problem with this "little shul on the prairie" that kept me from returning after three trial visits. The women's section was limited to only two rows in the back, curtained off way above eye level. The curtain was not transparent and I could barely make out the rituals going on in the men's section. The men appeared to me as puppets in an Indonesian shadow play. Clearly no one expected more than a few women to come pray at Ohel Leah. From the way the building was set on the hill, the women's rows seemed to jut out over the edge of a cliff. If there was a subtle landslide, the loss of the women's section could go unnoticed.

I didn't believe a God who wanted my prayers would prefer me praying like this. I knew a number of professional women in America who had no problems with settings like these, mostly women who had either grown up or married into Orthodoxy. They did not see sitting in the women's section as an exercise in self-effacement, but rather a pleasant opportunity to be in the company of women, praying some, chatting some about this and that: who got tenure, who was having a difficult pregnancy, who was being fixed up with a widowed psychoanalyst. These women, in charge at work and at home, were relieved to sit back in synagogue and let the men handle all the ritual. My complaints made them impatient. "What's there to see in a service anyways?" they would ask, as if to remind me that if I wanted to see a show, I should go to Broadway. "You're there to pray."

It seemed to me that if there was nothing in synagogue for *anyone* to see, then we should all be praying in the dark.

Sitting in Ohel Leah, I kept thinking about a jazzy sportscar my brother-in-law used to drive. It had two enormously comfortable reclining leather bucket seats in front. The seats had broad armrests and the leg room was luxurious. There was a hard bench in the back that suggested a back seat, a ledge wide enough to carry the slimmest attaché case. The back seat of my brother-in-law's car and the women's section of Ohel Leah carried the same implicit message: It is not that there is no place for you here. There is a place. A place of no honor, a place meant never to be used. When we rode in the back seat of my brother-in-law's car, we piled in as pranksters, hanging our legs out the window and hooting.

Each Saturday morning I would take Juliana, my elder daughter and the better hiker, in search of a synagogue that might be both pure and authentic like the "shul on the prairie" as well as respectful to women. So far I had discovered that the more progressive and egalitarian a synagogue, the fewer the congregants competent in synagogue skills. It seemed that if I wanted what I thought of as authenticity, I'd have to sacrifice egalitarianism. And vice versa. Either way I lost. Then I saw a notice tacked on the bulletin board at Pardes announcing a women's Sabbath morning prayer service. Many traditionally observant women accepted that when women prayed by themselves, it was permissible for them to lead services, read from the Torah, and have Torah honors. This service, as well as a vegetarian potluck lunch, would be held at the home of Penina Peli, a well-known activist in circles of observant women concerned with feminist issues. She was the chairperson of the Jerusalem International Conference on Halakhah and the Jewish Woman.

That Sabbath morning the streets were quiet. The only people out were those straggling into synagogue for the last parts of the service or secular Israelis out walking mutts and Irish Setters. I heard no noise coming out of the apartment where the services were to be held, and even though there was a welcome sign crayoned on a sheet of construction paper, I thought perhaps I had taken down the wrong apartment number on Brenner Street. Finally my knock was heard. An older woman wearing a long brown embroidered Arab dress and a long scarf draped over her short gray hair opened the door for us. I assumed this was Penina. She let us into the apartment she shared with her husband, the well-known professor of Judaica, Pinchas H. Peli.* Juliana noticed that the kitchen counter was piled with containers of salads and cakes. I was more intrigued to see that the living room had been transformed into a place for prayer. In front of the rows of chairs, the Peli family's small Torah scroll rested on a table covered with an embroidered cloth. It was cold in the room, and the few women who wore prayer shawls wrapped them tightly around themselves as though they were at a football game.

*Rabbi Peli died in the spring of 1989.

We were immediately enveloped in very soft, ringing sounds of women's voices: *Hallelu et shem Adonai,* "Praise God's name." We were twenty-one women in this room, some I recognized as rabbinical and cantorial students of the Conservative movement. The cantorial students sang operatic harmony, resulting in a sound that was part heavenly choir of angels, part Andrews sisters. I was shocked to hear prayer in this feminine key and found it wonderful to be able to join in at my natural range. I needed to instruct myself to accept that this pretty sound was as legitimate a vehicle for prayer as was the drone and mumble of men's voices. A woman I later learned was Esther's friend Yehudis swept me and Juliana into chairs next to her and wove us into the group. Yehudis frothed over with warmth. She was probably my age, but she reminded me of a great-aunt who always arrived with strudels and coloring books in plastic shopping bags. Juliana took an interest in Yehudis's bulky sweater, appliquéd with fruits and vegetables. Yehudis welcomed Juliana into her lap.

"How do you know this sweet child, this mamele, so well?" she whispered to me, wiggling Juliana's high ponytail. Juliana was inspecting Yehudis's long brown braid. "You seem to have such a lovely, close relationship."

"I've known her all her life. I'm her mother."

"I would never have thought that right off. That's sad, isn't it, that I assume all women in their thirties, like us, are single?"

The women in Penina's living room, many whom I recognized, were engaged in learning or teaching Torah at one level or another. That we had all come to this pickup service suggested that few of us had a comfortable regular place to pray. Some of the women were in their twenties; most were in their mid-thirties. With few exceptions, they were not married and had no children. I felt the matchmaker's concern, which I developed ever since my single friends stopped valuing their independence and started imploring with muted panic: Find me a good man before it's too late. If my highly educated secular friends were straining to locate good men, I worried that these women carving places for themselves in Torah

137

study—those interested in marriage, that is—were finding it doubly hard.

Only men learned in Torah would suit them as husbands, and I didn't know just how interested learned men were in dating women as or more learned than they. Unmarried women in the observant community nearing their late thirties I had met told me they felt like planes hovering over a control tower, hoping their clearance to land would come before their fuel ran out. These women felt another pressure: the observant community, whose supreme values were marriage, family, and home life, considered being single a temporary, unfortunate state that needed to be remedied. Single women who remain single beyond a certain age are considered satellites tossed out of orbit.

One woman, a Wesleyan junior studying for the year at the Hebrew University, began to chant the Torah. She forgot the melodies, stumbled over the words, and bungled pronunciation. Everyone cringed to hear dishonor being done to the Torah. Juliana squirmed. I feared she would conclude that when women took over services the result was ineptitude. I knew that if this woman chanting Torah had been educated as average Orthodox Jewish boys are, she never would have emerged from childhood without strong and practiced liturgical skills. You had to give her credit. She was determined to read Torah no matter how embarrassing the struggle.

Mercifully, another young woman, a Pardes student, took over at the next segment. She wore a white lacy *kippah* over her puffy blonde hair and chanted eloquently. She understood the meaning of the words and used the melodies for expressive emphasis. The content of the Torah seemed to be singing itself. I hoped the proficiency of this better chanter might blot out the ineptitude of her predecessor in Juliana's memory. When this better chanter finished, she recited the *Shehehianu* prayer for special occasions: "Blessed are you, *Adonai,* our God, King of the universe, who has kept us alive, sustained us, and brought us to this season." The women who surrounded her at the Torah kissed and hugged her, shook her hand, danced "mazal tov!" around her. "What is it?" people who didn't know her asked. "Is she engaged?"

The better chanter turned to face the congregation. "This is my first time reading Torah!" Her announcement divided the group into two camps of whisperers. One camp was irritated by her self-conscious self-congratulation, thinking it gratuitous and out of place. The other camp felt that if women didn't mark moments of joy and make up rituals where they were lacking, the time for celebration might never come. I sided with both camps. I vowed that Juliana would learn to read Torah at twelve, the proper age. Then she could stand before a congregation, chant as tentatively as all first timers chanted, and be showered at this appropriate time with packets of jelly beans and chocolate kisses tied up in squares of tulle.

Yehudis was called up to re-cover the Torah in its mantle after it had been read. She went up tentatively. Approaching the Torah, she wrapped a mohair shawl around herself. She might have been chilly. Perhaps she really wanted to wrap a tallit around herself but was uneasy with the maleness it evoked. Such a gesture may have enticed her. Was it too bold and potent to carry out? That's how I would have felt. I watched Yehudis bunch the Torah mantle up in her hands and then gently shimmy it down the sides of the scroll as though it were a baby's undershirt.

Walking home down Gaza Street, I felt jubilant. I was pleased that this was one Sabbath morning I could pray without anger welling up in my throat. Pity this women's prayer group was just a sometime thing, depending on Penina's initiative to organize and hold it together. I sensed Penina had been in the trenches long enough and was eager to turn the leadership over to other women.

I asked Juliana what she thought about the service. I knew she had enjoyed all the attention Yehudis had given her. "It didn't seem like a real service," Juliana said. "It felt like a class. That first woman who read Torah could hardly do it. She was awful. I would have died of embarrassment if I were her."

"She was learning," I said.

"Then she should wait until she knows how. She should have practiced at home. How come we didn't get to stay for lunch? That wasn't fair that everyone else got to. They brought such good food."

"We have a family to go home to and guests."

At home, Peter took one look at us and said, "Well I can see you finally enjoyed services."

I tried to convey how joyous I found praying with women. Peter wasn't surprised; he thought prayer was best in single-sex communities. What exactly about prayer did he find sexual, I wanted to know? If he could concentrate at a lecture or a play when women were in the audience, why couldn't he concentrate in synagogue?

He asked, "How can you make a declaration of affection to God and concentrate on your prayer with your spouse sitting next to you?"

Were we all temptresses in the women's section, the mommies stuffing their babies with Cheerios, the matrons with hankies tucked into their sleeves? How come no X-rated movies were set in the women's section of a synagogue? And how come no one worried that women were finding it difficult to pray and supervise small children in synagogue at the same time?

There was a knock at our back door. It was Raphael, taking off his bicycle helmet. The girls, who had heard me quote his jokes, raced over to inspect him. Juliana was confused. How come the man Mommy studies Torah with rode a bicycle on the Sabbath? I explained that not all people who studied Torah practiced all of it. Dede, who had heard Raphael was a clown, was disappointed that he didn't look like a clown. Peter looked him over with suspicion. Peter had once asked, "Who is this Raphael we keep hearing about?" in a tone of voice that reminded me of the way my stepfather used to speak of my high school boyfriends, quiet studious boys whom he considered perverts and sex fiends. "Are you in love with that clown? That masseur?" Peter had asked, kind of kidding.

I thought it best to diffuse everyone's curiosity about Mommy's study buddy by inviting Raphael over, thereby conferring upon him the status of "friend of the family." While Peter entertained other guests in the living room, Raphael insisted on staying with me in the kitchen to help dice carrots and make an avocado salad. He proceeded with professional flourish, adding seasonings and minced peppers and onions to the mashed avocado. My daughters took ringside seats at the kitchen table. Aside from the Frugal Gourmet, they had never seen a man so adept in the kitchen.

As Raphael cooked, I described the women's service I had been to this morning and asked him why he never joined the prayer services at Pardes, where the men run the show. Even when they needed a tenth man to complete the quorum for prayer, Raphael refused to join.

"I believe it's sexist," he explained. "I have to show solidarity with my sisters. If there were an egalitarian service and they needed a tenth person, then I would join in." Yet more than issues of sexism kept Raphael from praying. "I don't pray," he said. "I don't know how to. I don't see the connection between going to services and ethical behavior." At the kibbutz he had lived on, he said, "some of the biggest prayers were the biggest bastards—they prayed like sewing machines. Their prayer was not the expression of the ethical unity of the community; it did not come out of activism for a better world."

For Raphael, prayer was social activism. That was the core of his Jewish identity. "I'm an inheritor of optimistic energy for social justice," he said. His kind of Jewishness came from his grandfather, a bagel baker from Bialystok, who came to the States in 1905 and organized a bakers' union. It came from his father, a dentist, who opened a dental clinic for the poor of Glens Falls. It came from both parents, who organized meetings and a march against the war in Vietnam. "Jews believe in a better world and are responsible for social change. That's what makes someone a *mensch*, that's what it means to be a Jew."

The next week, on the morning I was to meet Yehudis at Café Atara downtown on Ben Yehuda Street, I pulled Juliana out of school, sensing Yehudis might teach her things she wouldn't otherwise learn. It was pouring out. We peeled off our soggy coats when we got to Atara, took a table close to a space heater, though it didn't do much good, and drank hot chocolate as we waited for Yehudis.

She finally arrived in chaotic flurry, her worn gray cape soaked, her braid dripping. She was exhausted from teaching, studying, and volunteering to feed and look after a family of thirteen Hasidic children temporarily abandoned by their parents, who had gone off to New York to arrange a marriage for one of their older children. "They had left a fifteen year old in charge," Yehudis said, shuddering. "And the last time they did this to arrange another marriage, they stayed away for three weeks." She had just come from doing their laundry and cooking up two pots of soup, one meat and one dairy. "That should hold them for a while."

She cupped Juliana's cheeks in her palms. "How beautiful this little girl is! Aren't I terrible? I always talk about children in front of them, as if they weren't there."

Yehudis, who had settled in Israel seven years ago, pieced together a living by lecturing on Judaic studies in various programs around Jerusalem for visiting foreigners, while she continued her own studies. She had just begun studying esoteric texts in Jewish mysticism with an American woman, a widow in her late fifties, who lived in a single room in the Old City. The woman taught privately for eight shekels an hour, a little more than I paid our baby-sitters. Yehudis said her teacher was charitable to an extreme. She spent every spare shekel she had buying food for Sabbath meals she would prepare for large groups of guests.

Yehudis was in awe of her teacher's capacity to learn.

She's a genius. Before coming to Israel and becoming learned enough in Jewish texts to teach others, this woman had been an economic adviser in the State Department in Washington. There was a point in our learning recently when she made me nervous. We were talking about natural order, exile, and redemption. Then she started to ask me, "What is God's plan for you?" I fear people who think they know you. You know you don't know yourself. Leave me alone, I thought, let's just do the text. I don't want anyone thinking they know how to unravel the secrets of my soul. I want to be respected because I was so disrespected in my life. I look back: there was so much agonizing. Still, I opened up to her. She's very special. She learns from six in the morning to midnight. She prays for hours each day on her roof. She's a mystic. She can contemplate nothingness. It frightens me. Even the stars make me nervous. Contemplating God overwhelms me with anxiety.

"Me, too," I said.

"You know, you remind me of a writing teacher I once had. She convinced me I had something to say. I would think: My life? My world? My life was so primitive to me. I thought you had to be from the Upper West Side to write." Yehudis couldn't fathom why Esther wanted me to meet her. In all honesty, she claimed she didn't know much Torah. "What does a Ph.D. in Judaic studies mean? It's a piece of paper."

I trusted Esther's instincts now, more so than ever. I felt Yehudis to be a soul mate. I wanted to be cynical together with her; to share certainty about only one thing—that we knew there was little we could ever know for sure.

"I'm very mixed up," Yehudis said, quenching her wild thirst only after she had drained a full pitcher of water and ordered another. "I see everything from a million points of view. I grew up turned off by my world. It's not all sweetness and bliss in religion."

"What was the world you grew up in?"

"Yiddish-speaking eastern European parents, both descendants of different lines of prestigious Hasidic rebbes, both Holocaust survivors, mother in Auschwitz, father in the death camps." Yehudis's parents met in Montreal after the war; theirs was an arranged marriage. On cold nights she often thought of what her parents' lives in the camps were like. There was one especially cold night when she was living in New York. She had only one blanket. All night she shivered. In the morning she telephoned her mother, "I know how it must have been in the camps." Her mother chuckled bitterly. "Blanket? Who had a blanket?"

Rarely did her mother talk about the war, as if she could protect her children from her memories with silence. When she saw Yehudis reading books about the Holocaust she became furious. "I went through it," she would say, "that's enough." Yehudis could hardly believe her mother was really in the camps, but there were the numbers on her arm. And summers at their bungalow, Yehudis would hear her mother crying. The sounds of building construction across the way reminded her of that same banging in the camps.

Yehudis thought she reacted to her parents' experiences in the camps by living intensely, for the moment.

It has a good and a bad side. When I'm cold, I think I'll be cold forever. Even with dieting, I can't connect that something I eat in the present will have any effect on me in the future. My childhood was very bleak. There was a lot of boredom. I hated *shabbos,* the Sabbath, with a passion. I would get nauseous, throw up. I survived my childhood by reading all day. Not great literature. Comforting books like *Little House on the Prairie, Anne of Green Gables, Little Women.* I had no trouble identifying with the characters, for in my mind all familiar people were Jewish. Ignoring all evidence to the contrary, I transformed their lives into Jewish ones. Books kept me going. They were my comfort, giving me a sense of security, normalness, and coziness lacking in my home. I always thought if I couldn't read, I wouldn't want to live.

Yehudis often dreamed of her grandmother, her namesake, who perished in a death camp. "In my dream she is alive in a cave in Poland and I bring her my brother's sons and say, 'Look Grandma, you have great-grandchildren!' People say my grandmother would wash windows with one hand and hold a book to read with the other. If only I could know more about her. She's a key to who I am."

Yehudis's family had been exceedingly poor. Her father cut diamonds twelve hours a day. She was crazy about him. He learned Torah with her, took her to museums, the circus, to see the store windows in New York at Christmas time.

"You walked down Fifth Avenue to F. A. O. Schwarz with him dressed in Hasidic garb?"

"He wore a big hat and a long black coat only on *shabes.* Even then, he never looked 100 percent like a Hasid. He was a Hasid with a twist. He's so brilliant. He took an *Encyclopaedia Britannica* out with him from Germany." His lighter, cosmopolitan side attracted Yehudis. She relished the great adventure stories he invented for her in Yiddish, setting them to melodies of Beethoven and Tchaikovsky. She heard that his branch of the family, attuned to culture unlike her mother's, used to sing songs from operettas in his house in Europe. They were all killed.

"My father wanted me to study piano, but my mother said, 'No, that's only for *goyim.*'"

Juliana, who had been half-reading *Mrs. Piggle Wiggle,* asked, "What are *goyim?*"

I said, "Non-Jews."

Yehudis said, "My mother meant nonreligious Jews. Real *goyim* don't enter my mother's world."

Yehudis had written an autobiography of several pages and was pleased to have me quote from it provided she remained anonymous. She called the autobiography an account of her struggle not to reject Judaism while still fighting the Jewish world's attitude toward women. The words of the poet Adrienne Rich fueled her own writing, giving her the courage to break her silence, to name herself, to "begin to define a reality which resonates to us."*

Yehudis reflected on her childhood:

What did being Jewish mean to me? I knew of nothing else. It was existence; my entire consciousness was determined by it. It was my world—suffocating, provincial, uncultured, primitive, unexciting, too familiar and ordinary—primarily, it was my parents. . . . All the people I knew when I grew up in Brooklyn were Eastern European Jews and their children. The school I attended all day was also strictly Orthodox. Closed on Jewish holidays and open on all the others, it enabled us to live in our own world. I didn't know until much later that Christmas existed outside of books. Every aspect of my life, all activity was determined by Jewish law. . . . Judaism is my mother: loud, enterprising, loving. Though entirely different, my father, too, is the very embodiment of Jewishness. He gives me my first substantial exposure to Jewish learning; for the Jewish studies in the girls' school I attend is so watered down, I learn almost nothing there. An unusual man, my father treats me the way others in his society treat their sons, learning Torah with me even though I am only a young girl. I study subjects as varied as *Sefer Mishley* [the Book of Proverbs], the exquisite poetry of the great Spanish thinker Yehuda Halevi, and even Hebrew grammar. . . . I am sitting at a table outside in a bungalow colony, learning with my father. A woman comes over to him and yells, "Why are you learning Torah with her? You're not supposed to; she's a girl." My father seems uncomfortable, embarrassed. He can't defend himself. I feel strange, singled out, in a world alone.

On Lies, Secrets and Silence: Selected Prose 1966–1978 (New York: W.W. Norton & Company, 1979), 245.

"What was it like to learn with your father?" I asked.

We sat under the trees. It was very relaxed. I felt his enthusiasm, the feeling of focus, of concentration, of fun. I felt the bond between us. I was eight, nine. It was not so important to me that I was learning Torah but that I was with my father. He gave me attention. More, oddly, than to my two brothers. He knew they were learning enough in yeshiva. I suppose I would have liked it if he had played a game with me, but this was real. I love to be with people who are smarter than me: this is a gift I got from my father. We always learned at the *shabbos* table. We still do. My father reads and then explains. My mother is good at it, too, but my father is brilliant. He knows all the allusions by heart. Learning Torah was a pure joy for him. When he came home from work, his fingers black from diamond dust, he'd go to the *bet midrash* and learn until three or four in the morning. When my mother was a newlywed, she'd be so proud he'd go to *shul* from six o'clock Friday evening until two o'clock in the morning. He learned in the camps; he learned underground with Nazis walking up and down over the bunkers. He studied with a tzaddik [a righteous man] ten, fifteen hours a day. Under other circumstances he wouldn't have been in a situation to study with him. Icicles dripped from my father's hands, but sweat dripped from the tzaddik's face, his study was so intense. For Passover, my father baked matzos in the camps. Do you know what that means?

Juliana looked deeply into her book, fearing Yehudis's question was addressed to her. She knew of Hitler. She knew Jews had died. But until now, they seemed dull facts of an ancient, traumatic history, lacking emotional reality.

Worried Juliana was being burdened with facts she could not yet handle, Yehudis turned back to her. "I couldn't even bring myself to say the word 'woman,'" Yehudis said. "I equated men with intellect and women with stupidity. My father would say, 'Yehudis, don't be a cow like other girls.' "

Late at night, Yehudis would watch her father pray. His eyes would be shut; he would sway with an intensity that frightened her. What kind of God is he praying to? she wondered. What kind of a God is it that would allow children to perish? She could not talk to her father about his faith or about her own doubts. "I know a Hasidic man who is an atheist," she told me. "Only I know. He can't tell even his wife. Still, he prays three times a day and wears a *streimel.*"

"Why does he go on with the masquerade?"

"We come from a world where no one leaves home. What other world does he know? It's his family, his friends, what he values. To not believe in God isn't such an important factor. If you were quarreling with Western values, you wouldn't start wearing a kimono."

In her autobiography she wrote:

As I grow older, Judaism becomes more and more of a cage. My father is squelching his own doubts and fears by not allowing me to think. I begin to question the sexism of Judaism, especially in reaction to my parents' fear that I am too intellectual to be marriageable. To marry is, of course, the most important order I have to fulfill—an unmarried girl is pitiful and a tragedy. My fear that I will have to obey my parents and marry some strange male creature who has been totally off limits till now is boundless—for despite all my seeming rebellion, I unwillingly believe in their authority.

Only by going to college (which Yehudis had to keep secret from her relatives in order to protect her parents from censure), and by studying Judaism as an adult, did she feel she could reclaim her Jewishness. She wrote:

At seventeen, when most, if not all, possibilities for serious Jewish studies are still closed for females, I hear Rav Soloveitchik lecture. The acknowledged Talmudical scholar of the Jewish world, he also has a Ph.D. in philosophy from the University of Berlin. His lecture enchants me. I have never heard anything that is so intellectually exhilarating and open, but he belongs to a modern Orthodox world, a world much less strict than my own, where boys and girls are allowed to socialize together.

Years later she felt she could dare to study at Bar Ilan University. Through those studies, she re-created herself:

I start to feel sophisticated, to see Jewishness as cultured, aesthetic, refined—uncolored by a Judaism of ignorant superstitions and blind beliefs.

She met Shlomo Carlebach, a composer—singer of Hasidic melodies and a teller of tales. She describes his impact on her:

The son of a prominent German rabbi, his upbringing, with its rational philosophical outlook and dry decorum, is the antithesis of the mysticism and joy of Hasidic life. . . . Openly fondling women in public, he earns the censure of the entire Orthodox world, as they mourn the loss of his potential leadership.

For me this is fortuitous. He can never become, as are other religious leaders, a feared demoralizing authority—those who wipe me out with their implicit message of "who are you anyway? You're just a female, you have no right to think or live your own life, you're not worth much. Just have our children and save us from sexual sin."

Rabbi Carlebach and his melodies opened Yehudis to a "loving connection to a divine presence." Through him, her own connection to God seemed possible. Still, her struggle to overcome internalized sexism persisted:

> To take myself seriously as a Jew even though I am "only" a woman, I organize a feminist Orthodox consciousness-raising group—all intellectual women, some with five, six children. And the passion, the anger, the pain that comes out, we cannot disband even after many hours. And I realize how much I, like the others, still feel insignificant, not a real adult, unentitled to achieve, unworthy of being a respected participant, let alone a contributor, in the Jewish world.

Having shared all this with us, Yehudis threw up her arms, knocking her glass off the table. "I'm just crazy about Jews," she said, picking up pieces of glass and wrapping them in napkins. Juliana got down on her knees to help. "No, mamele," said Yehudis, lifting Juliana back into her chair, "your fingers aren't tough enough to touch glass." She threw the glass out herself so the waitress wouldn't get hurt.

> I love Jews. With all their pain, and the anger in my family. I come from a place that's the opposite of phoniness. They're so rich in spirit, there's such passion. People gave so much for me. My grandfather lost everyone. Everyone. He's ninety. Now he learns Torah all the time. He's so happy. Torah is his connection to eternity. He devotes his life to charity; he's supported widows their whole lives. People trust him with thousands of dollars and he spends all his time distributing it. When I come to see him, he'll tell me, "I'm so busy with my bookkeeping, I can only talk a minute more." There's mystery, he's so alive. His religiousness is so natural, so organic. This is what has totally shaped me. It's in my blood.

When she took subways in New York she would fantasize: Someone would harass Hasidic-looking Jews like her father and grandfather.

She would come to the aid of all the fragile Jews, so gentle they cannot save themselves, and protect them. She would enable them to continue living their pious lives.

At our bus stop, heading home, Juliana wanted to know more about the numbers on Yehudis's mother's arm, the matzos. An old lady with only silver teeth in her mouth sat facing backward on the bench next to us. She leaned into Juliana saying *"Schnee!"* crooning *"Schnee!"* In Yiddish, she said to an old man walking by, "Tell me how can I tell the little girl what is *schnee."*

"*Sheleg,*" he said.

"*Sheleg,*" I said.

She shook her head, scraping off the snow that had fallen onto her sleeve, gathering it into her palm and offering it to Juliana like manna. The snow was light, nearly invisible, like October snow in New York.

I whispered to Juliana, "For her, it's as though glitter were falling from the sky, imagine that. Take it from her hand, tell her thank you."

It was the holiday of Purim, which commemorates the deliverance of the Jews from the villain Haman, as recounted in the Book of Esther. The rest of Israel had observed Purim yesterday. Jerusalem, because it has been a walled city since the days of Joshua, observed Purim today, the fifteenth day of Adar, just as the Jews did in Shushan, the capital of Persia. Yehudis had invited me to a party at her teacher's room in the Old City, a daylong open house for women. Yehudis's teacher could be someone with whom I could learn regularly. I liked the idea of private study, of progressing at my own speed. I was intrigued by what Yehudis had said about her teacher, although I did feel hesitant about the starkness and intensity of her piety.

I ventured into the Old City just as Purim was nearing its end. It was the eve of the Sabbath, and it would be a wild dash to make it home to Peter and the girls before public transportation stopped at sunset. Few people were around. Most Jews were already busy at home preparing for the Sabbath. As I walked through the Jewish Quarter, where parties were just winding down, I could hear tinny recorded Purim music coming from apartments. In the shadows of late afternoon, a few religious youngsters and yeshiva boys with bloodshot eyes were still delivering *mishloah manot,* little packages of holiday goodies.

I found the teacher's room on the third floor of a stone building on Misgav Ladach Street. I looked for Yehudis, but she was not there yet. Had she forgotten I was coming and left? Was this the right place? The room was filled with young American women in their twenties. They were dressed in costumes, a Purim tradition. There was a pregnant clown in a black wig, a blonde in some kind of Tahitian getup, two hoboes singing "Dona, Dona" while one strummed a guitar. No one I asked even knew a Yehudis. Still, I was given a two-handled cup to wash my hands according to ritual, and a South African woman dispatched me over to a tray of homemade whole wheat rolls so I could say the blessing over bread. I washed, blessed, took a crumb of bread and took a seat near the front door, hoping Yehudis might turn up. The room had been decorated for the party with streamers and crepe paper flowers. Ceremonial objects and bouquets of wilting flowers were grouped into little shrines on the tops of wicker bookshelves holding black sacred texts. There were unopened packages of *mishloah manot* scattered on every table and bookshelf, paper plates, and plastic bags containing squashed hamantaschen, a miniature bottle of wine, and a bruised piece of fruit. Many of the women seemed to be in a fog. One Madonna-like young woman, her hair in a bun, her dress rose-patterned, sat on a chair in the middle of the room. She cradled her hands in her lap, closed her eyes, and appeared to be meditating. Girls who had had too much horrid Israeli whiskey and chocolate liqueur that tasted like shoe polish were noisily wishing each other a good Sabbath, while the Madonna meditated deeply into her grace after meals (normally mumbled in a perfunctory way), carving out her sacred space.

I felt as though I were again back at those high school parties where everyone else would be in the basement making out, while I, a wallflower, thumbed through piles of record jackets just to look busy. No one talked to me.

Eventually I located Yehudis's teacher, gathering up used paper plates into a plastic garbage bag. She was the first mature person in the room I saw. Yehudis had told me her teacher's specialty was in guiding "difficult persons" back to Judaism. From all the sleeping bags piled up in the corners, I gathered that this party may have been a big event for difficult persons—at least, a respite from wandering.

The teacher, dressed in a plain gray skirt, a sweater, and a scarf covering most of her white hair, wore a metal crown and a green plastic sword stuck into a gold plastic belt around her hips. A cross between Queen Esther and Rambo. Hanging from her neck was a hand-lettered sign:

A concept. A woman is a CROWN to her husband.

The message was lettered in Hebrew underneath. Was this a joke? Sarcasm? For me, the line evoked an image of a little wifey nestled at home, her husband's glory—or Princess Di in miniature sitting on Charles's head as decoration—or dedications to "my wife, without whom this would not have been possible." Was the verse meant to allude to the Rambam's recipe for a wife's proper behavior as presented in *Hilkhot Ishut* 15:20?

[The sages] enjoin the woman to honor her husband as much as possible. She should be in fear of him and do everything according to his directions. She should view him as an officer or a king, complying with the desires of his heart, and eschewing all that is hateful to him.

Moreover, of what use was the concept to single women? Whom did they crown?

The teacher was urging the guests leaving her party to come back for the Sabbath, if not for the entire day, then at least to share what she called "the third meal" with her. The fancy-free, their lives so fluid they traveled with clean clothes and a toothbrush in their daypacks, said they would change their plans and stay. As meager as the teacher's earnings were from her private lessons, the more people she could open her home to, to feed and teach and give a place to sleep, the happier she was.

Yehudis, dressed as a Russian folk-dancer, finally arrived. I felt safer now. The Purim holiday, with its costumes and obligatory drunkenness, conjures up an aura of madness. For me, this party of vagabonds felt too mad, strung out, surreal. Yehudis had come in with a tough-talking, crisp Canadian woman in a jeans skirt and denim jacket. They had been Purim party–hopping—Yehudis had a million friends—and now were helping themselves to the remains of the whiskey. Yehudis hugged me, fussing that I had come.

We sat in a circle as the teacher, creating a salon-like intimacy, asked the woman from South Africa, "Please tell us the story of your reality." The South African, prim as a banker, said her father married her mother when she was fifteen. She had been an orphan whom he had raised. He worked for the department of roads and they sent him and his family into the bush, where they lived in a caravan. She said she always knew that her mother was a Jew and that she was, too. The teacher found this marvelous. "Even in the African bush your soul yearned for Jerusalem!" The teacher then asked the woman in Tahitian costume to share with the group the story of her reality in Guam, where she felt alienated as a white, female Peace Corps worker, not to mention as a Jew. The Peace Corps worker preferred not tell us the story she had told the teacher before, but she would summarize: until she had gone to Guam, she had never considered her Jewishness part of her identity.

Filling the silence, I asked the teacher, "What do your costume and your sign mean? Should I know who you are?"

The explanation, she said, was kabbalistic. The crown *(keter)* is the highest level of the ten divine emanations. It is also referred to as *nothingness.* In kabbalistic imagery, woman is moon, man is sun, both are necessary. A woman has a higher spirituality because she is closer to God. Why? Because she can create life.

I was following along marginally.

The pregnant clown asked, "What if a woman is infertile?"

The teacher said she still had a life-giving capacity.

The clown asked, "If you can't create on the Sabbath, why can you still make a baby on that day? Isn't that the ultimate creative act, to make another human being?"

The teacher said procreation was not one of the thirty-nine forbidden kinds of work necessary to erect the Temple. Therefore, it was permissible on the Sabbath.

"What's the sword supposed to be?" I asked, pouring myself an ample glass of ersatz Amaretto.

She pulled it out of her belt and swooped it up, slicing ribbons of air. *"Gevurah,"* she said, "the divine emanation that means strength, is a feminine principle—it means a woman's strength. Like God who creates the world out of shapeless nothing, a woman, too, gives form, creating boundaries in the world."

I could appreciate the poetry of Kabbalah, but I didn't think its symbolic images were meant to be taken literally—especially the male-female imagery—by people like myself, who have only a dilettante's appreciation of spiritual mysteries. Picturing *gevurah,* I saw Amazons chopping up the universe and making nice things out of it: frying pans, babies, apple pandowdy, rocking chairs, and library books. Treading in kabbalistic waters required a maturity, faith, wisdom, and learning that was out of my depth.

The Peace Corps woman said she resented hearing God spoken of as having male and female attributes. God had no gender. The

God of Judaism was experience. From the certainty of her tone, I could tell her knowledge of Judaism was limited to the few days she had spent in a crash course in one of the "yearning soul" yeshivot.

The Canadian, holding her head from so much whiskey, said, "You'd better believe it. God is a man."

I agreed. "If God were a woman, I don't think she would be invisible. You could touch her. She would come when you called. She would worry more, punish less."

The teacher listened to me politely, as a grandparent would tolerate the silliness of a beloved toddler, and resumed the exegesis of her costume: When the Messiah came, the sun and moon would be united and the moon would reflect the light of the sun.

I had to trust Yehudis's evaluation of her teacher's learning, since she was a better judge than I of what was and what wasn't profoundly, authentically Jewish. If Yehudis said her teacher had attained a high level of mystical understanding, then it must be true.

In some respects, I truly admired the teacher's lofty enterprise: to purge her being of dross, to ascend above the material world into godly realms, to become an abstraction. She had left the State Department, trading status and salary for what seemed like such a marginal existence. She prayed for hours on her rooftop, pleading for the redemption of the cosmos, praying to know God ever more intimately. When I could bring myself to pray, I asked God, the handyman, to do something about Aunt Shirley's diabetes, to make Grandma Sally's angina go away, to make rain when it was appropriate, to bring peace to all the trouble spots listed on the front page of the paper, and to reconcile Dede to the small smelly toilets in her nursery school so she wouldn't come home with a stomachache every day.

Yehudis said her teacher used to take off to go hiking in Eilat. She gave it up during one of her more thorough purges. Too bad, thought Yehudis. Before that catharsis, when she still cared about ordering the right hiking equipment from a catalog, she had seemed more real to her.

Something about the teacher—the way she saw the world—seemed amiss, unhinged. I bit my tongue for supposing this. But—and I could not push away the thought—what well person stands on a rooftop pleading for the redemption of the cosmos? Maybe all saintly people would seem strange to me.

I wondered: If Yehudis's teacher had been a man, would she have been directed onto a less eccentric track? Surely her intensive study would have won her rabbinic ordination by now. She would be teaching in a yeshiva. Because of her State Department experience, she'd have been made a yeshiva administrator. She would get a nominal salary, a place of respect. So I asked her if not having ordination was a concern to her. She said on the contrary, it was for the good. It intensified her conviction that one learned Torah only for its own sake and not to attain any tangible goals in this world. Did she have no desire for public recognition for her learning? None. The anonymity taught her humility; it enforced the continual shedding of ego. She opened her door to any Jew who wanted to learn. It was, she said, an unspeakable pleasure to start from scratch with a beginner and participate in the joy of Torah being discovered. She amply fit the Talmudic description of a genuine scholar:

> . . . meek, humble, alert, filled with a desire for learning, modest, beloved by all, humble to members of his household and sin-fearing. He judges a man fairly according to his deeds and says, "I have no desire for all the things of this world because this world is not for me." *(Derekh Eretz Zuta)* 1:1*

The Canadian searched her backpack in vain for aspirin. She shook her head, exasperated: "Why must the moon reflect the sun? Who needs the sun anyway? Will women always be willing to be reflectors?"

Yehudis seemed uncharacteristically meditative. She was drunk,

---

The Minor Tractates. Translated into English under the editorship of Rev. Dr. Abraham Cohen (London: The Soncino Press, 1984).

I thought. But then, perfectly sober, she announced, "Women have done enough reflecting!"

Her teacher was a little stunned by the outburst. "What makes you say that?"

Yehudis said she was prepared to name two hundred women in Boro Park, unwilling reflectors, all unmarried. "I find myself surrounded by all types of excellent women who want to marry, but to whom? The men are far inferior. At the very best, they are raw material that needs to be worked on."

An alarm clock went off. The teacher said that left them just enough time to get ready for the Sabbath. By waiting to the last minute, she would make the transition from the holiness of Purim to the holiness of Sabbath without cheating Purim of its due. She pulled out a list of things to do and read them off like a camp director at roll call. First, turn on all the *shabes* clocks, electric timers that would regulate the lights. Second, boil potatoes, steam couscous. I ran out, not wanting to be woven into this menagerie, which reminded me of the circle of women who gathered in the Old City in E. M. Broner's novel, *A Weave of Women.** I had yet to prepare anything for my own family's Sabbath.

The Peace Corps woman chased barefoot down the stairs after me.

"Please, can I ask you a question? If you're married, how come you don't cover your head? Does that mean you do or you don't tell your children Bible stories and perform all the lovely rituals?"

I suppressed my astonishment. In this land of experts, why was she turning to me, Jew of the boondocks, to clarify a religious matter? Her question meant I had to decide where I stood. If I told her I didn't do all the rituals yet, but *barukh hashem,* maybe I would soon, so there was still hope for me, I would not have contradicted the teachings she was getting in her crash course in Jewish practice and belief. Such courses, demanding stringency and promising

---

*A Weave of Women (New York: Holt, Rinehart, 1978).

certainty, did solid jobs winning souls. I hesitated to undermine her programming. Maybe it provided the right kind of healing—or whatever it was she was yearning for. She did, however, seem to be intelligent and mentally sound enough to be able to sustain the alternative point of view I felt compelled to give her. Why should she be offered only fundamentalism when she could more logically join me in the ranks of disenfranchised, but otherwise committed, Jewish women?

Purim is a holiday of coincidence and contradiction. I was surprised to hear myself sounding off for the first time so stridently, so sure of opinions I hardly knew I held.

I told her I didn't I cover my head. I didn't plan to. Ever. When I'm at the beach I wear two-piece bathing suits and swim in mixed company. But just because I didn't cover my head, I told her defensively, didn't mean that the Judaism I embraced and spread like a thick layer of butter over my family wasn't just as real and true and memorable as the other Judaism being served up to her at her crash course. (I didn't believe that altogether; why I was suggesting to her that I was confident in my Jewish well-being mystified me. Where was this coming from? Every pre-Purim lecture I had heard this past week stressed that Purim was the day we celebrated God's almost imperceptible intervention in our lives.) I continued:

> Those tales about the sun and the moon we've just heard are dear, and the women who tell and believe them have a kind of faith I'm sure I'll never know. I don't have much capacity for faith. Or it's a habit that was never developed in me. Fortunately, being Jewish doesn't require you to run up onto a podium and shout "I believe, I believe!" Acknowledging God's presence isn't a first or necessary step for a Jew. You live and learn and act like a Jew, and then you can start worrying about God. Talk to Yehudis. Ask her why "to not believe in God isn't such an important factor."

"Don't go yet!" she begged, snatching insistently at me. "What do you think about the way the tradition treats women?"

I told her I either ignored it mindlessly or faced it and it sickened me.

Running to catch the last bus out of the Old City, I called to her:

Learn everything you can here in this house over Purim and in the course you're taking, but don't let anyone force you into a Judaism that makes you deny what you value and suppress how you think. Do talk to Yehudis. Trust what she says. She has no fantasies. Beg her to let you read her autobiography. Nothing has yet to convince me that closing our eyes to modernity is a more sacred stance than coming to terms with it.

I raced off, getting to the bus at the Zion Gate in time to wave it to a halt.

I hoped the Peace Corps woman would indeed talk to Yehudis. She was the real thing, a Jewish woman who not only knew the tradition, but lived it. Despite her anger, despite her wounds. While I would not want to have lived her childhood, that background gave her an intense sense of loyalty to Jews and reason for being Jewish. I envied the massive learning she fought to attain, learning by which she legitimated herself in her own eyes. Then it mattered a little less that the tradition she loved had despised her and tried to make her invisible.

Yehudis would instruct the Peace Corps woman correctly.

Israeli soldiers carrying guns boarded the bus as it pulled away from the Zion Gate. They checked for bombs and unclaimed parcels under the seats. This was typical but always unnerving. "We're just here to prevent any problems," they announced as they ducked down in the exits, riding with us on the road just outside the walls of the Old City until they thought we were beyond danger of the fire bombs and stones that had been thrown on this bus route during the past weeks. The soldiers ran off the bus and returned to their posts under the cover of an eerie wind that twirled dust around everywhere. The stores downtown were already closed and the streets looked like a set for *On the Beach*. I took a quick cab back to Nayot. Only at home did the same wind and quiet seem less menacing. Peter was just leaving for synagogue by himself and Dede had begun to cry. I put her up on the kitchen counter while I chopped cucumbers.

"Daddy wouldn't let me go with him because he said it was too cold out. I have to go to synagogue to talk to God," she said.

I wished Peter were home. He could handle the God conversations in a more natural way, whereas I always hemmed and hawed. I felt I made up too many lies or not enough. "You don't need to go to synagogue to pray," I said, pulling this together as I went along. "God hears you everywhere. You can just find a quite place and talk. You don't have to talk aloud. You can whisper. Or you can just think it to yourself."

"God can hear even if you don't say regular prayers?"
"Yes."
"Even if it's a very, very quiet voice."
"Yes, yes."

She walked onto our balcony and had a fast pray. "What did you pray?" I asked. I hoped Dede would not bring up death again. Out of nowhere, it seemed, she had become preoccupied with death. Maybe it was the constant sight of soldiers and guns that made her fear our lives were in danger. I didn't know. Once she got going on death, there was no comforting her.

Dede said she told God she wanted him to bring the Messiah soon. When he came people would live forever and she wouldn't have to die. In tears, she went through the list of questions she had been waking up crying to ask each night this week: "Will they put me in a box in the ground? Can you go with me? How will they know I want to go with you in the same box? Will my nose turn to dust? Will there be food and supermarkets? Will I be an old lady or a little girl in heaven?"

Juliana piped in as she continued to step through her Chinese jump rope routine in the living room. "Why did Daddy ever tell you all that stuff about the Messiah anyways? I never made such a big deal. No one knows the answers, so stop asking Mommy. Only God knows."

Dede wailed, "I wish Daddy were home."

I had been hovering at the edges of religiousness for so long now like a tone-deaf groupie. In some ways I was jealous of the spiritual seekers who were nabbed at the Western Wall and whisked into the yeshivot, where they absorbed an instant connectedness to God. Maybe I envied the young women who studied with Yehudis's teacher for a few sessions and walked away filled with divine love and a conviction to live according to Jewish law. Perhaps I had no spiritual capacities, no ability to believe in the power and reality of anything greater and more enduring than human love. I identified too well with Indian women who leapt willingly upon their husbands' pyres. Better death than lovelessness.

I distracted Dede now with preparations for our Sabbath dinner, but in the middle of the night, she woke up crying. "I don't want to close my eyes in the box in the ground! What if the Messiah doesn't kiss us and make us all alive again?" Peter went to her room. I could hear him assuring her that the Messiah would come.

When Peter returned to bed, I told him I had no honest answers for Dede. Afterlife in paradise was a nice myth, a psychological aid. When people die, they're gone. All that remains is their belongings, their works, our memories that grow into myths.

"What if you lost someone close to you?" Peter asked.

I never had. "I might feel differently. To comfort myself in my despair, I might convince myself that spirits lingered and souls were resurrected."

"You mean you'd change your mind because a new understanding had been opened to you?"

"No. I think I'd opt for the most powerful psychological comfort. I'd believe in an afterlife because it would be too unbearable not to.

Isn't that why people suddenly turn religious after there's a death in the family?"

Dede was crying again. This time I went to her. I carried her into our bed, said nothing, and slept with her wrapped in my arms. Before dawn, she woke me again. "How does God talk to us?"

"Go back to sleep," I said, unprepared for a new round.

"God appears in my own ideas," she said, "and tells me, 'Don't be afraid.'"

Seven

While traveling home by bus from my class at the university, I had been looking through an English translation of the Yiddish *Tzena Urena,* the anthology of biblical commentary thought of as the "women's Torah." I was reading a legend in which the moon complains to God that it is the same size as the sun: no bigger and no brighter. The legend pulled me in powerfully, linked, perhaps, to all the moon-sun talk in the Old City. "Let me alone give light!" the moon pleads, and God, who does not ignore whining as a nursery school teacher would, punished the moon for its jealousy. The moon is made smaller and is given brightness only when it reflects the sun. And this works out fortuitously, the legend explains. For if the moon had its own brightness, we would not know how to differentiate night and day and we would be unable to mark the quiet, restful night that was designated for learning Torah.

It must have been soon after the moon was punished that I missed my bus stop in Nayot. I missed hearing what the lady behind me said to her seatmate after she complained, "My daughter-in-law thinks she can knit, so I told her . . ." If not for a teenager who squashed me as he craned to look out the window at hundreds of mourners following a shrouded corpse being carried down the street on a stretcher, I would have missed that dark procession altogether. When you enter the spiritual zone, where the moon talks to God, where earthly waters quarrel with heavenly waters, and the letter *alef* complains that it, and not the letter *bet,* should have commenced the Torah—then all the daily stuff around you starts to appear extraneous and distracting, cheap vanities and plastic shadows of the real thing. I caught myself enveloped totally by sacred lore. I had yearned for such an experience, or at the very least, I yearned to know whether I had the capacity for such envelopment. As soon as I became aware of the powerful draw of the text, I pulled away in panic, a sardine finding the one hole in the fisherman's net. Don't give yourself up to it, don't risk absorption, stay safely, cynically teetering on the surfaces of Torah. Come back to the world that is touched and felt, to the people on the bus who limp and have bad skin, to the soldier on leave dragging his cello and his gun to an amateur orchestra rehearsal. Come back to the smell of overripe persimmons in dangling string bags and to Ofra Haza's whiny hit song leaking out of the teenager's headphones. I tucked my *Tzena Urena* quickly into my satchel. What if I were to become completely oblivious to the startling views of Jerusalem? What if I no longer noticed even the most impressive sites: the Mount of Olives, the Valley of Gehennom, the Citadel of David? Already, in my weeks of Torah study, my map was becoming more private. Like a bee, I had two paths. Out from the hive in Nayot to suck nectar from the flowering circles of Torah learning, then back home to the hive.

Attend to this world, I cautioned myself. Pay attention to the details of *now.*

The Talmud, aware that the sacred texts can lure one too completely, too dangerously away from the material world, recommends that the individual hold on to threads that tie one to this world.

Jewish schoolchildren learn early on that Rashi derived his income from a vineyard in Troyes and that Rambam was a physician. I had become familiar with some sources on balancing the sacred and the profane while perusing volumes of Talmud in the Soncino English translation. I skimmed the volume the way I window-shopped through L. L. Bean catalogs, looking for nothing in particular, just letting my eyes land where they would in search of curious pleasures. Unlike the conventional student of Talmud, who learns with logical precision, I approached Talmud associatively, as if piecing together dream imagery. I read Talmud as Dede played Scrabble. She used the board, making up her own words or designs with the cubes. This may not be standard Scrabble but it was a game, a valid permutation.

In the tractate *Avot de-Rabbi Nathan,* Rabbi Judah ben Ilai presented a parable: If a man walks down a roadway, flanked on one side by a path of snow and on the other side by a path of fire, he should take care to walk down the middle so as to avoid being frostbitten or scorched. This image advocated holding Torah study and one's worldly affairs in rational proportion to each another, with Torah study naturally dominating.

I had confessed to a friend I had made at Aviva's class that when I took the bus home from the university, I would sometimes get off in Mea Shearim to trail after the married women who wore tight black kerchiefs over their shaven heads as they walked through mazes of courtyards and performed their errands. My friend, an Orthodox American woman who was an audiologist at Hadassah Hospital, said those women in their black scarves reminded her of Darth Vader of *Star Wars.* "Why the espionage?" she teased.

I explained to her that I needed to find out what it meant for these women to live in a world that had nearly no points of reference outside of Torah, a world whose roads all seemed to be paths of fire and snow. What did it mean for these women to experience this world only through the lens of Torah and to have no other impulse in life but to serve God? I kept dwelling on their baldness, which obsessed me most of all. It seemed violent, punitive, evoking images from prison movies in which women guards forcibly shaved the heads of new women inmates, an initiation rite into horror. How could these bald Jewish women look at themselves in the mirror when they unwound their scarves at night, itchy stubs of hair on a naked head? Did a man lying in bed with his bald wife say, "You are beautiful"? (Perhaps the women always kept their scarves on? Perhaps they were intimate with their husbands only in the darkest of nights? Was it true that these women had a certain way of getting in and out of their nightgowns that limited the amount of time they would appear naked in front of their husbands?)

My friend the audiologist suggested that before we resume our discussion next week after Aviva's class, I explore the texts for sources on baldness. This is what I found: In the Torah it is not stated but rather implied that a married woman must appear in public with her hair covered. The source is Numbers 5 and the issue is the *sotah*, the woman suspected of adultery by her husband. It is the wife who must bear the burden of proving whether or not her husband's fit of jealousy is justified. She is the one who must endure an ordeal of drinking bitter waters. If she is guilty, the waters will cause her stomach to distend. If she is innocent, the waters will leave her unscathed. Before the ritual begins, before her guilt or innocence is revealed, a priest humiliates her by baring her head. The Mishnah on the *sotah* describes this humiliation in lurid detail. The priest tears the woman's clothes, baring her bosom. If she wore white, she was forced to change to black. If she wore gold and silver jewelry, nose rings and earrings, they were taken from her. A rope of rushes was tied above her breasts. All who wanted to view her, excepting her own servants (who had seen her undressed and would not be shocked), were allowed. Her presence was a cautionary tale. The rabbis conclude from *sotah* (said to be a rite never actually enacted) that a woman's uncovered hair represents degradation. Later interpretations called women's head coverings signs of modesty, of dignity, or of respectfulness.

Why baldness, then, if Torah doesn't require it explicitly? Rules concerning the type of the hair covering used and when it is to be worn have always stemmed from the customs of individual communities. Over time, these customs took on the status of law. Often it is said that the praiseworthy daughters of Israel took additional stringencies upon themselves. Historically, then, different communities have adopted numerous variations on head coverings. Thus, some women have covered their hair only in synagogue; others, only in public; and yet others, always, in public and in private. They have worn scarves, hats, *kippot,* little lace doilies, and glamorous high-fashion wigs woven of the wearer's own hair. Other women who accept the virtue of modesty go bareheaded out of a belief that modesty is defined not by one's headgear, but by one's carriage and comportment.

Baldness plus a head covering, unquestionably a most severe variation, is said to have certain advantages. The bald woman needn't worry that any of her hair is exposed in an inappropriate place. She needn't fear that when she immerses herself in the ritual bath her hair will float to the top, making her immersion invalid. (Somewhat of a hysterical worry, since the immersion is always attended by a pious woman whose sole job it is to see that all hair gets immersed.) Yet megamodesty has its rewards. The Talmud says that righteous children will be born to the woman so scrupulous in covering her hair that even the "walls of her house" cannot see the "hairs on her head."

There is also an alternative point of view. *Halichos Bas Yosrael: A Woman's Guide to Jewish Observance* * by Ray Yitzchak Yaacov Fuchs teaches that a husband may object to his wife's taking baldness upon herself in order to be more scrupulous in her observance. He can do this because the rabbis, always savvy about the connection between

---

**Halichos Bas Yosrael: A Woman's Guide to Jewish Observance* (Southfield, Michigan: Targum Press, 1985).

sex appeal and procreative vigor, urged women not to appear un-attractive to their husbands.

When I saw the audiologist again, I reported my findings. Bald-ness continued to trouble me. What wisdom so enormous persuaded these bald women of Mea Shearim (and, apparently, their husbands as well) that their bodies were a temporary shell? Maybe they're really happier in their lives than we are in ours; maybe it's blissful to be an essentially disembodied soul. They seem like nuns to me: the way they dress, the way they have to submit to the authority of their husbands and their rebbes. And for all practical purposes, most of their lives are spent in the company of women. Following the bald women of Mea Shearim revealed nothing. They went to the cleaners and then to the bakery for bread and then they bought a few yogurts and went home. They didn't walk around in holy trances. Not that I really supposed they did—but I was hoping I'd get a glimpse of some outward signs, other than their headgear, of a heightened spiritual state. I'm never going to get to know any women in Mea Shearim, I complained to the audiologist. My friend Esther, who had been introducing me to the learned women, once knew a woman in Mea Shearim, but she was no longer there. How would I penetrate that insular community?

The audiologist said it just so happened that she had been treating the hearing-disabled son of a Mea Shearim family for five years and slowly the mother, Hava, had begun to trust the audiologist enough to invite her into her home. They had become friends, sharing recipes, worrying about each other, trading information. The audiol-ogist had most recently been at Hava's for Purim and was surprised not to find a single *mishloahic manot* package around. No goodies at all from friends or family? Hava had thrown them into the garbage as quickly as they were received, she was told. The family couldn't be sure anyone, anyone at all, was scrupulous enough in adhering to *kashrut,* the dietary laws.

"Can you take me there?"

"I think I can arrange it. Cover your head, wear long sleeves, and dark tights, and meet me in front of the downtown Hadassah Hospital on Strauss Street at nine on Sunday morning."

I had learned to slip easily into "religious costume," adjusting my dress according to the required level of observance. I never fully stopped resenting the need for disguise—and not only physical disguise. I believed my acceptability among the pious women hinged as well on my willingness to mask my thoughts. If in some crazy world I ever allied myself with the observant, I wondered if I would still have to remain in disguise, alienated from myself.

Sunday the audiologist and I walked together through the crushing crowd down the central road of Mea Shearim, past the stores selling ritual objects, past beggars, past the sign warning daughters of Zion to dress modestly if they entered these gates—gates that led into a world of various sects of Hasidim and other ultraobservant Jews, frozen in some past time in Poland or Russia.

We entered the deteriorated courtyard of a crumbling stone building. The poverty seemed overwhelming. Hava waved to us from her second-story porch where the old doors and bamboo poles for her family's sukkah (the little hut erected for the holiday of Sukkot) were stacked. She wanted us to hurry in. I assumed this was to keep her relatives who lived in adjacent apartments from gossiping about the modern women with whom she was about to associate. Hava wore a white scarf with flowers wound jauntily around her shaven head and a green-and-white checked housedress. "I told you she was a good-looker," the audiologist said. She was a knockout. Hava had porcelain features that needed no makeup, and she was svelte, a major feat for a thirty-two-year-old woman who had already given birth to six children. The audiologist said the women in the community recognized and took advantage of Hava's beauty and charm. When women received a suitcaseful of dresses or children's clothes from the States, they sent Hava out peddling them in the neighborhood. For this, Hava received a 10 percent commission on the sales.

The extra money helped. Hava had just convinced her husband to stop working in a factory and resume studying full-time in the *kolel,* the yeshiva program for adult males. "It is better this way," she said, meaning, more learning would assure the strength of his faith. Four mornings a week she carried her sewing machine across the courtyard to her sister's apartment, where she stitched black-and-gold striped caftans. The audiologist thought Hava earned about five hundred dollars a month for this work. This, in addition to her husband's stipend of around three hundred dollars and child allowances from the government, supported the family. Once in a while, she'd take a day off and go on an outing. That meant leaving the children behind and taking a bus to the gravesites at Meron, where she poured out her miseries to the souls of the righteous departed. According to the mystical *Zohar,* that information would ascend up the hierarchy of spirits until it reached God, who could choose to hear and have mercy.

The audiologist had accompanied Hava on one such excursion to Meron on the holiday of Lag b'Omer, when thousands come to mark the death of Simeon ben Yohai, whom they regard as the author of the *Zohar.* The bus was divided into two sections. Men sat in the front; women sat in the back. A sign faced the women, warning them that their talking was immodest. So the women whispered. Except for these trips to Meron and visits to doctors for the children, Hava rarely left the confines of Mea Shearim. Once she went to the Israel Museum, but when she got there, she was afraid to look around lest she gaze upon something forbidden. And so she returned right away. As for notable sights in the neighborhood, she was aware of an ornate, imposing building on the edge of Mea Shearim, but she did not know that it had once been an Italian hospital and that it now belonged to the Ministry of Education.

Hava chatted with us in the solid and idiomatic modern Hebrew she had picked up in the fabric and food stores. Rarely did she inject Yiddish phrases, although that was the language she usually spoke.

Hava apologized that she had not had time to tidy up after the Sabbath. What was there to tidy? The apartment was nearly bare. There were two and a half rooms for Hava, her husband, and their children, aged three to twelve. "Only six children," she confessed. "I have trouble getting pregnant." When she went to the hospital to give birth, she would tell the other children she was going to the dentist.

"Her children will grow up fearing dentists," the audiologist said, "because every time their mother goes to the 'dentist,' she stays away for a few days and comes home with a baby. Hava is a good mother, but she doesn't have much of a feel for child psychology. It wouldn't occur to her to prepare the son I treat when he has to have surgery. I suggest it to her, but she doesn't see what I'm getting at. At best, she'll say, 'My husband can do it.' "

Closet-size spaces held the kitchen and bathroom, and a vestibule was used as a dining room. The parents had a small bedroom with two separate beds pushed to opposite walls. The six children shared a large room with high ceilings. Six children in the house and not a single toy or ball or picture book. "They don't need toys," Hava said. "They have each other." There was nothing decorative anywhere, nothing frivolous. A wall packed with sacred texts, a glass cabinet of sterling silver ceremonial objects, a picture of a rebbe. Immaculate. Hava insisted on serving us bottled grapefruit drink and leftover Sabbath cakes. Just as we were sitting down, an old woman in a ragged housedress who seemed to be a maid lugged a mop and pail up the stairs and began to wash the floors around us. Apparently, there was a subtle distinction between chosen austerity and real poverty in Mea Shearim.

Hava wanted to show me around the neighborhood and excused herself to change. It took her a very long time. I had misread her earlier rush to usher us in. She didn't fear being seen with us. She feared being seen in houseclothes. She came out of her bedroom wearing the Hasidic equivalent of a figure-revealing Laura Ashley dress, elegant black spiked heels, a skintight black chiffon scarf knotted behind her neck, and rhinestone clip-on earrings. On the main street, she whispered that we were about to pass a cousin of hers. Trailing behind her husband, shuffling along in brown clod-hoppers, the cousin wore a heavy black crocheted scarf, its ends hanging over her shoulders like cobwebs. Hava barely acknowledged the woman, giving her only a nod and a grunt. "That's how our grandmother used to wear her scarf in the olden days. It's supposed to be more modest. But the rebbe permits women to wear the shorter scarves, so that's what I do. It's so much more modern." To be sure, even among bald, scarved women there are the stylish and the frumpy. Hava floated down Mea Shearim Street, the only runway this flamboyant beauty queen knows.

When she was seventeen, she told us, her parents feared she was asking too many questions. They took pains to marry her off quickly, believing that would squelch her rebellious nature. After her parents found a suitable match, she cried for three days. "All right," her mother conceded, "we won't force you to marry *him,* but you must marry now." If that was the case, Hava thought, she might as well marry their choice. He was just as good as anyone else. A year later, Hava's sister was spending her wedding day in hysterics. "I'm not ready to marry," she pleaded.

"Maybe your sister was really crying because her hair was going to be cut," the audiologist suggested.

"Understand," Hava said, "this is how we grow up. We know it's going to happen, and it's like anything else in life. Still, we put off cutting her hair until the next day. Too many traumatic things at once."

"Would you and your sister have felt better if you had gotten to know the men you were going to marry?" I asked. If I were talking to an octogenarian from a Greek fishing village, I might have been able to assimilate the bizarreness of an arranged marriage under the rubric of "that's how things used to be done in such places." But

Hava was just about my age, and in theory, we belonged to the same tribe. By the smallest fluke of genealogy, a shake-up of leaves on neighboring family trees, I could have been living Hava's life. I, too, would have cried for three days before my wedding, and if I knew no other life, I, too, would not have been bold or imaginative enough to run away.

"It's ridiculous to meet each other beforehand a few times," Hava said, beginning to weary of my questions.

These boys don't know how to talk to girls. They'll say stupid things like We want to have a home like this or like that. We all know we want the same home, the same thing. So what's to say? If you ask a young girl who she wants to marry, she'll say she wants an *ilui* [a young Talmudic prodigy]. But once she gets married, she realizes she doesn't want her husband off learning all day. She prefers him to help her with the children and wants him to pay some attention to her. I felt it in my flesh when I married that what I expected I would want before I married would be very different from what I would really need. When, *barukh hashem,* you get married [she told the audiologist] this is my advice to you. At first accept everything. Swallow it. Then, after two years, slowly bring things up. You understand, a woman runs the house, but God forbid your husband should think you do. The wisdom is for a woman to make her husband *think* that he has the last word.

I asked to see her children's schools. The boys' schools were off limits even to her. Given my own involvement in my children's schooling—the many times I ask a nursery school teacher How did it go today?—I couldn't imagine having no access whatsoever to a son's school, never to have conferences with his teachers. Were I altogether cut off, I would stand outside his window and suppose that he was being taught to despise women because they were fools who could know God only in the details of everyday life: stitching clothes made of ritually correct fabric, burning a corner of the challah dough. Hava said she didn't relate much to her five sons. She called them "beings of a different order." She had one daughter whom she thought of as an only child, her only companion. Hava felt sorry for her because she was her only help around the house. The daughter came home from school at one o'clock; the boys didn't get home until eight o'clock at night. "All the boys know is Torah," she said. "After four years in school, they know more than I do. I can't talk mundane things with them. I'd be wasting their time."

Hava offered to show us a girls' nursery school. She told the teachers, "Two young ladies from America would like to visit." The teachers beckoned to us to come in as though we were philanthropists bent on having squalor move us to make generous donations. Forty tiny girls holding rolls in their hands sat pressed together on chairs in a small, hot, windowless room. They were silent. Their eyes were dull. A dungeon brightened with children's paintings. Had only half the girls been there, it would still have been stifling. When in the Talmud, Rabbi Judah the Prince says, "The world endures for the sake of the breath of schoolchildren" (tractate *Kallah Rabbati*), I do not suppose it was to girls such as these in Mea Shearim that he referred, but rather to the boys whom we could hear shrieking out their lessons from the windows of their large, many-storied school. (What would I have preferred, I mused, to have been born a son or daughter of Mea Shearim? A girl. With enough hours of quiet, I would have spun out elaborate daydreams, and with enough girlfriends at my side, I would have whispered intimate and silly secrets—the whining rote over at the boys' school would have permitted me no inventiveness.)

"What was your own learning like?" I asked Hava.

In Yiddish, Hava answered, "Strangled." The word that emerged speedily and certainly from her throat, the bite of it, made her laugh. "Strangled," she said again, nodding her head. "It was very superficial. You could come out of our school knowing how to be a good mother. You wouldn't become a learned, enlightened person. We learned to read and write Yiddish, math, Torah, Rashi, laws, ethics, geography, sewing. All a little bit." Hava didn't appear to be angry in her recollection. At whom could she direct her anger? It just seemed ridiculous, a waste of her time.

"Do you learn now?"

What silly questions this American lady asks. "Who has time for learning? You see, I don't even have time to do my floors."

"There are no classes for women?"

"How many times can you go to the same two classes on *lashon hara* [gossip] and *taharat hamishpahah* [family purity]?"

As we walked in and out of the gates that have separated this quarter from the rest of the city for over a hundred years, the audiologist played the tour guide, having read the standard book, Zev Vilnay's *Israel Guide*. Hava said she felt foolish. She had lived here all her life, yet most of this was new to her. She would like to know the history of Mea Shearim. She said this as though the idea had just popped into her head, but I gathered that she had been practicing her request for some time, waiting for the opportune moment. If the audiologist would lend her that guidebook, Hava could have her husband read it. He would be able to tell her what was true and what was nonsense. "He knows a lot of history," she said.

"From where?" we asked.

"He just knows," she said, convincing me that just as an ill person believed doctors had healing powers, so she believed men had supernatural access to factual knowledge and could discern truth.

The audiologist would indeed bring the book—several Hebrew books on the land of Israel—next time. This pleased Hava enormously. Would she give them to her husband first so he could present his edited version? Or would she read them herself, on the sly? The audiologist explained that in Vilnay's book, Hava would learn that the name Mea Shearim comes from the Torah, a fact she was certain Hava already knew. Hava did not know. She was fascinated. It seemed too impossible, news too wonderful to be true. Hava had to see this for herself. We raced back home through the marketplace as fast as Hava's spiked heels could go. Before we could turn to the passage about Mea Shearim in Genesis, Hava insisted on feeding us once again: the commandment to offer guests some refreshment was renewed upon each entrance. Out came more cakes and bottled grapefruit drink. Hava took down a volume of Genesis and put it in the audiologist's hands. We three bent over to get a good look. The audiologist skimmed through to Genesis 26:12–13 and asked Hava to read aloud. She recited the text in what she called *lashoyn hakoydesh*—the holy language, pronounced and accented differently from modern Hebrew. It reminded me of the Hebrew spoken by old Mr. Shapiro, who recited the Torah by heart in my childhood synagogue. Torah pointed to each word: "Isaac sowed in that land and reaped a hundredfold [*mea shearim*] the same year. The Lord blessed him and the man grew richer and richer until he was very wealthy." Hava looked with suspicion at the audiologist, as if daring her to offer commentary.

"That's it," said the audiologist, for no commentary was necessary. "Just as I told you, the words *mea shearim,* they're there in Genesis."

Hava ran into the bathroom and returned with a slip of toilet tissue. She tucked the tissue into the book and returned it to the shelf.

"I must save the place and show it to my husband. Then he can see if it's really there and say if it's true." Hava could not take the word of the audiologist whom she trusted on so many matters. Seeing the text itself with her own eyes was not proof. Just as sensible people know not to take one look at a new person and say, "I have sized you up and know your soul!" Hava believed that what she saw in Torah was not to be taken literally. There was no such thing as an unmediated experience of the text. Torah existed only through the eyes of the authoritative interpreters. And even though she had studied Torah with Rashi as a teenager, it was to her husband, the ultimate judge when it came to Torah knowledge in her household, that she would turn.

When it came to the children's health, her husband ruled as well, although this was less easy for Hava to accept. The son whom the audiologist had treated suffered from unbearable headaches. Hava dispensed aspirin, but she wasn't authorized to help the child beyond soothing his bouts with pain. Her husband went to the rebbe to ask him what to do. The rebbe told him to say an incantation against the evil eye along with two other men and to take the boy to a certain neurologist. I was relieved to hear the rebbe sanctioned conventional medicine.

"What do you think of the evil eye?" Hava asked. The audiologist whispered to me in English that Hava had never as yet asked her an open-ended question about her beliefs. The audiologist hesitated to reveal her opinion, fearing it might complicate their relationship or make it impossible for Hava to continue pursuing it. She didn't want to say she thought the evil eye was a superstition in case Hava believed in it.

She fudged. "The evil eye? Who knows?"

Hava breathed in slowly. What dangers her friend the audiologist was exposing herself to by not taking precautions against the evil eye! It was as though an American college student had just learned her roommate depended upon luck as a method of birth control. Composing herself, Hava continued her account. Three men recited the incantation against the evil eye, and the boy was taken to the neurologist, the best in the city. The neurologist wanted to see the boy a second time. Hava's husband brought this issue before the rebbe. The rebbe said not to return to that neurologist, but to go to another.

At that time, Hava was picking up some sewing at the house of a woman who performed incantations against the evil eye. The woman could sense that Hava's son had a very big and powerful evil eye upon him, an evil eye that required a more potent incantation than the one prescribed by the husband's rebbe. "Only three men?" asked the woman. "The incantation will have no effect." Hava shared this with her husband. She pleaded with him. "I'll do what some lady tells me?" he said, turning away from her. The woman kept calling, begging that something be done immediately. The son's headaches became worse, and Hava could not persuade her husband to offer a more powerful incantation. She was frantic. She watched her son as he lay in bed, still and afraid to move. But then just today the woman called again. She told Hava not to worry so. She could feel the power of the evil eye lessening of its own accord. Hava still worried, but what could she do? It was completely out of her hands.

The audiologist listened. She said the first neurologist the son saw was considered the top man in Jerusalem. Was there no way of taking the boy back to him? Hava shook her head. Absolutely impossible. Her husband had scheduled an appointment with the second neurologist. You didn't question the rebbe's reasons.

As we readied to leave, Hava held us back to try out some ideas she had been mulling over. Talking about them gave her pleasure; her eyes flashed. If the audiologist had first been a conduit for information about the world outside, she was now also a sounding board for dreams and schemes. Hava had this plan for how she might learn to swim. (Wearing what, I wondered? A wet suit?) She had another plan for giving her daughter art lessons. Secretly. No one could know. No projects magneted to the refrigerator. Hava yearned to play the flute and to have the children play, but that was out of the question. In memory of the destruction of the Temple in the year 70 C.E., her sect forbids the playing of musical instruments, except on rare occasions. But maybe there was some way around the rules so that at least her daughter could learn, even a little . . .

"I have something to ask," Hava said. "Don't feel you can't say no. Do you think you could teach me—could you perhaps teach me English if you ever have an hour off? No one would have to know."

The audiologist was delighted and, fearing Hava might change her mind, said she would return tomorrow during her break when no one else was home. "English will be easier for you than you think. Some words you think are Yiddish are English: kitchen, dinner, nose, strangle."

Hava repeated in her new English: "Keetchen, deenner, nawz, schtrahngel." She had snuck in her first lesson.

I walked the audiologist back to the hospital, stopping in the restroom of a restaurant on the edge of Mea Shearim to pull off my scarf and undo my collar buttons. When I returned to the audiologist, she was in stitches: "You should have seen the face of the waiter. This was as close as he will ever get to seeing a religious woman perform a striptease." In two gestures, I had gone from prim to savage.

Being with Hava, the audiologist said, was like entering into the world of another century. When she accompanied Hava to synagogue and pressed her nose against the metal grating in the women's balcony, where it was too dark to see in a prayer book and too crowded to breathe, she felt as if she were not in her own life, but in a movie.

We live in the same city but have a totally different perception of it. I became so upset the first few times I visited her. Maybe she was the one who was living the right Jewish life and I wasn't religious enough. What if it was Hava, and not me, who lived more fully in accordance with God's will? Her community is convinced that it's possible to live in a society based only on the ideals of Torah. That attracted me. Then I began to think. The people in her community clearly follow all the laws between God and man, but I don't believe they think it's all that important to follow the laws concerning man's relationship to his fellow men. No, I think they don't. By not educating women. By not exposing anyone, male or female, to the modern world. It's as though they know they wouldn't be able to withstand being exposed. How strong, how much more correct, can their religious life be if they must stick to themselves to avoid the temptation of dangerous exposure?

Hava befriended the audiologist at great personal risk. Not the risk of censure. She had never been able to hide either her curiosity or her rebelliousness. By now her community accepted her wild, inquisitive streak as her defective nature. The risk of the friendship was more to herself: knowing the audiologist opened her up to ideas, to possibilities she couldn't realize. "I envy you because you chose your way of life and are happy," Hava had told the audiologist. "I'm happy with my life, but I grew into it."

My first impulse was to buy boxes of Fisher-Price toys for Hava's children, to tell Hava about the impressionists and Shakespeare and Japan and cross-country skiing and men walking on the moon. I wanted to take her to Lincoln Center to see the *Nutcracker* and watch her face as the Christmas tree grew and the snow fell on the Sugar Plum fairy. But on second thought, in the context of her life, my collection of worldly goods not to be missed seemed like so much trivia, like swimsuits in Antarctica.

No one was home when I got back. Like a frostbitten person who can't just jump into a boiling tub, I needed slowly to bridge the dissonance between Mea Shearim and my apartment in Nayot. I stood in front of my mirror and pulled my hair back tightly, trying to imagine being bald. It would save on shampoo, mousse, time blow-drying, the torture of making small talk with beauticians who ask, My lord, who did you last? I shook my hair wildly, my frizzy black hair that feels like steel wool, then plastered it down against my cheeks so I could smell it.

I turned on the news, went through the mail, pulled dry sheets off the line—anything to get back into my own skin. I couldn't stop thinking of Hava. Was it courage that Hava required to befriend the audiologist, or was her grasping for more knowledge an automatic reflex? Perhaps the audiologist was doing Hava no favor at all. Hava's world had magic and the audiologist, with her history books, with the cardboard dominoes she brought for the children, with English words, with the example of her life—a thirty-eight-year-old Orthodox woman who worked, studied what she wished, and lived all alone—was breaking into that magic, tearing away at the insularity that permitted Hava the joys she did know. "I wish you had been here to see the wedding of the rebbe's granddaughter," Hava had told us. "The children stayed up past midnight. To see all those children drinking bottles of soda with straws. It was remarkable. You'll never see anything like that in your life."

The audiologist had no intention of aggravating Hava's rebelliousness. The relationship served her own pacific purposes: "I want to understand her world and hope to give her a glimpse into mine—not to change each other, but to understand each other, helping in a small way to bring unity to this crazy nation."

Lacking the audiologist, Hava would have sought out another guide. Hava was well aware of being imprisoned by ignorance. The magic was wearing off on its own, antiquated ideas were extinguishing themselves. Her appetite for knowledge had been kindled long before she met the audiologist. Curiosity was her birthright. Sages say the Jew has a continual hunger for learning. Rabbi Hillel of the Mishnah studied every single word passed down by the sages, and it is said that he also studied "All languages, the speech of mountains, hills, and valleys, the speech of trees and herbs, the speech of wild beasts and cattle, the speech of demons and parables. Why did he study all these? Because it is stated (Isaiah 42): 'The Lord was pleased, for His righteousness' sake to make the teaching great and glorious' " (tractate *Soferim*). Swimming, art, English—Hava's wish to learn, all the more so after a strangled Torah education, was likely more enormous than she could bear to acknowledge. Did she truly believe that her husband, the warden who held the key to her learning, was capable of judging what was true, and that she was not? Or was that her "wisdom" to flatter him?

Through Hava, I understood Singer's character Yentl in a new way. "Yentl" was not about sexism in Judaism. Yentl didn't want to be a man, to have a man's strength, a man's sex, a man's life story. She disguised herself as a man only to steal the one thing a man had that she wanted: access to sacred knowledge. She wanted to hold the sacred texts that would recall her father's love for her and for his God. Hava, sneaking tidbits of secular knowledge, was every bit as hungry and cunning as Yentl. Like Yentl, she secretly pressed against the rigid distinctions her community imposed concerning what was worth knowing and what was trash.

I hoped I might get a clearer, or at least a less stark, picture of the lives of the women who belonged to the ultraobservant sects from a bright, articulate twenty-five-year-old woman who sometimes typed my manuscripts or baby-sat for the girls. She never became chummy with the girls or felt at home in our apartment as other sitters did. Yael seemed ill at ease, as if still overwhelmed by the pressures of growing up.

When I brought an article for her to type to her apartment, she told me that her parents, both originally from Mea Shearim, moved to Monsey, New York, where she was born and raised. She was sent to a Bais Yaakov school. Curiously enough, her parents then permitted her to apply and go to college at Stony Brook and live in a dorm. (This is highly irregular, almost as incongruous as monks hiring a a belly dancer to entertain at Easter supper. I hoped Yael would explain how she had gone from yeshiva to university.) Since graduating from Stony Brook with honors at nineteen, Yael said she had been in and out of graduate programs in computer science and hospital administration, back and forth and between New York City, Monsey, and Jerusalem, searching for herself in different careers and cities. Now she was staying with friends in a sublet apartment in Kiryat Moshe, halfway between Bruria and Angel's bakery. The four women she roomed with all had fixed up their rooms with religious posters and scarves draped over lamps, but Yael's room was almost bare, except for a mattress on the floor, a portable computer, and an electric coil for hot water. Everything about the room said "temporary." Sitting on her mattress, I felt as though we were camping outdoors. Yael spoke her words in a rapid whisper, making it hard to keep listening to her. She confused me. At first I assumed that since she had gone to a secular university, she had rebelled against her religious background. She looked like an American college student in unisex sweats, and I took it for granted that I would detect some gentle sarcasm in her voice as she tried to explain the prohibitions against women learning all of Torah. It seemed natural enough. A religious girl who had once worn white tights, a long skirt, and braids goes to secular, co-ed university, where she learns whatever she wishes, goes on unchaperoned dates—how could she not emerge angry at the society that had previously restricted her?

"The reason why it is forbidden for women to learn anything complicated is because of their nature," she said.

It's not an indication that they're stupid. The nature of women is that they read something and they think they understand it and so will not ask. And the importance in Judaism is asking. It's not that women don't have an intellectual capacity or that their brains are smaller. It's recognized that men and women have different control of emotions. A woman is prohibited from acting as a witness because of her emotions. You can't argue with that and say women are prohibited from learning because of male chauvinism. It's emotion.

Now here's a second point against women learning. Men learn because the Torah says they should study day and night. The commandment applies only to men because women are exempt from most time-bound commandments. Day and night means men must study any free time they have. You derive from this that you're talking about learning for *pilpul,* for intellectual reasoning, for the sake of learning itself and not necessarily for the sake of doing. It shouldn't be a woman's goal to learn day and night. Women should learn so they can *do.* This is the aim of Bais Yaakov schools: to produce women who are devoted to Judaism, who want to marry men who study in the *kolel,* who want to raise large families. They learn how to *do:* to keep a kosher home, to raise Jewish children. It's women who impart religion to the next generation. They give it heart, warmth, closeness, dedication. They're well educated. They've learned Torah with Rashi, prophets with all the commentaries, Midrash, legends, law. In essence, they've learned a lot of what the men learn.

The difference is the women didn't learn the Gemara page after page. They learn from the opposite perspective. They learn what the law is and then backtrack. Take the laws for separating challah dough. A woman learned the laws four years ago in high school and now she's a mother making challah and she wants to know what to do. So she looks it up in the Mishnah. To understand better, she needs to consult the Gemara. She looks at the Gemara. *Barukh hashem,* go ahead, that's what she's supposed to do and not start reading the whole Gemara. Bais Yaakov schools convey a love for Judaism and give you a *hashkafah*—an outlook on how to walk and dress, on what your role in life is, on how to perform the commandments and raise children. For girls, the attitude is: You've got twelve years to pack in what you're going to need for a lifetime. We hope that when you have your home and children and are busy working that you'll devote some time to learning, but the reality is you're not going to have much time. That's why there's no discipline problem in Bais Yaakov schools. Girls know they have their twelve years. Boys' learning is very different. They're going to be learning for the rest of their lives, so their approach to learning is different.

"What if a girl shows real scholarly potential. Is an exception made in her case?" I asked.

Yael said yes, kind of. Women such as Bruria fell into a rabbinic category called the *ishah hashuvah* (important woman), which exempted them from the normal prohibitions against women's learning.

Rabbis said that unlike the run-of-the-mill light-headed women, exemplary women should be treated by the scholars of their time with honor and respect and be encouraged in their learning. Yael showed me how the issue of the important woman was taken up in the *Kesef Mishnah,* the commentary to Rambam's *Mishneh Torah* and explained his four categories of *ishah hashuvah:*

First is the woman who doesn't have a husband and is the master of her house. Say a widow with five children who has the means and ability to run her own household. Second is the woman who is important because of what she creates with her own hands. Say she's a craftswoman. But maybe we could also understand that to mean a career woman who is recognized for her achievements. Third is the daughter of a great scholar of his times. She's born an *ishah hashuvah.* She's a woman of valor who fears God. Fourth is a woman who has a lot of servants who doesn't have to bother herself with preparing food and doing household chores. If you think about it, this could be a woman living in Woodmere, Long Island, who's very wealthy and sits around polishing her nails. That's a problem for me. So what makes a woman important? Lineage, money, status in the community, being the boss of her household. It leaves a lot open to interpretation.

"Funny," Yael said, slowing down enough to dart glances at me through her owlish glasses, "it doesn't even mention learning. I don't understand this. It's a problem."

"Explain this to me," I asked. "Does this suggest that an individual woman can say she was, or had the potential to be, an important woman, deserving exceptional consideration?"

"There's the catch," Yael sputtered.

The issue of modesty. Someone who is worthy of being a leader has to be modest. But she could be so modest and dedicated to Torah that no one would know she existed. She herself might know she was worthy of being a leader, but she isn't going to announce it. A woman who is dedicated to learning and keeping mitzvot *is* an *ishah hashuvah*. But for her to say Therefore I am exempt from this or that—that wouldn't go on in her head because she has reached a level where she doesn't think in those terms. She's so learned that when she's looking up a law, she'll look up hundreds of passages in the Gemara. She knows the whole of Gemara. Of course, the restrictions against women's learning no longer apply to her because she wouldn't use her learning for the wrong purposes. As the Talmud states: "Do not seek greatness for yourself: so that you should not say, 'Behold I study the Torah and what a great man I am!' Should you do so, the consequence will be that you occupy yourself with the Torah not for its own sake" [tractate *Kallah Rabbati*].

"Yael, do you think there are such profoundly learned women now? Is there a Bruria among us?"
She paused to think. "No. Today I can't say I've heard of such women."

Later, I would pose a similar question to Esther: "I know you wouldn't measure a Talmudist's greatness—male or female—by publications, but what criteria do you use to say this one's a great, and that one's not?"
"Torah learning is dialogical," Esther said. "Torah personalities have an experiential impact. Of course one doesn't measure their greatness by publications." Her husband, Reuven, home for a moment between classes, added, "In the Soloveitchik line of rabbis, the tradition was to publish only after death. Perish, then publish. The greatness of the current Soloveitchik is based on a single lengthy essay, "Ish ha-Halakhah," published in English as *Halakhic Man*.*
The Vilna Gaon, the great eighteenth-century Lithuanian scholar,

Halakhic Man (Philadelphia: Jewish Publication Society of America, 1984).

published nothing in his life and is known through his teachings that were passed on by his students to their students."

Esther interrupted: "Even if you were to publish transcripts of the classes of a great teacher, the transcripts wouldn't replicate the experience of learning with him, just as a photograph gives you only a partial experience of a person. The reason women are not among the *gedolim,* the great scholars of the generation, is because that stature is achieved after, say, fifty years of learning."

When Yael had described the restrictions against women, I still couldn't tell if she was comfortable in that ultrastrict world or if she spoke with a sense of irony. Say she had been her brother, would she be sitting in a yeshiva learning now?

"That's what my brother does," Yael said.

He's still in Monsey with my parents. He's a Hasid. He wears a black coat, *peyes* [sidelocks], a *streimel.* He works in the diamond district and still *lerns* five to ten hours a day. He *lerns* on the bus from Monsey to New York two hours each way, he *lerns* when he gets home. If I had been male and not gone to college, that's what I'd be doing now.

Looking back, Yael regretted her rebellious phase and regretted that her parents gave in to her.

Stony Brook was a waste of time. What I did there, I could have done on my own. What you're supposed to get out of education is *hitlahavut:* strong devotion, dedication, direction. My professors were cold and into their careers. The rabbis have a saying: "And your eyes shall see your leaders." That's why when you go into a religious home, you see the pictures of important rabbis. At college I used to think of that saying a lot. My teachers at Stony Brook were intelligent, they had book smarts. But they were closed-minded in their openness. No one had *hokhmah*—wisdom. I studied history in college. It's disillusioning because you discover history is what each author determines it is. But if you're studying Torah and you believe strongly that Torah is all truth from God—well, then you get a lot more pleasure out of it.

"And," she wanted me to be sure to know, "I only wear pants when I'm at home."

For Yael, Jewish learning was like the show you wanted to watch on TV; secular learning was a commercial with bright colors and a catchy jingle promoting some junk cereal. Unless you were extremely vigilant, you'd end up humming the jingle, buying the cereal, eating it, and becoming forever addicted to it.

"See," Yael said,

we're talking about a process that started almost two thousand years ago. For two thousand years, people weren't agitating for women to go to schools like the men. Women learned at home from their mothers. Who learned in the Talmudical academies in Babylon? Men. That started the tradition of yeshiva learning in Europe, where young men would leave their wives and children behind and come from far away to learn with the great rabbis. Where do women fit in? *They don't.* There was never a tradition that women learned in a formal setting. There was a Mishnah that said it: You can't teach her Torah. I don't think it was disputed. The Rambam was living in an Arab society. I don't want to say he was misogynist. That would be unfairly harsh and sharp. But you have to understand that the twelfth century wasn't the height of women's lib. You have to take all he's saying with a grain of salt. No one argued with him in his lifetime because it didn't matter. It didn't become an issue till it mattered.

"Did it ever matter to you?" I asked.

I think I felt the world I came from deified men, and women were their servants. All my girlfriends were always cleaning and helping, and the boys did nothing. The brothers would make a mess in the kitchen and walk out, and the girls had to do everything. It bothered me. I started to have problems in school. There were things I wanted to learn that weren't available. I had never seen a lab.

It was television that made her aware of the world of which she was deprived. For years Yael fought to have a television, and when her parents relented and finally permitted one, the house changed. Yael's father, convinced that his daughter's hunger for television and newspapers would seed problems, was nonetheless unable to curb their influence. "He was right about television," Yael said. "That's where I was getting all my ideas from, because I certainly wasn't getting it from Bais Yaakov."

"What kind of ideas?"

I had discovered that there's a world out there and I wanted it. I wanted to go to the movies. I wanted to be something, a career person, a lawyer. I must have seen that on TV. I'd go to the public library for hours and read tons of stuff, whatever I could get my hands on.

She dropped out of her yeshiva high school after her teacher complained that she had abandoned her braids for a Farrah Fawcett hairdo. "I'd take the bus and explore New York. I went to Gimbel's, Bloomingdale's. I had the time of my life. One day the weather was horrible and I came home early. My mother was there, and she said, 'Why are you home so soon?' She called the principal and he said, 'Yael hasn't been here for a month.' "

Yael said the rebelliousness had worked its way out of her system.

The ideal life I want is a yeshiva life, where Torah is what life is all about. I yearn for that world. But there's going to have to be a little better treatment of women, at least on the personal level. The wives of yeshiva men believe fervently that they are *ezer knegdo,* their husbands' helpmeets. Their husbands are doing all the spiritual stuff, and they're doing all the physical stuff to help. And in the world to come, they'll both get equal reward. Well I don't agree with that. OK? There could be a source for that in Torah, and Torah is from Sinai, and it is God's will. But it doesn't make sense to me. God made human beings who have the same brains and the same capacity and desires for learning. OK, men and women are different, but compared to all the other beings in the world, they're so much the same. Yet He wanted there to be such differences between them. That's the trouble I have. I would want a household where the spiritual and the physical can be everybody's task.

"How would you educate your daughters?"

"I'm going to shock you," she said. She would send them to the strictest schools to be sure they would emerge with absolute love and fear of God. She had wanted to be a lawyer once. She now no longer wanted to. She wanted to have ten kids. A career was a waste of time, illusory—it would never lead to understanding what life was all about. She would raise her children, work out of her house on a computer, take Torah classes when she could.

"I'm not married. That's my only problem. Now I'm going out with I don't know how many guys, but the only one I'm interested in is a yeshiva boy."

We stopped talking abruptly when Yael heard her doorbell. It was an Orthodox sales manager from Spring Valley, New York, coming by to bring Yael a contract that needed to be typed immediately. "Wait a minute," Yael called to him, then flew into a long skirt.

Yael was, in certain respects, like Yentl in reverse. She had gotten access to the knowledge she wanted—and when she saw what it was, dumped it like so much unopened junk mail.

As I walked over to Angel's bakery to buy the muffins my family had become addicted to, I reviewed what I thought Yael was telling me: A person who knows Torah (and it is never mastered—it is always possible to delve more deeply into the text and beyond it) is not just in possession of a body of material. Torah is a way of being, a way of knowing God. Torah sculpts the personality, it defines how to relate to others, what to yearn for. Ideally, a lifetime of Torah study refines one's ability to make judgments, to understand human nature well enough to prescribe paths of action for others to take.

It was true that all of Jewish learning was not open to women, but that was a moot point. There was sufficient permissible material to last a woman her whole lifetime. Hava had picked up more of Rashi's commentaries in her strangled education than I would probably ever know. Yael, in her Bais Yaakov school, had become adept at decoding Torah with all the commentaries, Mishnah, Midrash, codes of law. Many women who complained loudly about limitations in women's learning had never learned at all.

Yael was not oblivious to the problems for Jewish women, but they were like a small tear on the inside hem of her Sabbath dress. While she might finger the tear and lament it, she would not throw away the dress. With what could she replace it?

I felt for the choice Yael was making. I suppose her choice of the ultraobservant life could be interpreted as a Band-Aid, although I think it was not. There was great clarity underlying her decision to accept the strictest observance. She was choosing to live at what she believed to be the highest ethical level. But for myself, still, still, I could not imagine any scenario that would compel me to give myself fully to a Torah society that seemed to me to ignore the intellectual capacity of women or, at best, to acknowledge us as "important exceptions" only if we educated ourselves and stood out from the crowd. There was the bottom line: any Jewish man had all of Jewish scholarship offered up to him on a platter; a woman stole what she could. Jewish boys were treated like princes for breathing— as for girls, we're valued if we're good, quiet, cooperative, tame; if we serve, make babies, keep society going. Even in those modern

Orthodox schools, where girls and boys studied sacred texts along-side each other, I still wondered if girls were encouraged to see themselves as future leaders in Torah learning.

For me, Torah was like a dress with a disfiguring stain. I couldn't wear it, I couldn't throw it out. It would hang in my closet, and I would look at it, sadly.

Eight

At 8:30 in the morning, I joined Raphael, who was fixing a cup of coffee for himself in the lounge outside the *bet midrash* at Pardes. I was glad to have my classes at Pardes each week these past months, and I was glad to see Raphael. He, like my family, was a respite from the eccentric worlds that had attracted me of late. In one respect, these outings were alike. I always found myself more drawn to each religious milieu than I would have anticipated, but in time, a ghoulish threat of being absorbed in alien territory always sent me retreating to the blander and safer ground of home. I had come to count on Raphael to joke and jolt me back into perspective after my zigzags between attraction and repulsion. He wasn't surprised I found it provocative to watch others leap into faith as I stood riveted to the ground. He understood that it was not sufficient for me to be plodding away at Pardes or basking in Aviva's presence each week. He understood there was still something else I hungered for, something I couldn't put my finger on.

Raphael said spiritual experiences fascinated him, yet he insisted he had not come to Pardes for a spiritual experience of his own. "I'm not a seeker," he avowed. "I'm not good at following organized paths, and so I'm turned off to those paths that are available."

If that was so, I asked, then why was he spending this year studying full-time at Pardes? Pardes, however unconventional, was a yeshiva!

He explained:

Because after being in Israel for more than eleven years, I still felt a hole in my education. For observant and nonobservant Israelis, the Torah is the source of Jewish culture. Even the yeshiva's style of argument is central to Israeli life. To be an Israeli without knowing Torah would be like being an American who had never watched TV. I went to a Reform Sunday school. We read about Judaism and we were tested on the names of the major Jewish books, but we never opened the books themselves. Pardes offers me the opportunity to take a seat in the study hall where Jews have been arguing for thousands of years about how to live righteously, about how to create a just society.

Even before I studied Torah, I thought it would touch me deeply. It does. The rushes I get reading Torah . . . It feels right—I can't explain it—it's like falling in love. I feel that Torah was written for me. I feel so many associations reading the text; even the plagues awaken memories. At Pardes, I have an overwhelming feeling of returning home, of being magnetically rooted to my place and people. At Pardes, I reclaim a vital, missing part of myself.

Raphael and I enjoyed being together, we were committed to each other's well-being, we established an adult working relationship, we got on with the tasks at hand. I took comfort in knowing that we atypical yeshiva students were both trying to forge paths into the sacred texts, however different those paths were. Now I laughed at my hypersensitivity about gender on our first days. If our modes of arguing were male or female, the distinction eluded my notice. As my confidence in handling the texts grew, I had a better sense of when my comments were valid and worth pressing and when it was wiser for me to defer to Raphael's point of view. We corrected each other without rebuke, bullying, or screaming. We learned to curtail discussions that lapsed into metaphysical bull and to stay tight with discussions that led to insights connected to the text. If we were best at Pardes in anything, it was in rapidly recognizing our shortcomings and being impatient to address them through our own efforts. We were the study partners most compulsive about calling the tutor over to clarify the text when, to our eyes, it appeared too opaque or too trivial to be taken at face value.

I had grown fond of Aryeh Ben-David, our redheaded, red-bearded young tutor who had come to Pardes via Vassar College and the Yeshiva Gavoha of Mevasseret Zion. It was clear to him that neither Raphael nor I was on the brink of committing to a life governed by Jewish law or devoted to Torah scholarship. Nonetheless, we were Jewish souls, and a little Torah was better than none. Aryeh would kneel or pull a chair over to our study table. He alternated addressing us, turning his head from side to side to make equal eye contact, transfusing his enthusiasm for the text to us in equal portions. The more familiar Aryeh became with our personalities and backgrounds, the better he was able to bring the depths of the texts into our grasps.

Raphael would be going off during Passover to do his reserve duty in the army. I was relieved to hear he had been assigned to patrol the beaches of Eilat, an assignment less politically problematic for him than service in the occupied territories. (I needn't have worried so; on his return he was well tanned. Joking, I asked if he had enjoyed his off-hours checking out the beach for nonterrorist activity. He said that my remark was sexist and undeserved. He had spent his free time reading and drinking cappuccino. The darkest moment of his stint had been the day the cappuccino maker at the King Solomon Hotel went on the blink.)

The army—that remained the big difference between Raphael and me. "What do you snipers do?" I asked him.

"We're called when a clean, surgical shot is needed."

That's it, I said to myself, picturing Raphael scrubbed for surgery and waiting for an army nurse to slap a gun in his hand. Men can change diapers and women can fly into space. But I could not picture myself with a machine gun in my hand, the enemy in front of me, and the fate of my comrades, family, and nation behind me. I didn't doubt that I, good enough at darts and archery, could learn to shoot and to shoot well. I did doubt that I could shoot calmly when staring at an enemy, and that I could shoot to kill. When Raphael left for reserve duty, mustering up any ruthlessness and courage his gender either possessed innately or learned or faked, I would still be at Pardes studying, still at home bathing children, making soup.

Perhaps because of the centrality of military service, Israelis—despite the myth of women plowing fields and men scrambling eggs on the kibbutz—hold a dim view of egalitarianism. The impact of feminism has come late to Israel. Issues of women's inequality under Israeli civil law, of day care, of family violence, and of pornography are just beginning to be addressed by a growing group of activists. Only in 1984 was the Israel Women's Network, the leading advocate of women's rights in Israel, founded. My Israeli friend Shanit, a therapist in her forties, married and the mother of four, described how her perceptions of feminism had changed:

When it first came to Israel, it was only Anglo-Saxon women who were feminists. They were divorced, single, bitter, unhappy, vulgar women, many of them lesbians. Things they said didn't apply to me. But that's all changed. Look at Leah Shakdiel in Yeruham. She's a happily married Israeli, she's a mother with a family, she cares passionately about the welfare of her community, she's a career woman, she's religious. When soft, caring, family women became feminists, then I could identify with the cause. I went to the meetings that were held when Leah was first denied a place on the Yeruham religious council. I wrote letters to the head of the rabbinate. What's happened to Leah will open up doors for all women.

Still, the old stereotypes are firmly in place. In Israel, men fight the wars, women nurture the babies who will become soldiers. "Israeli women know what they must do," says an Israeli nurse, the class mother of Juliana's third grade, whom I knew only as *ima shel netta,* Netta's mother. Each time her son comes home from the army, she takes his shirt, and using the most durable thread in her sewing box, reinforces each one of his buttons. It is as though she were giving him a coat of armor, the metaphor of her protectiveness. She and her daughter stay up all night baking for him. When the son dresses in the morning, he finds his pockets and his duffel bag lined with sweetmeats and love notes. "You would do the same," *ima shel netta* told me, pushing away tears with the sleeve of her sweater, "any mother would—otherwise you would never be able to let the boy leave your sight."

The reigning Israeli vision of what each sex is supposed to do had been vivid to me at the Purim party for parents and children in Dede's nursery school in Nayot. The music teacher opened up her bag to reveal plastic pistols. She skipped around the circle handing out the pistols. My beliefs were about to mark me as socially deviant: to refuse a gun in Israel was to refuse a reefer in the sixties.

I rehearsed what I would whisper when the music teacher came to us: No thank you. My child does not play with guns.

Next to me was an American mother holding her Israeli-born son on her lap. "We do not play with guns in our family," she reminded him.

He threw a tantrum. "I want the gun! I want the gun!"

He got the gun.

"You're a cowboy," the teacher told him. Everyone eyed the immigrant mother with disdain.

Just as I decided that Dede might as well take the gun, the music teacher skipped over us. Only little boys got guns. The teacher had no intention of giving guns to the girls. I was ashamed of my enormous relief. "Girls never play with guns," said Dede, who knew all along she wasn't getting one. "Guns are gross."

We clapped along as the boys mimicked the teacher performing a macho cowboy strut in time to accordion music. The boys shot at their feet, the guns were collected, and another bag was brought out. Bangle bracelets, for girls only. The gist of their dance was "Look at me in my splendid finery." The mother of the adamant little cowboy shrugged her shoulders as we watched my daughter and all the other little girls imitating the teacher as she wiggled her hips and slinked around as a femme fatale. "In Israel they don't have a problem with sexual stereotyping," said the mother. "They get right down to business."

Like most Pardes study partners, Raphael and I permitted ourselves a first few minutes to share current bits of our lives. I told him about the guns at nursery school, he told me about his friend Nina the masseuse who had just come to Jerusalem and was looking for clients. (That day, I made an appointment with Nina. She said she would be using the massage table at Raphael's apartment. I made Raphael promise that he and his roommate would not be home when I had my massage. He agreed, accepting my inhibitions just as the crowd at Pardes tolerated his nonobservance of ritual.) The chats Raphael and I had before class bridged daily life and sacred study and served, in part, as a little ceremony of intimacy and caring.

Sometimes the moments of personal sharing leaked into our learning. Studying the plagues—always studying the plagues—an issue that troubled us arose: How could Pharaoh have remained unmoved by the first nine plagues? Lice, frogs, and death were everywhere. A normal leader would have said: Enough, leave us alone, get out of here! But each time Moses presented increasingly compelling evidence that his powerful God existed, Pharaoh more stubbornly refused to allow the Israelites to leave. Rashi suggested that Pharaoh was unable to relent—even if he had wanted to—because God had hardened his heart. And even if that had not been the case, Pharaoh's alternative, to acknowledge the God of Moses, was pushed into his face. "You can change your point of view," Raphael said, "only when you believe you have discovered an alternative yourself." To retain his integrity, Pharaoh clung furiously to his own ideas, risking the dangers of even more odious plagues. This, in a roundabout way, reminded me of an encounter with a woman whom I called "the knee lady" that had been troubling me for some weeks, and Raphael, who relished a tangent, listened hard as I unburdened myself.

I had been telling Esther about my encounters with women of the more insular sects, and she feared that these encounters were not serving to bring me any closer to Torah. She was alerted to a growing skepticism in my voice. It seemed to her that I was drawn to the closed sects because that made it easy for me to conclude: I clearly don't belong here if this is how Torah tells women how to conduct their lives.

I suppose Esther also recognized some positive potential in my interest in the closed sects. It indicated I was beginning to grasp that Torah study was more than an intellectual pastime, that it seeped into how you constructed your life, from the minutiae of every day to the way you conceived of your place in the cosmos. Studying Torah was not like studying Baudelaire—you could become an expert in Baudelaire's life, you could know *Les Fleurs du Mal* by heart. But the knowledge didn't necessarily change who you were or how you lived. Secular knowing provided a charge, but a charge that was temporary and superficial.

Striving to nudge me into a direction that was right for me, Esther urged me to learn about a woman's perspective on Hasidism from a member of the Habad community, a solidly learned woman called Nechoma Greisman.

The name *Habad* is an acronym for the Hebrew terms for "wisdom, understanding, knowledge," types of knowing that lead to a perception of God. The Habad movement was established in the 1700s by Rabbi Shneur Zalman of Lyady (also called the Alter Rebbe), author of the *Tanya*, a guide to the contemplation of Godliness that serves as the keystone of Habad philosophy. In a word, contemporary Habad Hasidim favor an intellectual Hasidism steeped in Torah study, and they work relentlessly, often in far-flung communities, to bring nonpracticing Jews back into the fold. Even in Hamilton, New York, a Habad rabbi, dispatched with his family to bring the light to Syracuse, once drove to the Colgate campus in a sukkah-mobile, a portable hut on a truck, and parked on the quad in front of the gold-domed university chapel. He attracted curious stares and not much business.

Habad Hasidim teach that all Jews can potentially be brought back into Judaism. Despite the intensity of their alienation, no Jews should ever be considered lost, for who can know what *gilgul* (reincarnation) their souls are in or what atonement they are making for their pasts? For the Habad follower, every Jewish soul is as pure as the soul of the highest *tzaddik* (righteous person). Who can say what will arouse an alienated soul? It need not be a tragedy, but a flash of insight that changes all of one's perceptions. A Habad follower believes that a most effective way to bring someone close to accepting God and the commandments is through *hasidus* (Hasidic teachings): "that part of Yiddishkeit that deals with philosophical issues. There is," as Nechoma Greisman would later explain, "no reason to feel defensive when there is *hasidus* to explain *emunah* (faith or belief)."

A good many Habad Hasidim in Israel live just south of Tel Aviv, in the village called Kefar Habad, founded by the Lubavicher rebbe

Rabbi Joseph Isaac Schneersohn. Each Monday morning, Nechoma Greisman, pregnant with her eighth child, took a long taxi ride from her home in Kefar Habad to reach the Israel Center at 10 Strauss Street in Jerusalem. She needed to be there by 9:45 so she could teach her class in English, advertised on flyers as "Hasidic Insights into Torah: A Class for WOMEN of all ages, dealing with themes from PARASHAT HASHAVUA and special CALENDAR DATES, made relavant to our times, sponsored by Becky Farber of Miami Beach, Florida." The Israel Center, sponsored by the Union of Orthodox Jewish Congregations of America and the National Conference of Synagogue Youth, was located in pleasant enough second-story quarters with lounges, a lecture hall, and library, just two blocks north of the center of town. It offered a long roster of classes calculated to appeal to every taste and background, from the American Orthodox college student studying in Israel to travelers stopping by to retired people. In one week, one could choose from thirty-five offerings, including: "What the Torah Says About . . . ," "The Cheeseburger and the Jew: Textual Study of 'Milk and Meat,' " "The Writings of Rav Kook (for Serious Students)," "Timely Torah Topics," and "Let's Learn a Page! Gemara Applied to Modern Life."

This morning Nechoma Greisman was late. Her taxi had been stuck in heavy morning traffic at the entrance to Jerusalem. I joined the crowd of slightly disheveled-looking women waiting for her. One wore a nurse's white skirt and nurse's shoes, but judging from the white leather cowboy hat she had tied onto her head with a white scarf, I felt sure she was no nurse. The chiffon scarf on the head of the friend sitting next to her seemed to have floated, via a big wind, from someone else's head onto her own. She was guzzling down a bottle of cough syrup and going over the notice for this class that she and the nonnurse had clipped from the *Jerusalem Post*. One young mother was using a yellow marker to highlight passages in *Raising Children to Care*, a guide written by an observant woman that wedded popular child psychology to Torah values. Grandmothers sat together knitting elaborate popcorn-patterned dresses and cable-stitched sweaters.

When Nechoma finally appeared, breathing energy into the hall, the women asked her and two women wearing matching Cher wigs who filed in behind her, "How's everything?"

"Barukh hashem," said Nechoma, thudding hard on the *r* sound. She was lively, confident and pretty in her blue maternity jumper and pert wig. Today's class was in basic understanding of *hasidus,* but before proceeding she asked the newcomers to the class to introduce themselves. If I heard correctly, the women carrying the ad said they were a Miss Peeper and Miss Harmony and they were passing through Jerusalem. I introduced myself as Esther's friend and won an approving nod. Nechoma warmly told us newcomers that if she used unfamiliar terms or if we got lost, we should stop her or see her at the end of class.

Almost immediately, Miss Peeper stopped Nechoma as she was describing, with both love and clarity, the three categories of laws that appear in Torah. First, *mishpatim:* totally understandable laws, civil laws, laws even atheists would follow—not killing, or stealing, or bearing false witness. Next, *hukim:* all those commandments we observe—like keeping kosher—not because they make ethical sense or have scientific validity, but because they are commanded by God and constitute the Jewish way. Finally, *edot:* groups of commandments, such as eating matzos and not eating bread on Passover, which serve to commemorate events in Jewish history.

"Who wrote the laws of the Torah?" Miss Peeper wanted to know, her challenge well rehearsed. A tremor passed through the room. This woman was a gentile, the class was sure. Had she come here to make trouble? The two women in Cher wigs rolled their eyeballs. The grandmothers clicked their tongues. One didn't ask such a question. You knew the answer in your heart. But what, everyone seemed to wonder, about Nechoma? What would she say? Were this a soap opera, the music would heighten, and we would need a commercial to relieve the tension.

Nechoma, unflustered, reminding me of a high school teacher pressed unsuccessfully to reveal some facts of life, calmly and patiently explained that the laws were from God and that Moses wrote them down. Before Miss Peeper could pursue this further, Nechoma set the ground rules. The purpose of the class was to study a Hasidic discourse by the Rebbe on the Torah. "Let's not get too far afield!"

Often the implications of Nechoma's points of view—if I understood them as she intended them to be understood—seemed too narrow to me. She explained that it was important to observe all commandments completely and accurately. This was particularly important with laws classified as *mishpatim,* for since we believed we could grasp their rationale, we would be tempted to modify them to to fit our private ethical concerns or the mores of our generation. Thus, the commandment "Thou shall not murder" means no killing at all, with battle and self-defense being the only exceptions. No aborting a deformed fetus. No pulling the plug on the person in pain who begs to be allowed to die. Nechoma explained:

> I believe according to the Torah, the body of the person is not his property. It is a sacred creation of God; therefore, the person does not have a "right" to do with his own body as he chooses nor does a woman have the "right" to abort her fetus. Since a belief in Torah and God incorporates the premise that everything in this world fulfills a distinct purpose and nothing is created in vain, a Torah Jew humbly admits that "despite what may seem to be merciful in my eyes, if Torah forbids the doing away of life, then to do so is not truly and ultimately merciful."

Our perception of kindness is necessarily based on a finite human understanding of the present. We have no conscious knowledge of previous reincarnations and afterlife—the world to come—and what is happening this very moment in the spiritual realms. All these are integral pieces to the puzzle called life, and part of every Jew's faith. For example, there is much support in Torah for the understanding that pain suffered in this life—whether physical or emotional—is an atonement for transgressions in this or a previous life. It is for the person's good to suffer this pain and thus "pay up the bill" rather than have to be spared the pain and suffer in the world to come.

I couldn't accept Nechoma's approach to abortion and mercy killing. We Jews are trained to spend so much energy trying to be ethically correct—how could there not be any situations in which euthanasia was the ethical and compassionate response? I found Nechoma's approach too unbending, too disrespectful of each human's potential to make wise and ethical choices. I thought of Torah as a guide, not a shackle. For her, the great potential of a human being was to acknowledge the absolute nature of the yoke of God's law. It would have been one thing if Nechoma's faith had prohibited just those of her sect from aborting their deformed fetuses. But the antiabortionists of the religious parties, believing they have morality on their side, seek to make the restriction universal. What if abortion were denied to all Israeli women?

Yet there was a flip side. I respected the unusually loving stance toward imperfect children held by Nechoma's community. A woman in the lecture hall asked if it was true that some Hasidic rabbis stood in the presence of children with Down's syndrome. Nechoma said the rabbis consider such children docile, sweet, and incapable of being bad, for they possess no evil inclinations. They were the reincarnation of lofty souls. A mentally handicapped young person in a Habad community was not considered a tragic aberration but, rather, one intentionally created that way by God. Such a young man could be an integral part of the life of his synagogue and have a role that suited him: arranging chairs, tidying up prayer books, setting out the plates of fish at a bar mitzvah.

Not only did Nechoma dismiss the possibility of abortion and euthanasia, she also appeared to dismiss the validity of the State of Israel until the Messiah showed up. According to Nechoma, certain strictly observant Jews did not celebrate Israel Independence Day because the foundations upon which the state was established were not Torah foundations and its rulers were not enlightened by Yiddishkeit. How could she say that? I wanted to shake her, to tell all those who shared her attitude: If you don't accept the legitimacy of Israel, then don't live there. Don't accept government stipends for children and the military protection of all the secular sons while your sons sit studying in yeshivot, exempt from military service, as if their share in the war effort, speeding up the coming of the Messiah through the merit of their prayers and Torah study, were in any way equivalent.

But here again, if I could put politics aside (and in Israel, many relationships were possible only when friends averted their eyes from each other's politics), aspects of Nechoma's understanding of the relationship of Jews to the land of Israel were instructive to me. While she accepted that her own present mission, as defined by her rebbe, was to teach Jews in Israel, she upheld the value of life in the Diaspora for Jews. As she explained:

Galus [exile] is important because God wanted *elokus* [godliness] to be revealed in every part of the world. Every point of the world is elevated with spirituality when a Jew lives like a Jew, when a Jew in Australia builds a sukkah and makes an effort to eat kosher food even when it was hard to get. But *galus* is not just a place on the map: it is a spiritual distance from God.

Nechoma illustrated:

Take the example of a perfect teacher and a perfect student, an analogy for God's relationship to the Jews. Say the teacher wanted to teach the student something deep and difficult, something that would be important for the student to know. The art of teaching is to bring knowledge down to the level of the student so he can absorb it. The teacher asks himself: What words will I use so my student will understand? He has to stop and think and go off into his own world to come up with a solution. The student is bewildered. He can't know what's going on in the teacher's mind, and, what's more, the teacher's temporary retreat makes him feel abandoned. The student wonders if he's being ignored because of something he's done intentionally. He feels lost, and this is at the very moment when his teacher is thinking so hard about what to give the student, he loves him so very much.

"This," Nechoma concluded, "is *galus*. The length and severity of *galus* is only indicative of what will come. It is like a shadow. The taller the object—the redemption—the longer the shadow—exile."

I thought I might be able to dismiss those of Nechoma's views that I disagreed with and retain those aspects of her teaching I found valuable. I might eventually be able to discuss my differences with her. This distinction wasn't possible for me when I first came to Jerusalem to learn. Then, in my rigidity, a teacher was either all right or all wrong. I had since developed a capacity for more flexibility. Nechoma opened something up in me. She lived a poetic metaphor; for her, spirituality clothed itself in physicality. Nechoma's knowledge of Torah and *hasidus* had transformed who she was. She was not just a teacher of Torah, but through her life, she was Torah. Christian theologian Paul van Buren describes such a person as "a Torah-saturated person who . . . is a living response to Torah."*
Nechoma's talk of *olam haba* (the world to come) aroused within me awe for the depth of her conviction, conviction rooted in a lifetime of complex spiritual training, not superstition. For her, the world to

*A Theology of the Jewish Christian Reality, Part One (San Francisco: Harper & Row, 1987), p. 138.

come was not a reward for good behavior but a state of ultimate pureness, the most intense intimacy with God. Her voice conveyed such certainty as she spoke of her world to come, it was as if she had been there for summer vacation and had the photographs to prove it. This kind of certainty used to cause me anxiety; now I viewed it as strength. If Nechoma led a moral life, if she possessed happiness, clarity, and the will to act in an ethical way, I believed it was because such goods came to her through knowing and living Torah. This is how her education was given to her, she said. She was obliged to live as a Jew who illuminated the world around her with godliness. Nechoma's Jewish life was systematically thought out—that's what made it so palatable to me. It felt good to be in Nechoma's presence, reassuring. And it motivated me to quit sitting on the fence.

For the Habad Hasidim, ritual that organizes one's personal and home life and bestows aesthetic grace represents the lowest level, the nursery school, of spiritual life. Study must lead to practice, observing more, sanctifying even more scrupulously, and in this way coming closer to knowing God. I wasn't yet prepared to abandon my theory that I might be able to go from Torah study to knowing God, skipping over all the tedious practice of ritual. But there Nechoma was—she truly illuminated the world with godliness. I was convinced of it. She had power, she empowered, and the medium of her power was practice. The Jewishness she held was so full with knowing and belief. Even if only a trickle filtered down to the next generation, it would be sufficient sustenance.

Then, in the middle of one of Nechoma's classes—just as I was poised to hear Nechoma tell us how we could make what we were learning in class today relevant to our own lives, just as I felt myself on the verge of a discovery that might make me change my entire orientation—something happened that kept me from ever returning. This was the story I told Raphael at Pardes.

There was a woman in the class, say, in her sixties, who had a strange air about her. During the entire lecture, she kept reaching into a red plastic child's lunch box for food. She popped open a can of Coke, ripped the wrapper off a chocolate bar. I knew Israelis were compulsive, constant eaters—mothers at playgrounds shovel spoons of mashed bananas into their toddlers' mouths as they zip down slides, and moviegoers need an intermission after an hour to purchase a snack and drink in the lobby.

But this woman was chomping away in a Torah class.

She whispered across the room to me several times. Something about keys? coat? I'd dropped my keys? She was freezing and she wanted to borrow my coat.

"Here," I whispered, holding out my coat, hoping she'd stop annoying me.

"Cover *your* knees with your coat," she hissed.

"Oh," I recoiled. What was the matter with my knees? I inspected myself. I had a run in my stockings, but who didn't? I was wearing a proper long-sleeved dress, my legs were modestly crossed. Yes, here was the problem: my dress had pulled up a little on my right knee. Reluctantly, I laid my coat across my lap. Either I did that to keep the woman from disturbing me again, or I stomped out of the room and missed the rest of Nechoma's lecture. "Is that better?" I whispered. I'm sure I was glaring. Had my knees, which no one ever noticed, suddenly become so alluring as to break her concentration? Were they more of a distraction to her than her own vigorous chomping was to me? If she wanted to teach me about modesty, could she not at least wait until class was over? I couldn't retrace my steps back into Nechoma's words. I wished I had walked out, but that would have been rude to Nechoma. I stewed in humiliation. Here, just at the moment I was straining to achieve glimmers of some spiritual perception, this lady was saying I was my body, my female seductive body, I was breasts and legs and knees.

The knee lady made me lose more than several moments of Nechoma's lecture. She made me lose my equilibrium. What was happening to me? Was my thin skin tripping me up again, my inability to receive reproach graciously and benefit from it? I recalled an editorial in the *Jerusalem Post* written by Rabbi Riskin, co-dean of

Michlelet Bruria, which explained why my encounter with the knee lady disturbed me. Rabbi Riskin wrote:

> Maimonides in his Mishneh Torah (laws of Proper Ideas 6) teaches that chastising a fellow Jew is a special art. He interprets Lev. 19:17 ("Reprove your fellow, so you will have no share in his guilt") to mean that you must be aware lest you incur guilt by publicly embarrassing the person you are reproving or by causing him to move even further away from his present religious position.

Therefore Rabbi Riskin concluded:

> God's covenant must be accepted voluntarily and not be imposed by any form of coercion. . . . The Torah was meant to be accepted as a matter of free will.

Nechoma, the teacher, hadn't been disturbed by the flesh of my knee. If she had been, I'm sure she would have found some sensitive way to talk to me about it. This knee lady was ill-mannered—why couldn't I simply dismiss her rudeness?

After class, this knee lady came over to me as if she were my long lost cousin. "I hope you didn't mind my asking you to cover your knees."

I considered saying: Not nearly as much as I minded your barnlike eating. I considered saying: If you are a Habad woman, is this what you call reaching out to a lost soul? I tried to control myself. It struck me why my reaction to the knee lady was out of all proportion. I believed the ill-mannered knee lady said straight out what all the other women were thinking: I didn't belong here, who I was and what I believed in had no value in this place. It was all or nothing. If you wanted Nechoma's knowledge of God, you banned abortion, you spat at the idea of the State of Israel, you worried about your neighbor's knees. The knee lady robbed me of the illusion that I could slip into this Habad world, take what I needed, and slip out.

It was as though she had said: Girl, you get no Santa, no tooth fairy, and no chance at heady sanctity unless you join the clan, play by our rules, and pay the dues we exact.

If I couldn't accept the rules of the Habad women, I had no business studying with them here.

At that moment, my fantasies evaporated. Until my encounter with the knee lady, I had figured that if I could swallow enough, if I could diminish my needs enough and sufficiently disguise my identity, I could have access to learning Torah in the context of a spiritual life within a religious community. But just because I was skilled at accommodation didn't mean the falsehood of it all hadn't been gnawing at me. What was I searching for in Jerusalem? I no longer knew. If learning Torah and decoding Talmud was what I wanted, I should have marched right back to the Jewish Theological Seminary on Broadway and 122nd Street in Manhattan, wearing whatever it was I pleased, and gotten down to work among Conservative Jews who accepted me with my naked knees. If it was a woman's perspective on text I wanted, I could have studied at the Seminary with Professor Judith Hauptman or one of several women now on the faculty. Just because all my relatives, with the exception of my parents, disdained non-Orthodoxy didn't mean I had to be self-loathing. I could have had Jewish scholarship up to my ears.

Who needed Esther's learned women, who needed to learn Torah within the context of such blind faithfulness and with such disdain for secularism? If, according to a saying, Jerusalem held nine parts of the world's ten portions of beauty and nine parts of the world's ten portions of suffering, then Jerusalem also held nine parts of the world's ten portions of craziness. Yearning for holiness made people crazy. Or it was the crazies who yearned for holiness.

The knee lady was checking me over, almost sniffing me.

"Why did you tell me to cover my knees?" I asked, almost wanting to see how far this would go, wanting to be aggravated. "My knees seemed to upset you a great deal."

"Once when I was visiting the house of Rabbi Moshe Feinstein, of blessed memory, the Rebbetzin Feinstein came up to me and said, 'You know, your knees are showing. Pull down your dress.' So I did. I was glad she told me. It meant she took an interest in me."

She inspected me as though I were a roach in a sugar bowl. Could it be that I really didn't know what she was getting at? It struck her she may have mistaken a *goy* for one of the tribe. Perhaps I, too, was a friend of Miss Peeper? She grilled me. Where did I come from? What kind of people did I come from? What kind of schools did I go to? Were they Jewish schools? Did I belong to a congregation? She stepped even closer to me. I stared at the unmoving hairline of her frosted wig and at the deep perspiration stains the size of cantaloupe slices in the armpits of her sweater. She said if I really wanted to learn why my knees had to be covered, I would do best to go to the bookstore down the street and buy myself several books in English on Jewish women and modesty. "But wait. I want to show you something. Follow me to the library."

Down the hall in the small library a Jewish man rocking in his chair hummed Talmud and an Arab man peddling sprigs of mint hawked, *"Nana! Nana!"* The knee lady took down the Book of Psalms. Although it was Psalm 45 she wanted me to see, the book had opened by chance to Psalm 22, so she insisted we engage in bibliomancy, the practice of using the Bible for the purpose of divining, and search the psalm for the private meaning it would yield.

She pointed to a verse of this psalm attributed to King David: "But I am a worm, less than human; scorned by men, despised by people." She struck her heart with her palm. The verse was a natural for my situation! "If King David is a worm," she explained, "then what are we? A worm doesn't even have feet to show off . . ."

"Let alone knees?" I completed.

The knee lady, convinced she had scored this preliminary point with me, then flipped to the passage she was looking for, Psalm 45:14: *"Kol kevudah bat melekh penimah."* The new Jewish Publication Society translation of Psalms says that the meaning of this difficult verse is uncertain (it now translates, "The royal princess . . . is led inside to the king"), but older translations read, "All glorious is the king's daughter within the palace." The knee lady, unfazed by the oblique text, translated: "All the glory of the king's daughter lies within her." I didn't grasp what the verse so clearly revealed to her. "This is why the rabbis tell us," she said, "that all Jewish women must be modest and humble and belong within the spheres of their homes."

I was reminded of a refrain in Muriel Spark's novel *The Mandelbaum Gate:* "People who quoted the Scriptures in criticism of others were terrible bores and usually they misapplied the text. One could prove anything against anyone from the Bible."*

"Thank you," I said, masking no frigidity. "What is your name?"

"Name?" She waved my question away.

What did it mean that she refused to tell me her name but could ask me all about myself and tell me what to do with my knees? That she saw herself as an angel, too modest to take credit for saving my soul? That if I knew her name, as the queen eventually knew Rumpelstiltskin's, she would crash through the ground? I said, "My name is Vanessa. I have to go now to get my daughters at school."

She was shocked. "You have children?"

"Yes."

"Then does that mean you're married?"

"Yes, I'm married."

This seemed distressing news. She was more shocked than relieved to hear my children were conceived in wedlock.

"Then next time you come to hear Nechoma—and you must come back, you know—she can be like a rebbe for you—you mustn't go from teacher to teacher—you have to pick the one who's right and stay. What a rebbe says that is right for someone else isn't necessarily right for you. Next time I'll nudge you to cover your head."

Next time, never. I didn't dare expose myself to the knee lady

---

The Mandelbaum Gate (New York: Alfred A. Knopf, 1965), p. 19.

again. And a pity, because something about Nechoma was so right for me. If the knee lady had ever brought anyone back to Jewish observance, it was surely a most desperate person who thrilled in public chastisement, a happy alumna of pillory boxes and scarlet letters.

I walked down the street to the bookstore, curious to see what books the knee lady had in mind for me. I hoped what I found would annoy me. A woman was asking the salesman if he had anything for her to give a twelve-year-old girl as a present on her bat mitzvah. He asked what kind of school she went to. "Religious," she said. He look all around the shop, which specialized in religious books in both English and Hebrew. Of the hundreds of books, so many suitable as beginnings for anyone's private collection of sacred texts, a single book seemed right to him, one about a woman's role in Judaism. The lady inspected it. It had a feminine dust jacket, pink and fuchsia. "That's all you have? What if she already has that book? I'll get her a bracelet."

The salesman asked if he could help me, pointing to the shelf of English books for women on family, modesty, and marriage. I ran out, dodging cars to get to the other side of the street, where I took refuge in a kiosk that sold trinkets. I bought Dede a Mickey Mouse sun visor for a few shekels, thinking touching it might help me switch back into my own world more quickly.

I meant to take the bus home, but every bus stop smelled of stale, deep-frying oil coming out of the falafel and shwarma stands, so I kept going. I started to run, chased by my nausea. The knee lady left me shell-shocked, as if in the aftermath of an assault. When I reached the park near Herzog Street, I stopped to pull off sprigs from a rosemary plant. I crushed the leaves between my nails and breathed in the strong fragrance like smelling salts until I reached my own backyard.

When Raphael heard me out at Pardes, he urged me to exercise some cross-cultural compassion. I should see the knee lady simply for what she was—one boorish, intrusive person. I didn't have to exclude myself from the Habad lecture just because one woman had tried to bully me into observance.

I listened to what he was saying, but I still couldn't go back to the Habad lectures. Neither had Peter been able to coax me back. "Why didn't you tell the knee lady to mind her own business?" Peter asked, wondering why I had come home from Nechoma's lecture with such a large handful of crushed rosemary.

I didn't belong to that circle of learners, I told him. The knee lady was tolerated on that turf, not me.

My argument sounded weak to him. Peter suggested that if I really wanted to hear Nechoma out and if I was ready to accept what she taught—that the consequence of Torah study would have to be a Torah life—then I should have suffered the foolish knee lady more gladly. He thought I blew the knee lady episode out of proportion just as I had considered dropping out of Pardes when I had to fill out an application. The knee lady gave me an excuse not to return to Nechoma's classes and act upon what she taught. "You're afraid it would trivialize you to take greater pains in your ritual observance."

Maybe I was afraid it would. Maybe I thought getting absorbed in ritual would take me away from the work I needed to do, becoming more learned in Torah just for the sake of knowing it. But what was the point of knowing Torah if not for the purpose of living Torah? I felt confused, unsure of what motivated my learning or my observance. I wanted to escape to movies at the Cinematheque, to show Juliana the exhibit at the Israel Museum of products designed by graduates of the Bezalel art school. The holy world was getting on my nerves. Was it so impossible to learn Torah and have the privacy of my life respected? I thought I needed a vacation in a land of abundant profaneness. The best I could come up with was spending a day walking along Tel Aviv's Dizengoff Street and splurging on a pile of Penguin paperbacks. The fiction filled me up but didn't tell me how to be or what to believe. Unlike the Torah world, it was unintrusive.

Something peculiar was happening. The more Torah learning I acquired, the more intense were my temptations to abandon the whole project, to loosen my commitment, to dump it all back into Esther's lap. I wondered why I had ever let her lure me into a way of life incompatible with my nature.

Nine

The first time I saw the Jewish laws concerning the menstruant in print, I was watching the "Mickey Mouse Club" on TV by myself in my grandparents' living room and eating fish sticks and mashed potatoes on a folding tray. I had never seen the word *menstruation* in print. My uncles had been cleaning out the attic and had brought down books from their yeshiva days that seemed worth saving. An English translation of the Mishnah survived their triage, and, out of curiosity, I inspected it during a cartoon. The more I read, the more I hoped no one would catch me reading this stuff. I was sure I had discovered my first dirty book. It fascinated me in the same wonder-ful-horrible way the photographs of rare rashes and disfiguring diseases in medical journals did, a second body of literature I consulted surreptitiously. Why had this religion of ours once been so fixated on secret parts of women? I was sure the menstrual practices, like animal sacrifice, had long been abandoned. Someone was coming downstairs. I hid the Mishnah under the *National Geographic*s also rescued from the dump and feigned absorption in Mickey.

Pardes announced a women-only field trip to a mikvah, a ritual bath that women immersed themselves in the week after their menstruation ended. I penned my name onto the sign-up list in broad strokes. I joined the trip, in part, because the mikvah evoked the lurid curiosity of my childhood. But there was another reason. These days I alternated between hostility and ambivalence toward my Torah learning, which I kept up, but with limited appetite. I joined the mikvah trip to ignite my fury. Could anyone convince us bright Jewish women that we should adopt the menstrual laws of our own free will, these laws that seemed so very man-made, laws that defined women by their corporeality?

We gathered in front of Pardes. Fourteen Pardes women usually clothed in sweatshirts and jeans had transformed themselves, with knee-covering skirts, necklaces and earrings, into a group of young ladies who appeared to be about to stroll down to a 1950s fraternity party. Anxiety hung over the group, as though their action verged on treachery. Their voices were uncharacteristically twittery, and they fidgeted like adolescents, unsure of where to position their hands and feet as they stood.

These were women who claimed they had been born into a world in which the principles of feminism were accepted or, at least, acknowledged. I asked Linda Gradstein, the journalist who studied Talmud, what she meant when she said she came from a feminist background. She explained:

My parents treated me much more like a son than a daughter. I was the oldest. My parents had lost two children before they had me so I was the center of attention. I had sports lessons, which I hated, karate lessons from the time I was five. I have a younger sister, much cuter and more feminine than I am. I was the intellectual of the family. I could be whatever I wanted to. There was no question of "women's" professions: Go as far as you can, I was told. Push yourself intellectually, physically, whatever way you can. I thought: I'm as intelligent and capable as any man; it doesn't make a difference that I'm a woman. Still, I used to think that if I had been born a man, it would have made my life a lot easier. When I was twenty, I knew that I wasn't going to get married and have children. To have the kind of career I wanted, I would have to make sacrifices in my personal life.

For many Pardes women, the conviction that they, as women, had every right to learn and master the sacred texts was what had led them there in the first place. However, upon immersing themselves in the texts, these Pardes students, in particular those who were not already observant, felt compelled to acknowledge that these texts supposed Jews would live the law and the lore not only with their minds, but with their lives. And if they took the laws respectfully— meaning they accepted that the law is the law—then they'd find it inconsistent to say they'd observe the laws they liked and ignore the ones that didn't appeal, or were invasive of their privacy or not the stuff of liberated women. Precisely a problem I had been wrestling with. For some Pardes women, encounters with observant women in Jerusalem (often the wives of Pardes instructors) significantly altered their views of women's roles. Linda Gradstein recalled meeting an observant, well-educated, articulate mother of four children and asking her, "How can you stay home taking care of kids? Aren't you absolutely bouncing off the walls?" The mother answered, "I have four souls entrusted to my care, and I don't want to mess it up." For many of the women Linda now admired, going to mikvah—seen as a key factor in a harmonious family life—was de rigueur.

For me, the mikvah is a most troubling ritual, representing the extent to which obedient Jewish women would go and do what they were told. If rituals to sanctify menstruation were coined by women, I doubted menstruation would be called an "impure" state.

In my own extended family, all serious public religious celebration was connected to men. The birth of a male baby meant relatives from all over the eastern seaboard would travel to celebrate a circumcision, and a month later, they'd be back on the road again for the ceremony that marked the redemption of a firstborn son. There would be prayers, singing, a pillow strewn with jewels to carry the newborn, plates of smoked fish, challah, iced petits fours, cartons of cream soda and seltzer. The women would be in the kitchen, replenishing the food trays. By contrast, the birth of a female baby meant people could stay home and send musical lambs and Carter's pink stretchsuits by UPS. (We held naming ceremonies for our daughters, to which our parents came.) A female baby undermined the virility of her father. "Ha ha!" the relatives would say, "Cousin Izzy has *three* girls." A girl baby was a practical joke; she was a financial investment that yielded no interest; she was a blot on her father's manhood. When we gave birth to our second daughter, along with the lambs and stretchsuits, relatives sent my husband loose-fitting underwear, thinking it might help create a boy next time.

Only once in the life of my family do I recall being part of a powerful woman-centered public ritual. It was apparently a folk ritual, of what origin I didn't know. For all I knew, it might have been coined by the Long Island division of the daughters of Israel. This was my sister Susan's wedding, a day of profound delight. After the ceremony and a hefty amount of eating, the ladies of our neighborhood rushed to weave my mother a crown of freesias harvested from the centerpieces, and set a chair out for her in the center of the hall where we celebrated.

"What's going on?" Susan and I wanted to know. Nothing like this had happened at my wedding.

"Your mother has married off her last child. Thank God she's done!" From their expressions of empathetic relief, one would think a pogrom or epidemic of meningitis had just skipped over our town.

Was having an unmarried daughter left at home so shameful that one danced when the burden was lifted? How satisfying was it to be rid of us? Mesdames Bernstein, Gottlieb, Schildkraut, and Radlauer escorted our mother to her chair as if she were royalty. Shimmering in purple chiffon, she celebrated her moment in the sun. Though our mother would never abandon the responsibility of worrying about her daughters, she must have been convinced that having one more skinny, level-headed son-in-law would at least help ease her worries. Not wanting to be party poopers, we daughters did what the ladies expected of us. We danced around our mother, kicked off our shoes, stepped slowly, and then whirled, a flurry of pink and white chiffon.

And in that whirl, we spun out the history of our interconnectedness: all those languid afternoons lying all together in my mother's bed while considering the helpful hints in women's magazines, peeling the skins off mushrooms, and watching "Lost in Space"; all those evenings washing and drying dirty dishes, debating if bells indeed rang when true love came along. That chance to dance together was a prayer, each step articulating another memory, binding us in trust and memory, solidifying the knot of our kinship even though we were now established in three separate households. And it heralded a shift. Before, it had been our mother who circled our lives in embracing protectiveness; soon it would be we daughters who encircled her. By this public ritual, by performing the "Dance of Bobbie's Daughters," all this was made intensely clear to us at that moment and could linger with us forever.

This experience alerted me to be on the lookout for women's rituals I could willingly embrace, although I had my doubts about finding any. I knew that Jewish women in places more hip than Hamilton, New York, were creating new rituals to acknowledge and communally celebrate female life-cycle occasions—the onset of menstruation, pregnancy, birth, weaning, and menopause. I wondered whether I would be more attracted to scrupulous observance if I had available to me rituals that clearly addressed the events and cycles of my life. I felt uneasy about most of these and other women-made rituals I was hearing about: smearing red clay on the face of a young girl to mark the onset of her menses, eleven women coloring in a mandala for a pregnant woman to use as a focal point while having natural childbirth. Some of the new ceremonies appeared to me primitive, hippielike, or new age gestures not rooted in tradition, but grafted on like paper menorahs on Christmas trees. Something about the rituals suggested Jewish women dancing naked in the moonlight. If these rituals were relevant to our times, then our times were shallow, we were childish and self-centered, and our Judaism was another "touchy feely" sign of the times. Did substituting *Elah* for *El,* Goddess for God, make a difference? While the male term "God, King of the Universe" had an irritating ring, did switching to a Goddess Queen emancipate the cosmos from feudalism? To bless God the King at least had the advantage of sounding familiar. It was, after all, the incantation spoken in every synagogue around the world. A Jew who went along with the crowd, who avoided the impulse to transform, was a Jew who could find a common language with Jews everywhere. I was hesitant to relinquish such a generous passport.

How readily I dismissed the handiwork spun from the female religious imagination. How quick I was to make fun. If I had eagerly honored the artistic and literary accomplishments of women and drew strength from them, what blocked me from acknowledging Jewish women as religious authorities? Perhaps this was the catch. I didn't accept that women disenfranchised from traditional Judaism could create rituals that had the aura of authenticity I demanded. The new rituals seemed self-conscious, the creations of women who were adept at feminism but amateurs when it came to Jewish learning. If Aviva Zornberg had been cooking up new rituals sensitive to women's lives, I would have joined her cult. Her knowledge would have imbued the rituals with authoritative sanction. But the learned women I had met so far were glued tightly and happily to tradition; inventiveness seemed unnecessary to them. If a pro like Aviva didn't need to invent woman-friendly rituals, why should I? I wondered whether having the depths of the sacred texts at her disposal was sufficient resource for her spiritual life.

So I decided: No new rituals until my learning had increased.

The Pardes women, especially those who had newly embraced observance, wanted to be able to see the mikvah as a beautiful ritual, an opportunity for sanctification, a privilege and not a punishment for women. Particularly because men seemed to have the bulk of ceremonial acts for sanctification—reading Torah, praying in public, sitting in the yeshivot and in the rabbinical courts, wearing fringed garments—it seemed important for these women to find a female ceremony that they could enthusiastically embrace, a ceremony that could be a conduit to divine encounter. For them, the mikvah was rich in possibilities, and they went with high hopes. The mikvah was connected to private biological rhythms, lunar cycles, marriage, birth, the return to sexuality after birth, the wish to abstain periodically from sexuality and retreat into one's private space, the wish to know one's husband again with freshness, the wish to perceive one's body as a vessel for holiness. The mikvah was old, authentic, sanctioned, and hallowed by tradition. It took a mundane, recurring bodily function and turned it into a regular opportunity for sanctification.

I just couldn't keep an open mind. The mikvah saw us as prisoners of our bodily functions; it defined us by the activity of our wombs.

I tried to convey this to Peter before I went off to the mikvah: "Would a man be satisfied if one of his central Jewish rituals involved sticking a white cloth into his body for seven days to see if he was still bleeding?" He saw my point.

"Your big rituals are learning Torah and talking to God," I said.

"Wait," he said, "what about circumcision?"

"You were eight days old. You had no awareness, except for the pain, which made you cry. It doesn't count."

I had dipped in a mikvah once on an earlier trip to Jerusalem, almost as a lark. I had been writing a story about a mikvah attendant, and

a woman I had met—through Esther, of course—convinced me that
I needed to go myself, at the very least, to get authentic details for
my story. I knew she had ulterior motives. She thought that once I
went, I would like it and start to go regularly. I did go, to see for
myself where it was that generations of Jewish women had gone. But
I was uneasy about participating in a ritual that left one so unbearably vulnerable—naked in public, even if only in the presence of the
mikvah attendant. The nakedness aside, the mikvah did not turn out
to be so awful. Dipping in water evoked a lightness and purity I had
never before experienced. I finished the story and never returned to
a mikvah. Its negative connotations still outweighed my positive
experience. At that time and still, I couldn't see taking any ritual
upon myself linked to menstruation and the control of sexuality.

I asked my poet friend who studied with Aviva how she brought
herself to go to the mikvah.

"The mikvah is one of those places I take pleasure in and have
conflict with because it suggests things about the relationship between a man and wife and about the female that I'm not sure are
true—for me."

"But you do it?"

I do it. It's been nineteen years we've been married. I do it. I
found a place in Bakka that is really easy. The women there
bless me. "Kosher!" they say, and suddenly I'm kosher. That's
the unbelievable statement. Something spiritual is present there.
Aviva always makes the careful distinction between impure and
unclean and something spiritual and something physical. The
woman isn't necessarily unclean—but there's something impure going on, and it just has to be cleaned up. I'm compelled
by the mikvah, and yet I always feel I'm the one who doesn't
belong there. The women bless me doubly, "Kosher! Kosher!"
and go on and on with their blessings. They're lovely women.
They perceive me, I guess, the way I look. They don't see "in,"

they don't see the questions I have. I go in there wearing one of my floppy hats. I usually take my shower or bath at home. I get all ready, cut my nails, and I go in there with sopping wet hair. Because I like to go in quick-quick. A lot of women go to the mikvah to relax. They spend a luxurious evening taking a bath at the mikvah. I go in and out. So they perceive me not only as one of them, and therefore as doing the right thing, but also as tremendously efficient. They don't know I'm doing it quickly to get through. There's a certain repulsion to the place that I feel. Maybe that stems from feeling I don't belong there—one repels what one isn't connected to. Why do I picture myself the outcast when I'm doing the thing that brings me more "in" than many people?

I asked the poet if she could make the connection between performing a ritual act and serving God; that is, did ritual acts such as the mikvah create an opportunity for God to make an inroad into her life?

Can something I do, wrong or right, affect more than the little world in which I live? Something says yes. Something says there's a scar as a result of a fall. There is reverberation, an echo. There is the idea that one white spot on the soul can change the blackness, and therefore my sense of God in the world is related to this idea of repentance, of changing oneself. It's an enabling force. Ritual acts connect me to change, to be conscious and alert, which is what I am in my poetry. The ritual acts say: Open your eyes, see yourself now.

We traveled to the mikvah in a convoy of two cars and a cab to a village in the hills just outside of Jerusalem, right off the highway to Tel Aviv. A young woman, delicate as a flower child, was sitting behind me in the cab. She said she had been studying privately with the wife of a Pardes teacher because she was going to get married soon and needed to master the laws of family purity. The other women were eager to know if she would observe *kissui rosh,* that is, if she would cover her head as a married woman.

The bride-to-be said she had already found herself in the Sabbath and in *kashrut.* She admired women who covered their heads and admired the kinds of families they raised. She hoped she might feel ready to observe *kissui rosh* when she married. It would be a big step, a powerful symbol of her commitment to traditional observance.

A Pardes woman who had been studying Torah for some time filled the bride in on the history of head-covering traditions. She said Orthodox women in America used to cover their hair for prayer and study only. Even the most devout. (This is true of my own grandmother. Now, when the wig-wearing wives and children of her yeshiva-educated grandsons come to visit, my grandmother puts on the beret she has crocheted for such occasions, lest the great-grandchildren become confused by inconsistencies in observance. My grandmother explains her usual bareheadedness, echoing the words of so many Jewish immigrants: "When my mother came to America, her sister who was already here told her, 'In America you don't need to wear a *sheitl* [wig] to be *frum* [religious]': So she took off her *sheitl* and never wore it again.")

The new strictness, the older Pardes student said, reflected a contemporary trend toward fundamentalism. The bride disagreed, miffed that her thoughts about head coverings could be construed as trendy. She said Jewish women who went around bareheaded did so because they were still rejecting the restrictiveness of the European shtetls. Now Jews, both men and women, could be proud to identify publicly as Jews by their head coverings. The older student, continuing to press her sociological analysis, added that by wearing a certain kind of head covering, by tying your scarf this way or that, you conspicuously identified with a specific community. It was like a code word, like a camp T-shirt.

The bride did her best to conclude the matter: "When you cover your head, you honor your husband. Only he knows your loveliness."

At the village we got out of our cars just below the staircase to the mikvah, a building indistinguishable from the other tan cement houses. A house of prayer, a proper cemetery, a mikvah—the necessary ingredients for a place where Jews could live. Peeking out the door of the mikvah was the attendant, in charge of the mikvah and in charge of educating the town's brides-to-be in the laws of family purity. I would describe it as an intimate curriculum. She taught the brides how they were to inspect themselves for evidence of staining and what constituted staining. (The rabbis of the Mishnah and Talmud were expert in the varieties of menstrual blood, apparently delivered by husbands to them for inspection on "test rags." The rabbis specified five kinds of blood as unclean: red like blood of a wound, black as ink sediment, bright crocus color, the color of earthy water mixed with wine. The school of Rabbi Shammai added two other unclean shades: the color of water in which fenugreek had been soaked and the color of juice that comes out of roast flesh. Can it be that rabbis spent Saturday nights tinkering in their kitchens, soaking paprika and saffron in water and asking their wives: Is that the color? Try cinnamon. How about now?)

The attendant signed the forms that attested to the fact that she had instructed the bride in family purity, as required by the rabbi who would perform the wedding ceremony. She looked like an American Indian ballet dancer. No makeup, hair tightly scarved, and wearing one plain gold ring. We Pardes women, modest by American standards, felt overdone and gaudy in her presence. She greeted us, voice soft and clear, her Hebrew poetic.

Our guide, a former Pardes student, now married to a man on the faculty, said we would be overwhelmed by the degree of purity the mikvah attendant had achieved, a level of purity that we might consider outside our range. Not that it was impossible for us to achieve such purity, our guide assured, but given our attachment to values in the secular world, such purity was not exactly what we yearned for.

We filed into the mikvah and sat on benches on either side of the tight corridor that was the waiting room. Because it was Friday morning, and Sabbath would be coming soon, the little table in the corridor was covered with a white tablecloth. On it were three artificial roses in a vase, an embroidered challah cover, and a basket of the beauty aids that were permitted for use in the mikvah on Friday nights. There were notices everywhere. No smoking in the mikvah. A prayer for the mikvah attendants so they would approach their tasks with the appropriate religious intention. A price list: so much for the mikvah, for a shower, a bath, a shampoo. Special introductory instructions to brides-to-be and blessings of welcome. And a note to women who needed to use the mikvah on Friday nights when it was open for just one hour after sunset: they were to do their preparations at home and to prearrange payment.

The attendant leaned against the outside doorway and spoke to us as if sharing precious treasures. She hoped we might one day experience what she felt the first time she went to the mikvah and what she continues to feel. Filled by a light. The mikvah was a beautiful opportunity to achieve closeness to God, whom she called "the Holy One, blessed be He." She achieved this closeness both through her bodily preparations and through the actual immersion in water, the source of life and purity and a metaphor for Torah, which descends from a higher to a lower level. The seven days after a woman's period—the days in which she continues to abstain from intimacy with her husband—were a special time for a woman, she explained. Always we women are rushing about. And so these seven days are not just a time for physical inspection but a time for making a spiritual accounting, a self-analysis of one's soul. It was a time to review and perfect one's relationship with one's children, husband, self, and God. The holiness a women then brought back into her home would fill her husband with the energy to learn more Torah.

The attendant omitted any negative connotations of the mikvah. From her presentation, one wouldn't know that Jewish women in central and eastern Europe once recited this *tkhine,* a women's Yiddish supplicatory prayer, as they put on white underwear for self-inspection after menstruation:

So we women must suffer each time, and have, basely, our periods, with heavy hearts. Thus, I have had my period with a heavy heart and with sadness, and I thank Your Holy Name and Your judgment, and I have received it with great love from my great Friend.*

Nor would one know—or want to know—that in another *tkhine* intended to remind women that they ought not to have intercourse with their husbands for the twenty-four hours *prior* to menstruation, that women believed the reward for such observance would be having "good, pious and clever male children who will be rabbis."†

One Pardes woman confessed she was troubled by the idea of a menstrant being *tameh,* ritually impure. Wasn't the mikvah washing away a woman's putrefaction? The attendant said a dead body is considered *tameh,* and menstrual blood expels a life that was not brought to fruition. She said her own mother put it simply: When a woman has her period, her womb cries for the child it didn't hold. Just as Jews gave ceremony to the passage from death to afterlife, so the mikvah ritualized the death of one cycle and the birth of another.

We filed in to see the mikvah itself, a deep, oversized bathtub one stepped down into, containing a prescribed amount of pure rainwater. Standing along the edge of the mikvah, we watched the attendant as she demonstrated the posture of a woman immersing herself. Contracting her stomach in Martha Graham style, she bent

---

*Chara Weissler, "The Traditional Piety of Ashkenazic Women," in *Jewish Spirituality,* ed. Arthur Green (New York: Crossroad, 1987), p. 261.
†Ibid., p. 259.

her knees and reached out with her arms, "like reaching to take a baby out of a carriage," she said. If we were willing, she would train us in spirituality, developing our potential for a woman's mystical experience. The possibility was there.

The bride-to-be wanted to know if a bride going to the mikvah before her wedding for the first time could dip with friends. The image of the bride and her friends in a holy hot tub made some of us giggle.

But the attendant shook her head. The bride-to-be was onto something. Ashkenazic brides come quietly and shyly to the mikvah, by themselves or with their mothers, but certain Jews of Sephardic origin make a festive bash of their prenuptial mikvah rituals. A Sephardic bride comes to the mikvah accompanied by her mother, mother-in-law, aunts, friends, cousins. The guests wait alongside the mikvah while she dips into the water, and when she comes out, they shower her with blessings and sweets. They bring along liquor, cassette tapes; they dress the bride up, parade her like a queen. While I would hardly would have wanted to encounter my husband's aunts Sadie and Dottie for the first time along the edge of a mikvah, this prenuptial ceremony seemed less derivative than my own ladies-only surprise bridal shower, complete with a paper parasol centerpiece, Jell-O molds, a frilly peignoir, and a keepsake bonnet constructed of bows and wrapping paper.

I drove back to Jerusalem in our guide's car. A Pardes woman who had just been to a mikvah the week before as part of her conversion to Judaism said she wished she had had friends poolside. She also wished the attendant at her mikvah had been as saintly as this one. Her mikvah attendant wielded a comblike weapon and made her comb through both her hair and pubic hair for tangles.

Our guide said this was a matter of luck; there were all types of attendants. She had once been a mikvah attendant herself. Overzealous intervention was not required. All an attendant had to do was check for complete immersion. If she clips cuticles, yanks off scabs, and provides tools for pubic combings, it should be because these services are requested. She must learn to look aside, to consider the human body a vessel for *kedushah,* sanctification.

I asked the convert if she had been bothered by the pubic hair episode. She said it had amused her. I, by contrast, would have run out of the mikvah, screaming that I refused to join any religion that cares a fig about pubic hair! What did tangled pubic hair have to do with a ceremony that marked one's passage from one spiritual state to another?

The Pardes women asked a lot of questions. Mostly they wanted to know how our guide experienced the monthly period of abstinence and physical separation between husband and wife. She said she'd be lying if she denied that the abstinence was hard: "Imagine if there's a death in your family and you really need to be hugged and comforted. No dice." There were times of feeling very alone, lying alone, wanting the contact of a touch, even the intimacy of being able to pass your husband a drink you knew he'd enjoy.

A Pardes woman who had taken lately to wearing a *kippah* said that if she ever married and took the laws of family purity upon herself, she'd want her husband to culminate his own seven days of introspection and preparation for togetherness by going to the mikvah himself. Our guide said she knew couples who did just that: both husband and wife immersed separately before resuming intimacy. They found their own ways to keep the spirit of the law, and while no rabbi sanctions private innovations, people do what they will. She was happy that her husband devoted some of his last day of enforced chastity to studying issues concerning *shalom bayit,* maintaining peace within a household. "He's discovered his own medium for sanctification."

One woman timidly asked, "Does this mean no sex for half your married life?" There was a collective shudder.

Not according to our guide's estimation. Her face glowed with the good news. Sexuality was permitted during pregnancy as well as during the time a lactating mother had yet to resume menstruating. Since women in the observant communities were almost always pregnant or lactating, that left a lot of opportunity for kosher sex. (Aside from our guide, I was the only mother in the group, and therefore, the only one not comforted by her good news. Considering how absurd sex is for a good chunk of pregnancy and how exhausted and continually interrupted a nursing mother is, this boon of kosher sex leaves much to be desired.) And, she added as an afterthought, you were released from going to the mikvah after menopause. (I didn't know when the Pardes women imagined that occurred, nor did I have any idea myself of how interesting sex from ages sixty to ninety was—it seemed a long time to wait.)

Some Pardes women were feeling huffy about all the restrictiveness. One woman said she could understand abstinence during menstruation, but why the added seven days? Our guide wanted to make this perfectly clear. It had not always been seven additional days. The daughters of Israel felt they couldn't be absolutely sure they could observe the colors of their staining with absolute accuracy, so they took it upon themselves to wait these extra days. These daughters of Israel must have been ancestors of the knee lady, with the self-abnegating personality of a Saint Teresa of Avila.

Our guide wanted so badly to convince us that the seven days of waiting were a time of sweetness. She called the days "a time for myself . . . a time for introspection . . . a time to creatively explore alternative means of being together, like taking walks and hikes."

I said I doubted the sweetness of seven days of checking one's secretions. She asked me to remember that in college the cool thing to do was to "get in touch with our bodies" and perform internal self-examinations with a mirror and speculum. (This had never been *my* definition of a cool thing to do.) The mikvah obliged a woman to stay in touch with her body, to feel unafraid about touching herself. I was glad our guide had found a way to make the ritual tolerable for herself. But I did not see such a way in for myself.

I shared the disturbing thoughts that came to me with the student sitting next to me, a studious young woman who would be returning to the States to do her doctorate in women's studies and marry her

Orthodox fiancé: If I recalled college biology correctly, the seven days of menstruation and the seven after were, from a procreative point of view, useless. If a woman doesn't ovulate until the fourteenth or fifteenth day of her cycle, sex before that time would be unproductive. Jewish men would do better to study a few more pages of Talmud. What's more, some researchers suggested that abstinence until ovulation favored the making of boy babies. I asked the young woman if she had thought about the connection between biology and the laws of menstruation. "How about you," I asked her, hoping I had given her something new to think about, "will you go to the mikvah after your marriage?" Probably, she said. She had accepted the yoke of the law, which meant she'd follow them all, whether they appealed to her or not. Of course, she said she was troubled that Judaism was born out of a patriarchal society that excluded women from learning and communal worship. But what more powerful model of ethical living would any of us ever know? Surely we weren't so audacious as to think that any system we could evolve on our own could compare with Jewish tradition. As for the laws of family purity, there were the benefits she had heard about. Two weeks of abstinence made for better sex, maybe even a cancer-free cervix. Each month was like a little honeymoon, your husband didn't take your body for granted. He saw you as his bride again. The mikvah kept the Jewish family together, it warded off divorce.

She was such a discriminating student. In our class in Exodus, she was the most attentive to subtle nuances. We listened to her bore holes through any poorly constructed theories. Now I was dismayed to hear her spouting off the jargon characteristic of the guides for Jewish brides circulated by the observant. She, in turn, felt sorry for me, because I had permitted my prejudices to cut me off from both a rich experience and an opportunity to serve God.

My suspiciousness about the laws concerning the menstruant remained solid, despite the appealing purity of the mikvah attendant. I needed to remain on guard, for, as Judith Baskin explains, "In virtually all societies, women have tended to be defined almost exclusively in terms of their biological characteristics (fertility, menstruation, maternity and sexual attractiveness)," which explains "the anxiety of rabbinic Judaism to circumscribe, defuse and control the sexual attributes of the female as both potential polluter and possible temptress."*

If I wanted to know the life of the Jewish mind, I would have to resist being classified by my female body.

---

*"Rabbinic Reflections on the Barren Wife," *Harvard Theological Review* 82:1 (January 1989): 101–102.

Ten

I walked up the hill from Nayot to the Jewish Theological Seminary's Jerusalem campus, Neve Schechter, in order to consult the Talmud in their library. But first I stopped in their dormitory to say hello to Miriam, one of our baby-sitters we especially liked. Miriam was a Columbia University junior studying Mishnah and Talmud this year at Neve Schechter. She told me she was going to lead prayers at Neve Schechter the next morning. She was a little anxious because most of her fellow students, male and female, were studying to be rabbis and cantors. On Miriam's dresser, alongside hair conditioner and a photograph of her boyfriend, were her prayer book and tallit and tefillin bags all set to go. I asked if women were counted in the minyan at Neve Schechter. Miriam said yes, but only if they'd voluntarily obligated themselves to perform the set of commandments otherwise reserved for men, such as saying daily prayers and winding on the leather tefillin straps.

These commandments are referred to as being time bound, which means they must be performed during a set period of the day. While women are not released from all time-bound commandments—they still must sanctify the Sabbath with the kiddush over wine and eat matzo on Passover, for instance—they are exempt from most. This is first stated in *Mishnah, Kiddushin* 1:7: "Every positive precept dependent upon a set time, men are obliged to observe but women are exempt." Rabbis have rationalized this exemption in three ways. The first rationale, intended to enforce the husband's perogative over his wife, is rooted in Genesis 3:16. God punishes Eve, saying: "Yet your urge shall be for your husband, And he shall rule over you." The rabbis explain that if women were preoccupied with performing God's time-bound commandments, their husbands would have have no authority to tell them: But I want you to help me *now!* By freeing wives of these time-bound commandments, the rabbis gave husbands, and not God, authority over the way wives spent their days.

The second rationale, the enforcement of domestic tranquillity, is closely related to the first. If women were released from certain obligations toward God, they could devote themselves without interruption to the needs of their hungry husbands and crying children. Women's home duties are thus given priority, even holy, status.

The third rationale suggests that women, angelic by nature and sequestered by culture, simply don't need to perform these commandments. The nineteenth-century German rabbi Samson Raphael Hirsch explained:

Our women are imbued with a great love and a holy enthusiasm for their role in Divine worship, exceeding that of man. The trials men undergo in their professional activities jeopardize their fidelity to Torah, and therefore they require from time to time reminders and warnings in the form of time-related precepts. Women, whose lifestyle does not subject them to comparable trials and hazards, have no need for such periodic reminders. (*Commentary to Torah,* Leviticus 23:43)*

The Jewish Theological Seminary, in order to sanction the ordination of women as rabbis in a way that minimized conflict with Jewish law, came up with a curious legalistic twist. It was proposed that two classes of women be created. Those in the first class chose to retain their exemption. (Most observant women are more than happy to do so. The exemption eases their daily burdens—how many women want to wake up half an hour early to get to synagogue to say the morning prayers? Especially when they've been up all night with a baby, the idea of a morning prayer regimen has little appeal.) Those in the second class of women—those who can become rabbis—voluntarily obligate themselves to perform men's commandments. They are essentially women who decide to be like men. There is historic precedent for such behavior, the earliest being King Saul's daughter, Michal, who wrapped herself in tefillin. This aberration troubled the rabbis, who felt the precedent should not be used to encourage other women to wear tefillin. Michal, they said, was exceptional in her virtue and her cleanliness. Any woman who likened herself to Michal branded herself as haughty and conceited. Did this include the pious daughters of Rashi, who also wore tefillin?

Miriam had evidently joined the second class. "Are you saying that each morning as you enter the synagogue you get grilled on the status of your obligation?"

"No, we just know," she said. "The community knows who considers herself obligated and who does not."

"So, in order to be counted in a minyan, a woman has to be consistently and publicly pious, but all a man has to do is show up?

*Quoted in Getsel Ellinson, *Serving the Creator* (Jerusalem: Torah Education Department of the World Zionist Organization, 1986), vol. 1, p. 41.

Even an unlearned and nonobservant Jewish man who has never before stepped inside a synagogue counts automatically?"

"Yes," she said.

"Having a Y chromosome can really open up doors," I said.

"Saying it bluntly."

As I was about to leave her dorm room to consult the Talmud in Neve Schechter's library, I added, "Or having money of one's own."

I had first assumed that denying women complete access to Torah in our days was an extension of ancient taboos. Men extended the taboos because they were convenient and preserved their higher status. Women accepted the taboos, convinced they expressed God's will. But the continued denial of access to Torah was surely also a matter of financial power, certainly nowadays. Women's access to Torah was linked to Jewish women's having hard cash, having the authority to delegate where the family's money went, and believing that Torah education for women was a valid cause to fund. Jewish women are not strangers to money. Jewish women have been shrewd businesswomen for hundreds of years, a fact often lost on the generation that knew its Jewish mothers as 1950s homemakers. The earnings of the Jewish women permitted husbands and sons to ensconce themselves with the holy books.

I had been hearing stories of wealthy Jewish families that made handsome donations to men's yeshivot, yet sent pittances to women's schools, even when the wives and daughters of those families were devoted in their learning. The stories were related by female Jewish philanthropists who were turning their money and connections into power that would reshape the Jewish world exactly as they saw fit. I met these women through the Orthodox Talmud teacher Malke Bina. In Hebrew, her name is both funny and fitting for her profession, much as the name I. M. Fine suits a physician. Loosely translated, Malke Bina means "Queen Brain" or "Queen of Understanding."

Though Malke Bina had been high up on Esther's list of learned women, I postponed seeking her out. I had heard one person refer to her as "an apologist who exalts the lower status of women" and "a strong woman among weak men." Another called her "a *weibl,* a Jewish wife who teaches girls to go to the mikvah." And someone else said, "Malke Bina does not see the problems Jewish women have. She should have her glasses fixed." I didn't think Malke Bina would offer me what I was looking for. She sounded like a lightweight who dabbled in Talmud. But then I heard others speak of her in a totally other vein. A male teacher in a women's yeshiva had complained, "What does Malke Bina think she is, a rabbi?" Someone called her a "well-disguised, quiet time bomb who opened up doors for women to study Talmud." And yet another referred to her as "Jerusalem's best-known woman Talmud teacher."

My curiosity was piqued. I would meet Malke Bina for myself and see just how serious an item she was. I would go to her Talmud class. The time had come, I had decided, to stop running away from Talmud. Otherwise, I would justify postponing it forever.

Nothing I had heard about Malke prepared me to meet a woman thickly engaged in what her right-wing Orthodox community might call subversive activity. Nothing I had heard suggested that Malke's students, both young and old, were devoted to this quietly spunky teacher who had no instinct for self-promotion. Meeting the older students in her private class did not, at first, lead me to suppose that these women, headstrong, well-to-do, and well connected, could conceive, staff, and finance an institution for women's sacred learning in the blink of an eye.

Malke had been teaching her Talmud class Sunday and Thursday mornings for the last year and a half at a home on Alfasi Street, deep in the heart of old Rehavia's Ashkenazic upper middle class. The idea for the class originated when a Frenchwoman and her American friend were running a fund-raising dinner for Yad Sarah, a charitable organization that loans out medical equipment, like oxygen tanks, for home use. The Frenchwoman told her friend that she was going to study Talmud privately with Malke Bina, with whom she had previously studied. She admitted it was no good to learn alone.

So they gathered up their interested friends, agreeing on a maximum of ten women who could study in Hebrew. The Talmud lesson would eventually be followed by a lesson on the Bible portion of the week with Fruma Gurfinkel, a teacher who had earlier approached the Frenchwoman about getting funding for her project of translating Rashi into Russian. Both classes would be run entirely in Hebrew.

Starting up an informal women's learning circle in Jerusalem was common enough. Even I could name a dozen such groups that met weekly to study *parasahat hashavua*. But Orthodox women studying Talmud? Were there others?

On a street of elegant apartments, this was an elegant private home with the trappings of luxury one found in the homes of Westchester County: leather armchairs, Oriental rugs, a silver tea set, lithographs, and tapestries. In the kitchen, a maid was preparing a tray of hot drinks and cookies for the 10:30 break. Sacred Hebrew texts were piled on the fine credenza in the dining room, references for the women who came to study.

To me, this affluent environment didn't suggest serious intellectual endeavor. A cocktail party, maybe. Women consulting their decorators about whether to reupholster the ottoman in chintz or to spring for a new one. I felt out of my element here. My friends were teachers and writers, grown-ups who subsisted on graduate student economies, our walls decorated with museum posters and our books and knickknacks shelved between milk crates and cinder blocks. I checked the bottom of my loafers to be sure I wasn't tracking dirt on the carpet.

Malke had told me that most of the women in this private class could afford not to work and, therefore, had the leisure to devote themselves to an in-depth study of texts. Fancy ladies keeping busy, I thought. How serious could this be? Batya Gallant, a teacher at Michlelet Bruria, described some of the sophisticated women's studying groups she knew: "The women's groups offer intellectual stimulation, but they're not sufficiently serious. It's different for men. For them, Torah study is their job in life. It's a man's work, not his pastime. Even though a man in yeshiva has no degree or published papers, he has competitiveness. For the woman in a study group, learning is recreation. A man has a formal framework for leaning in the yeshiva: it's considered serious."

Malke said the affluence of some of the students in this class posed an attendance problem. Whenever they went away on vacations and or took trips back to their families in America or France, they missed class. Malke was realistic about her clientele: "If I want them to prepare, I give them an assignment from Sunday to Thursday because they're busy on weekends. I gear the class to their needs."

Some of the women gathered here were influential forces in establishing institutions for women's advanced Torah learning in Israel, both as financial angels and policymakers. They know how to get what they want. Through them, I would meet Belda Kaufman Lindenbaum of New York. Belda, whom I spoke with in Jerusalem and later in New York, suggested that philanthropy was in her sisters' blood: the girls had grown up with a father who wished he were a millionaire so he could give it all away and with a mother who always wrote checks "to take care of things."

The women sitting here around the dining room table ranged in age from forty to seventy. Some American, some French; some covered their heads, some didn't. Since immigrating to Israel, they had become fluent enough to study in Hebrew. Some reminded me of Mother's upper-middle-class friends, who wore lovely perfumes and who harvested *Vogue* for tricks that restored youthfulness and enhanced glamour. With one difference. My mother's friends shopped, went to Broadway matinees, and did volunteer work for their synagogues. Even those most committed to Jewish life would not have dreamed of spending Talmudical mornings. It had no cachet.

One woman at the table stuck out from the group. Wearing a wig with a librarian's bun and a demure Old World print dress, she could have appeared in a movie about immigrant Jewish life on the Lower

East Side. She was ageless: maybe thirty, maybe fifty. This had to be Fruma. No one I spoke with in the group seemed to know much about her, although they were sure that for a few years she had been a Jerusalem Fellow, one of an elite group of international Jewish educators supported by The World Zionist Organization for a period of intensive study in Jerusalem. The consensus was that Fruma was ultraobservant in practice but liberal in outlook, that she was a disciple of the world-renowned Bible scholar Nehama Leibowitz, that she lived with her parents, that she taught Bible to new Russian immigrants, and that like her mentor, she guarded her privacy and made a point of speaking only in Hebrew although she was fluent in many languages.

Malke arrived. Malke's entrance did not make activity freeze as Aviva's did. A student would have gone on talking about her vacation if Malke hadn't opened her Talmud and cleared her throat a few times. Malke reminded me of an earnest Irish Catholic schoolgirl. A round open face, hair parted in the middle, a jaunty beret, a black knit vest, a Mickey Mouse watch. Though she was not oblivious to fashion, she was not nearly as au courant as her students: if they were *Vogue,* she was *Woman's Day.* Her skin was so white. She was a creature of the indoors, impossible to imagine running along the beach in shorts. I couldn't help notice that her eyeglasses, mended with tape, needed to be fixed.

Finally Malke weaned her student away from her travelogue, introduced me, and got the group going on Talmud. The issue at hand concerned a husband's giving or withholding a *get,* a writ of divorce that a wife must receive if she is ever to marry again. Line by line, Malke explained the material. The women, busily annotating the margins of their texts with translations of unfamiliar Aramaic terms, asked the same questions about the passage that students of Talmud have always puzzled over. If the students were clear about the text, certain of the issues, and how they hung together, Malke was satisfied and moved on. The students were sharp, wide awake, hungry to gather information, and committed to getting a knack for

the methodology. Holding together the threads of logic was tough
but not impossible. The learning seemed tremendously concen-
trated, and the hour and a half flew by. I was surprised by how much
of the Hebrew and the Talmudical thinking I could now follow.
When I got lost, Malke slipped me a few key words in English. The
women were very kind to me. My roles in the secular world as writer
and college teacher had a status they acknowledged. They seemed
pleased to have me join their classes when I could and later welcomed me as a guest into their homes.

Malke said she found teaching this group very rewarding.

I was telling one of my former teachers what I was doing and
he said, "But it's not really a full-time job," intimating maybe
I could do more. I said I really saw this teaching as a main part
of what I'm doing. I prepare, I give classes in Talmud twice a
week. I've learned a lot of this on my own and put a lot of time
in preparation and see it as a very big accomplishment, a rewarding and productive experience. The preparation spurs me
on, motivates me to learn the material well, to anticipate the
questions I'll get. You can see the women really understand
beyond the simplistic level. I don't go for this idea that men
learn Talmud totally different from the way that women learn.
This is a group of women who've seen the world. They want
to know the bottom line, what's the law. These women taught
me to bring the Talmud down to earth. Do the learning, do it
well. The theoretical, the analysis. But in the last ten minutes,
bring it down to earth.

Was there anything special about women teaching Talmud to
women?

Malke thought women studying Talmud might be offered a more
practical thrust. "They're not only interested in conceptional analysis. They want to know when push comes to shove, what is the law?
And men may be able to put that out of their minds. They can be

satisfied dealing only with the higher ideas. Women grapple and deal with the higher ideas just as well as men, but then all right, they'd like to translate it into something practical."

Adjourning to the living room for tea and coffee, the women shared stories of how their personal libraries of sacred books had grown. One woman acquired books abandoned by her husband and sons. One received books as a gift from her son who called them "a bat mitzvah present." All modern Orthodox women, they were tickled not only to be studying Talmud, but by the very idea of it. Said one American, "I like learning with women. I feel less inhibited, I don't feel threatened. I'm basically insecure. The boys always seemed so much more articulate. They had no inhibitions about speaking in class." At the beginning of their studies with Malke, the women came to class apologizing that they were unprepared because their husbands or sons had not been able to help them. "Now," the American said, "I love knowing sometimes I can catch myself getting the Gemara as fast as my husband."

Belda Lindenbaum would later tell me this story. In the late seventies when her daughter Vicky was in the fourth grade of a New York yeshiva, the boys were taught cantillation and the girls were taught sewing by the principal's wife. Belda told the principal, "You're not a trade school. If you think sewing is so important, teach it to the boys." Belda pulled Vicky out of sewing and hired whatever private teacher she could get—as it happened, a French teacher—to instruct her. When a school administrator called Belda to solicit money for a special program, Belda explained that her contribution was impossible. "I'm sorry," she said, "I'm spending that money for a private French teacher." The next year, sewing and cantillation were replaced by a co-ed "Jewish living" course. Everybody learned cantillation. The principal's wife went back to graduate school and got her degree in reading. Belda says, "She owes her master's to me."

Each week, Belda and her sister Carol Kaufman Newman studied Jewish texts with Orthodox women at Drisha Institute (where Carol is president) in New York City, just as Malke's students studied in

Jerusalem. When I spoke to Belda, I asked her how she came to interpret being actively Jewish to mean committing herself to study.

On my thirty-sixth birthday I was jogging in the country. I remember thinking this was the most perfect time in my life. My kids are well, my parents are alive. This was a charmed time. I knew it wouldn't last forever. It's almost as if I knew my father would die six months later. When one loses a parent, the wholeness in gone. I felt it was terrible I hadn't been learning. Jewish people study. That's what it is to be a Jew. When my father died, I wanted to make a statement. I said, I'm going back to learning. That's how I had to show respect, to live better and more fully, to make my life more straight. That's what I did in his memory.

During the break after Malke's class, as we sipped our drinks, the women got busy talking about the details of creating a new women's school. I asked Malke to fill me in. Malke explained that Jewish educational institutions in Israel were willing to provide programs for eighteen-year-old girls because that's a money-making operation, but they were unwilling to support the full- or part-time study of adult women. When it came to men's learning, the institutions were willing to have money-making operations subsidize the non-profit segments. The problem in Israel was that there were four hundred men's schools and one school for adult women. Malke's students had suggested, "Maybe we should start our own institution." Malke had agreed: this was the thing to do.

Someone would go to America to raise money for a women's institute for Torah studies that would be conducted at a sophisticated level in Hebrew. Unlike Michlelet Bruria, it would be a school run *for* women *by* women. Malke Bina would be its educational director. Her private students would sit on the board. There would be many women on the staff. There would be two levels of study: part-time courses for women who could apply themselves to learning Bible, Prophets, Talmud, Midrash, or Jewish philosophy in their free time, and a *kolelet,* a program of full-time paid study for advanced young women who could be groomed as future leaders of women's Torah education. The full-time students would be given high-caliber teachers, a *bet midrash* atmosphere, study partners, and a monthly stipend. Malke would tap young women with intensive Jewish backgrounds in Jewish education who wished to continue studying at a high level in a yeshiva environment. They'd learn to prepare texts on their own.

It was late in the afternoon when I visited Malke at home. She was with four of her five children in the Old City apartment she shared with her Israeli-born husband, Rabbi Aharon Bina, dean of foreign students at Yeshivat Hakotel. It was an enormous modern apartment, Scandinavian in its brightness and clean lines, yet cozy, a place where people could study, live, and play in comfort and dignity. There was none of the dreary inattention to aesthetics that I associated with the yeshiva world. I felt elevated to be welcomed into a house that evoked the proverb: "A house is built by wisdom/ And is established by understanding;/By knowledge are its rooms filled/With all precious and beautiful things" (Proverbs 24:3).

The Bina household was always open. Malke's former Bruria students would drop by to consult about their lives as though she were a combination of spiritual adviser, therapist, and big sister. Boys from Rabbi Bina's yeshiva would come in at eleven or twelve at night to help themselves to drinks or fruit. Malke recalled the time she and her husband were strolling in the Jewish Quarter and met one of Rabbi Bina's students with his father, who was visiting. The father asked Malke what she did, and the son proudly answered for her, "Don't you know, Daddy? I always come in late at night and Mrs. Bina is sitting at the dining room table and learning. She teaches Talmud."

We started out in Malke's kitchen, surrounded by a rows of cabinets and the good smell of root vegetables in a boiling soup. Malke was telling one son to see if there was something good on TV, advising another son on the phone to buy himself a slice of pizza while he waited for his dental appointment, and fixing bowls of soup for yet another son and his friend. She was going to set aside time to teach Mishnah to her only daughter, Chaya, because it was not taught in her school. "I agreed to teach her Mishnah *Pesahim,* to get ready for Passover. But you know hard it is to teach your own child."

The predinner chaos was only marginally controlled, as it usually was in my house. Seeing the chaos relieved me. Malke didn't float in a bubble of holy knowledge. She was a working mother of four sons and a daughter whose job was Talmud. She didn't compartmentalize her life. She was whole: always a mother, a wife, a teacher.

Malke fixed us some herb tea and fed me a spoonful of the soup. It was good. "Take down the recipe," she advised.

Malke Bina's Vegetable Soup for Winter

Fry onions in 2 T oil.

Brown 3 T matzo meal for added body.

Dump in any vegetable: stalks of celery, carrots, potatoes, squash, red peppers, kohlrabi.

Cover with water.

Add ½ cup barley.

Simmer 2 hours.

To know Talmud, to know cooking—for Malke, all knowledge was valuable, all could be integrated. Surely, the Vilna Gaon had not whipped up many pots of soup in his day. It is true that making nourishing and tasty soup took time away from Malke's learning, but it didn't diminish her scholarship. Soup organized experience: soup was a poem of love, of sustenance, of celebrating plenty, of surviving the cold. Torah fed life, so did soup.

"This is my Talmud teacher's Malke Bina's soup," I told my girls when I prepared it at home over the weekend. I did not burn the soup or let it overboil.

"Lima Bina, lentil Bina, Malke Bina soup," Juliana chanted as she and Dede stirred their soup cool. For the first time, they felt my Torah study was of some direct benefit to them.

Malke was from Baltimore, the daughter of Rabbi Boruch and Leah Milikowsky. At the Talmudical Academy of Baltimore, her father was the *mashgiah,* a rabbinical supervisor whose duty it was to monitor and motivate the intellectual and spiritual growth of the boys in his charge. As a child, Malke didn't have set periods of learning with her father, who was always busy with his yeshiva boys. "My father would sometimes bring the boys home to talk with them in the house," she recalled.

I would be kind of sitting there. I liked to listen to the discussions he had with the boys. When I had a difficult assignment in school—the Bais Yaakov school of Baltimore—a Hebrew essay to write or a chapter in Bible to understand, he would help me with it, and when he helped me, he would go *beyond* the assignment. He would make it very enjoyable. So even if I knew how to do an assignment myself, I would sometimes go to him and ask for help because he would show me an additional Midrash or commentator.

Did your father study with your brothers?

"Maybe a little more, but not too much. He helped them out with their Gemara—I didn't study Gemara when I was younger. The overriding picture in my mind is of my father helping his students, through discussions with them, as to what they wanted to do with their lives and what Torah meant to them."

Did you have anything to do with these boys who came to your house?

"When I got to a certain age, there's that natural kind of association, you know, talking to them, meeting at the library. I was a good girl, so I didn't do much more. But every once in a while, there was one boy I liked a little, so I would talk to him a little more."

Did your father influence your profession?

"My father didn't encourage me specifically to go on with my Jewish learning. I think he might have liked for me to be a math professor or a psychologist, but he didn't discourage me either. He's a very practical man and he thought: You're a woman. Something in the secular world might be a better career."

At seventeen, Malke came to Israel to study for three years at the women's seminary, Michlala. She decided to study religious subjects and math and to decide between them later on. The sister of her future husband, Aharon, studied at Michlala. She had seen Malke around and was impressed. Malke seemed a potential match for her brother, then studying in the prestigious ultra-Orthodox Ponovezh yeshiva. The sister was too shy to play matchmaker herself, so after clearing the plan with her mother, she asked her friend to tell Malke, "Look, this suggestion has come up . . ."

Why not? Malke thought. What was there to lose? She was nineteen then, twenty when they married.

It appeared that the relationship of Malke and Aharon Bina was unlike the typical marriage in their yeshiva world.

"We have a special relationship," Malke said,

the relationship I've always dreamed about. To be married to a person who is very open-minded and treats people for what they are and wants to hear their opinions. We don't actually sit that much and learn together. We would like to. We feel we should learn more with the children independently. But our schedules don't allow for it. In our relationship, we take each serious point and really discuss it with each other, not just to get approval after a decision is made, but to get the input of the other person. Let's say we're making a *sheva berakhot* (a festive celebration during the week after a wedding) for a student. Even if I do a little more of the preparation than my husband, I'll discuss the menu with him in a very natural way. Or if he's going to hire someone for the yeshiva, he'll tell me about the person.

He has a deep respect for me; he's interested in what I'm doing. Even though each of us has our own area of expertise, our area of greater responsibility. It's not that everything is done half and half. You can't do that in life. There's a lot of cooperation. Sometimes I'll be busy, so my husband will do more. Or he'll be busy, which might be more often, and I'll do more. Nursing, things like that, I wanted to do. I'd know my husband could look after the other children if I were nursing. I don't want to hold him back from going ahead in his learning Torah, teaching, his work with the boys—his "career" so to speak. And he wants me to go ahead. I get help from the outside sometimes. If he can't help me or I can't help him, at least to get some other help to take over, trying not to leave the other person in a difficult situation. So we take someone to do it. Baby-sitting, help in the house with the laundry, ironing. That's why we really have no money saved. The money goes for help so that we can pursue other things that interest us. That we could devote ourselves more to our learning, even to people. A lot of what we do is talking to people and hearing what they have to say.

Malke had taught Bible and math in a junior high school, then began to teach Jewish learning to American high school graduates in Israel. She enjoyed her work with eighteen year olds and decided math was something other people could do. Back in the States, she got a master's in Bible studies from Revel College of Yeshiva University. Since returning to Israel at twenty-two, she had been teaching at various women's institutions: Machon Gold, Shappel's, and then ten years at Michlelet Bruria, which she helped found with Rabbi Brovender in 1976. That means sixteen years of experience teaching Bible, Talmud, and law to adult women, and learning Talmud on her own with guidance.

I asked how she got going in Talmud.

I had studied Mishnah at Michlala (a women's seminary in Jerusalem). That whetted my appetite for Talmud. Rabbi Brovender, then at Shappel's, asked me to give a preparatory course in Talmud for women. On my own, with Adin Steinsaltz's explanation and Jastrow's dictionary always at my side, I plugged through the logic, the questions and answers. And as you know, if you're going to teach something, you have to know it. I happen to like Talmud. I have a facility for it, or maybe because I like it, I feel I have a facility. I like math, law, logic.

Malke had loved the enthusiasm at Bruria, particularly during its heyday. She loved the sense of creating a unique atmosphere, guiding women from eighteen to twenty-five, getting their input. Her responsibilities and the extent of her authority at Bruria eventually became unclear. She felt that the unwieldy administration could no longer attract serious students. "I felt frustrated in my desire to build up a strong place for women's learning."

I had heard a rumor that there was about to be a major donation that would rescue Bruria from its doldrums (as it turned out, Belda and her husband, Marcel Lindenbaum, would be the angels who would turn Bruria into the better-endowed Midreshet Lindenbaum), and I was curious to see if Malke would choose to return to Bruria or choose to become the educational director of the new school her students were hoping to create, which would be called by a Hebrew acronym, *Matan,* or in English, Women's Institute for Torah Studies (WITS).

If the Women's Institute for Torah Studies materialized, there would be advertisements and posters, and it would soon become public knowledge that Malke was the educational director. I asked Malke if her affiliation with such a progressive institution would bring criticism from the more right-wing yeshiva community of the Jewish Quarter of the Old City in which she and her husband lived. Did Malke fear ostracism enough to think twice about accepting the position?

"The school won't be here in the Jewish Quarter," she said. "We're thinking about the German Colony. We will put up posters. What you have to do, you do. But we wouldn't do something beyond, just to glare and make something conspicuous and ostentatious when it's not going to help get more students. Putting up posters in the Jewish Quarter or Geula could catch the eye of someone who's a rabble-rouser and could make more trouble."

"So you're saying that as the wife of a yeshiva rabbi, it would be impossible for you to teach Talmud here in the Jewish Quarter?"

Malke was not one to rock the boat. "Maybe I'd want to check it out before. The only reason I wouldn't is because my husband teaches here, and I wouldn't want people starting to say anything in his yeshiva. It might not be looked upon favorably; not everyone in the yeshiva would approve of it 100 percent. They may say about my teaching Talmud in Rehavia, 'All right, it's further away.' I wouldn't want my husband to suffer in his work in the yeshiva because of it. Then again, maybe I could teach Talmud to women here in my house. It might be accepted. Sometimes you don't know what's accepted and what's not. My husband says not to worry so about him. But why make trouble if you don't have to? *I* know my teaching Talmud is OK, but it's not acceptable by everyone else."

"I want to make sure I have this perfectly straight, Malke. You're saying that according to Jewish law, it's perfectly permissible for women to teach and study Talmud?"

"Yes," she said.

"And acceptance of women teaching and learning Talmud is based not on law but on cultural, communal norms?"

"Right. It depends on which opinion you follow. Some communities are more negative on the issue of women going ahead in all areas of Torah study. Or some have the idea, 'It's OK, but why does she have to do it? Why can't she do something else?' "

"Does your father know what you're up to?" I asked. "How does he feel about it?

She smiled. "Yes. Oh, nice. Very happy about it. He said, 'I hear you give a class in *lamdus.' Lamdus* is a more analytical type of learning. Not just the Gemara itself, but with commentaries, with discussion, conceptional analysis. On the one hand, he's very proud. On the other hand, it's like Oh, this is—uh—something—new. He knew all along I was advancing in my studies."

Malke's voice held enormous reserve. "But I'm really getting up there and I'm able to give a class in such difficult materials. My father was proud. And my mother, always proud of my achievements, wanted me to advance and go ahead. Talmud never particularly interested her—she herself went on in Hebrew literature and Bible and Jewish history. But she always felt a woman had to be well versed in Jewish subjects."

Given Malke's extreme respect for religious authority and her resistance to causing a stir, I wondered what motivated her to go as far as she did in learning and teaching Talmud. She had been telling me about her friend—the granddaughter of a *rosh yeshiva* (the rabbi who headed a yeshiva, a position of great status) and the wife of a learned rabbinic judge—whom she admired for her broad-mindedness. When I asked how this was possible given her lineage and marriage, Malke explained, "Many times the children and grandchildren of the big scholars have a broader outlook than the lay people in the yeshiva. Maybe they feel they're 'above' in a sense and can make their own decisions. They don't have to go by what others are doing. They themselves aren't scrutinized because they have the umbrella, so to speak, or protection, of the scholarly father or grandfather." While Malke was far too humble to suggest that *her* lineage gave her special dispensation, that was the conclusion I drew.

I asked if she wouldn't mind reviewing a point in the Gemara we'd been doing in class in tractate *Ketubbot,* which concerns wedding contracts.

The cadences of Malke's speech switched to Talmud singsong. "The claim is that the husband has the right in certain situations to come to the court and say 'I found my wife not to be a virgin because it was too easy for me to have relations with her.' *Petah pituah*—the vaginal area was too open."

Malke assumed I recalled the argument better than I did, and so represented it to me in shorthand. I strained to follow.

There's a lot of "How can you accept him when there really isn't proof?" Remember the term *mego* means "since." *Since* the wife wanted to lie, she could have lied better by claim A. Here she said, "I'm a virgin." She could have said claim B: "We had relations after we were engaged in the area of Judah," where it was permitted. If she wanted to lie, she could have said claim B, which would have been believed. But she said claim A—"I'm a virgin." So we believe that to be true, because if she were lying, she would have thought to lie better.

My head was swimming. This was as hard for me as trigonometry. I was embarrassed to admit that I wasn't following too well. I listened on, hoping I would eventually get it.

Here was the new point Malke wanted to make.

At the end of the Gemara they mention a case that actually happened. A young man comes to the court and claims, *petah pituah.* What was the reaction of the judge? He ordered the young man to be whipped. One explanation: The young man was believed by the judge. But if the young man knew his wife was not a virgin, *how* did he know? Because he had promiscuous relations with whores. Or another explanation: The young man was not believed and was whipped because he had the audacity to think he knew this was an instance of *petah pituah.*

He thinks *he* knows anatomy and what it should be? Well who does he think he is?

Now I think I understood, but I was troubled by the assumptions such an argument made about the material value of a woman's virginity. "Whether the bride was a virgin or not, the position she's being put into is humiliating. She's seen as either marred or acceptable property."

Malke went back down into the text, the end of the first chapter in the tractate *Ketubbot.*

We're talking about a husband who accuses his wife of having had relations with another man during their premarital period, a time in which they are already considered as if married. If the husband's accusation is true, there's a standard legal procedure. The husband goes to a court and the marriage is dissolved. If there's proof, that is, if two people actually witnessed the wife and another man going into a closed room by themselves, then the court can impose other penalties. This is adultery, so the consequences are severe. Death even, for the wife and the man.

Now here was the point Malke wanted me to pay special attention to. "There's a second legal issue we must look at, one that's equally as important. What if the husband has *falsely* accused his wife of having had relations with another man? Then we really punish the husband for his arrogance, for humiliating and giving a bad name to the woman."

When teaching this Gemara, Malke felt it was important to clarify that when a man claims his bride isn't a virgin, he isn't automatically believed. That was the conclusion of the elaborate reasoning, simpler than all the complexities that led up to it. "It's important to see the whole picture. Men are so busy analyzing the process of what goes on—which is also important, for we do have to analyze in depth—but then you have to come down to the ground."

I blurted out what was on my mind:

I read novels by women because I find it illuminating to see the world perceived by women's minds. Writers like Virginia Woolf and Grace Paley and Doris Lessing tell me things I need to know in language that clicks with my experience. They also tell me: Take yourself seriously. You have a legitimate voice to make stories, too, to make art, to tell your version and make it be heard. I know Talmud isn't a woman's novel. It's the world perceived by generations of men, except for when Bruria does her brief walk-ons. The tiny peeps of a woman's voice in Talmud are like squeaks in a roaring engine. I need to know what it's like for you to subsist on a steady diet of the world perceived by a male intelligence and a male concept of law. The Talmud is men creating laws by which women have to live. It doesn't reflect female thinking, female experience, or a female voice. Talmud is the way men have mediated between sacred text and life. Doesn't that bother you? Isn't it an enormous problem? Sometimes I wonder if women should even aspire to becoming "masters" of Talmud. I don't like the idea of separatism, but maybe we'd do better to create an oral lore that reflects women's sensibilities.

Malke was a good listener. She truly appreciated that the maleness of Talmud could bother me so, given who I was and where I came from. She, who spent her days poring over Talmud, was untroubled.

Talmud may have been a bit different on certain points if women had been involved. If that would have been the case, I'd enjoy it more and find it more fulfilling. *But it didn't happen.* Women in those days weren't studying Jewish law in the depth and with the intensity it requires. Up to a hundred years ago, women were hardly involved in Jewish scholarship. There's a popular expression in Hebrew that translates as "If grandma had skates." It means you can't ask What if? It would have been nice if women had also contributed to the Talmud. But it didn't happen. I feel Rabbi Akiva and all the other scholars had the absolute integrity and truth of the law behind them to create the best Jewish society for all. This is what was uppermost on their minds. I hate to make an issue of sex. These were the people who were studying then and for whatever reasons women didn't study then. I'm sorry, if it had been, it would have been. We're dealing with people who had the Jewish nation so much on their minds they wouldn't go down to sexist issues. If I were making a law, I wouldn't want someone to say I'm making it from a woman's perspective only.

"Do you realistically see that happening, women like you making Jewish legal decisions in our times?

I want every woman to develop to her fullest potential. In the internal way. On the other hand, I'm a practical person and I'm not a radical by any means, and what's going to happen externally I don't know. I don't like to create ruckuses. There's already so much friction and division in the Jewish nation that I don't want to cause any more. There will be many women *able* to write legal opinions, many women who know more what to do in their lives, how to instruct and tell other women. Whether it'll be time to do it or if it will be accepted by society, I don't know.

"Why do you think the power remains male?" I asked, thinking afterward that my question was as inane as asking why people liked chocolate.

But the question seemed reasonable to Malke.

In order really to be a rabbi of a community and a legal decisor, and to do it properly, you need full concentration, eighteen-hour days devoted to study and community work. No organized schedule. Only because of the importance of family in Jewish life, that's not suggested for women. You couldn't raise a nice family doing that and have normal children. Nothing to do with a woman's intelligence. I want to have the time to be with my children at meals, have discussions, and talk to my daughter about her ballet. Not that my husband doesn't want that, too, but he removes himself more. We are women. Women can do so many things. But this idea of ultimate power—in the rabbinic sense—and devotion to the community, the way it should be done properly—I think it's something a woman could do if she wished but naturally wouldn't want to. Up above, the scholars and the whole system think it's not healthy. Those women doing it will definitely suffer. Their families will suffer a lot.

Malke seemed satisfied to live out the "the woman's role" as defined by her religious community and did not see that role as limiting her aspirations in any way. She told me a story of a woman she admired, her brother's mother-in-law.

The rebbetzen is articulate and well versed in rabbinics, politics, history. She's well-read, meticulous, and very gracious. She has the charm of a woman with what the world would call "the solid knowledge of a male." But every bit a woman in her caring for the house. You don't feel like you're speaking to a woman who couldn't fend for herself. She was married to a brilliant Talmudist, and they had four children. They were such articulate and dominant personalities that their marriage didn't work out and they were divorced. She then devoted herself to taking care of her ill father during his last years. He passed away, and she kept herself busy taking care of the children and maybe even had a little position here or there. The husband meanwhile remarried for a few years to a very fine woman, but the woman died and he was widowed and got sick with cancer of the lungs. It was very difficult. The four children, most of them with their own young children, were taking turns caring for their father. Their mother came to help take care of the children so they could go take care of the father. The father really needed someone with him around the clock and he didn't want a strange woman taking care of him. So he and his former wife remarried. She remarried him to help take care of him. Even if they couldn't get along on a day-to-day basis, she still had great respect and admiration for him. And it helped out her children. For a year and a half or two years she took care of him. It was very difficult. Then he passed away. A woman knew what she had to do and was able to do it.

Malke thought it was realistic to envision the possibility of a woman becoming a religious judge. A judge would have normal working hours, and there was the precedent of the biblical judge Deborah. "She seemed pretty busy," Malke said.

She had a husband, Lapidot. We don't know about children. One opinion says that she was permitted to do the judging. Another says it was permitted only in her time and not now. The question for us now is how would being a judge fit in a natural way with what else a woman wants to be doing? We don't want to upset the whole pattern of the world that God created and make women freak robots. We want life to go on and children to be laughed with.

I told Malke that her stance on "women's nature" would strike women, particularly those studying for the rabbinate in the progressive movements, as hopelessly conservative. That's how she struck me. Yet she spent her days learning and teaching Talmud. Regardless of her acceptance of the constraints of conventional wifely and motherly roles, regardless of her care not to do anything that could be construed as "bad for the Jews," she was, in the context of her community, a radical activist. Not only was she fashioning herself into a Talmudist, but she was also empowering other women by giving them the tools and the confidence to approach the texts themselves.

It wasn't clear to me whose glasses needed the fixing.

Malke smiled at my description of her as a renegade. It didn't mesh with her own self-image. Still, I think she was flattered. She said she had been invited to Pardes to give a talk, and afterward, she was told she presented a paradox: You say you're not a feminist, but you say the daily prayers, you keep the commandments, and you study and teach Talmud. What's not feminist about that? She didn't disagree.

"Why do I do it?" Malke asked, impishly. "Because I love Jewishness."

I took her to be saying that she had her hands filled with children to raise and a lifelong commitment to living, learning, and teaching as Jew. She didn't have the time or inclination to fuss over the issues of egalitarianism. Because Malke knew Jewish law, she knew stretching and straining it to conform with modernity was possible and even ethical. She had no appetite to press for social change by negating the Jewish law by which she was bound. Why would she want to do such a thing? To maintain the letter of the law in a world where it was so tempting to abandon it was a blessing, a duty, a challenge to self-perfection. To negate the law would be like murder, like betraying all that was beloved.

When I got around to making Malke's recipe for soup again, instead of winter kohlrabi and turnips, I substituted spring peas and green beans. Frying the onions and matzo meal together—her special trick—I recalled the last of her classes I had been to. Before she began to teach, Malke addressed us calmly, as if she were about to give an assignment. Her father had been suffering from back pain, and his doctors had decided to operate soon, to remove his kidney. Until the day of the operation, she assured us, he planned to go right on studying and teaching Talmud. It was clear from the way Malke presented the matter to us that her main concern was to alleviate *our* worry.

"The doctors will do all they can," a student said, "and the rest will be in God's hands."

Malke agreed. Resting her hands on the open pages of her Talmud, she announced, "I'd like to dedicate today's learning to my father."

Once Jewish women could offer up only their prayers, good deeds, and charity to plead for the recovery of a loved one. Malke believed it was just as effective for a daughter of a Talmud scholar to offer Talmud study as a talisman for her father's health, so the merit of our learning might intercede for him in heaven. Unorthodox though the gesture may have been, Malke felt sure it was appropriate, for her father had always encouraged her to develop her intellect. When she was five, she told us, he would give her a difficult math problem such as nine times nine, and challenge her to work it out.

I tried to picture the energy of our learning transported into the hands of the surgeons at Johns Hopkins, causing them to be wiser in judgments, more cautious with sutures and stitches, luckier. We returned to the tractate *Ketubbot,* to honest virgins, to lying brides, and to grooms deprived of their marital rights who wanted revenge. Out of respect for my teacher Malke, I postponed fretting about the problems I had with the maleness of Talmud.

Did I really believe our learning could have any effect on the health of Malke's father? I believed it would be irresponsible and disrespectful of my teacher not to consider that there *could* be some connection. We women in this house in Rehavia were engaged in sacred study, an act of devotion. We strained to learn well. When my attention drifted, which it inevitably did, to my family or to my teaching or to the texture of the upholstery that rubbed against the back of my legs, I tightened the screws of my concentration until no distractions could filter in. Now was not the time to decide if I could ever accept the Torah, this construct of reality made by God and men, as a structure for my own life.

I felt the light of our learning rising.

If there was a divine scheme of things, this surely counted.

"The beginning of wisdom and understanding," says the Torah, "is the fear of the Lord."

My soup burned some, but the family enjoyed it nonetheless. Over the years they have grown accustomed to a burnt flavoring, like vanilla or curry, the spice of my distraction.

Eleven

I had rescheduled my own class at the university today so I could stay for both classes in Rehavia, first Malke's, then Fruma's. After Malke left, Fruma taught the section of Leviticus called Behukotai, which began with the words "If you follow My laws and faithfully observe My commandments. . . ." I noticed that Fruma looked different today. She wore delicate earrings, an olive green sweater with a lacy collar and a cuter, shorter wig which allowed me to see she was a young woman. Fruma started reading the blessings God promised the Israelites if they followed the commandments, and she continued with the curses that would be brought upon them if they were disobedient. As Fruma read, she touched the words with her hands as though the letters were raised, like Braille, as though she were reading a letter from her lover and wanted to connect with him through the ink that had flowed from his pen. She delighted as each word formed in her mouth, shuddering as her consonants broke into the air. Her power of visualization seemed strong enough to conjure up her own presence at the giving of the Torah.

Midway into the curses, Fruma caught her breath and stopped. "I tremble when I read these. I don't have the strength to go on." Someone had to finish recounting the miseries: eating the flesh of sons and daughters, cities in ruin, sanctuaries made desolate, consumption by enemies.

I wanted to know more about this woman. As soon as I felt confident I could carry on a cogent conversation in Hebrew, thereby respecting her desire to speak only Hebrew, I asked if I might visit her one evening. I hoped she could tell me how she had become so intimate with the Bible, how it had come to be so beloved to her.

The evening I was to go to Fruma's, the family was eating dinner, when Peter proposed we elevate that evening's table chatter. He asked me to tell the children a Bible story.

I froze, I blanked. Telling Bible stories was what *he* did. That, and doing taxes, fixing toilets, vacuuming, and buying red meat. We had a rigid division of labor in our household. You got stuck with a task in one of two ways. Either you did it well or the other person simply refused. I tell a Bible story? I couldn't, I didn't know any well enough. I could do Noah's ark from Peter Spier's picture book. That was it. I had worked out children's versions of *The Metamorphosis, Madame Bovary,* and *The Sufferings of Young Werther,* which the girls adored, but the Bible? Peter reminded me I was the one who had studied Bible every day for the last few months. While I might not yet feel confident about participating in learned discourse, I should be able to come up with something for children. That did not build my confidence. Learned discourse was actually a snap. You grabbed on to a theory, you blabbed on, no one listened much anyway. My daughters listened. What I told them, they believed.

I stalled until I had served seconds of chick-peas to everyone. They were all looking at me, waiting. I would try. Sometimes in the Bible, I said, the same story is told two different ways. Take the story of the creation of Adam and Eve. In one version of the story, God made Adam first and then decided Adam was lonely, so a woman was made from his rib.

"How could Adam have been lonely?" Dede asked, primed by her father in habits of faith these last three years. "He had God."

"He needed someone to see and touch, Dede. Sometimes you're happy to play with your dolls and make things up with them and you don't feel alone, but other times you say, 'Mommy, can I have a friend over?' That's how Adam felt. Then there's another version of the same story of Adam and Eve. In that story, the first person God made was a man-woman creature."

Although disgusted and incredulous, Juliana still speculated, "With a beard and bald like Daddy, bosoms like Mommy."

"Maybe. It's hard to say for sure. It means," I concluded, "that back, way back in our minds we each have a memory of what it's like to be a mommy and a daddy, a girl and a boy." I think I wanted to tell them about possibilities for mental androgyny. I'm sure I wasn't getting that across by describing an androgyne. Rephrasing Colette's *Vagabond* would have been more effective.

Juliana said my story was gross and smashed away at her chickpeas. Dede seemed relieved by the story. She said there was a half boy, half girl creature in her nursery class.

"Who?"

"Yosef. She wears boy pants and has girl hair."

Yosef was the only child in class from a highly observant family. His parents, who adored his long yellow curly locks too well, kept finding reasons to postpone his hair-cutting ceremony. As a result, not a child in the class was clear about Yosef's gender.

Peter shook my hand just as he shook his students' hands after they had given a *devar torah,* an informal interpretation of Bible, at our table. Had I taught Bible? My lesson seemed quirky, like *National Enquirer* material. I wasn't ready. I needed more information, more confidence. I needed to know what I wanted the girls to learn from the Bible before I tried to teach them. And what I wanted to draw from it myself. I was a little proud, nonetheless, a little embarrassed. I didn't want Peter to know how worked up this tiny recitation had made me. I was glad I had to run off to Fruma's.

I took a bus that went through the ultrareligious Geula neighborhood and then on to Ramat Eshkol, where Fruma lived on Achinoam Street. For a few moments, I sat on a stone ledge in front of her apartment, rehearsing my questions in Hebrew and watching little girls wearing twin braids and religious school uniforms lining up outside the neighborhood grocer to buy bread while boys cruised teasingly close by on their bikes. As I entered the apartment building, I noticed many Russian names on the mailboxes. I thought I could smell fried farmer's cheese, meat pastries, and baked fish in the air, the same hallway smell I remembered from the Brighton Beach apartment of my stepfather's relatives whom we used to visit.

Fruma's parents were sitting in the living room watching a TV documentary about the Warsaw Ghetto uprising. Sad and rousing music played the entire time we talked. Her father kept glancing at Fruma and pointing to his watch as she sat with me at a small dining table in the corner. She assured him she had not forgotten there was something else she had to do.

Fruma was happy to share her special connection to Torah with me. Her only worry was that it would be hard to articulate it. Perhaps it would become clearer to me if we were to study together. "Studying together eventually creates closeness and understanding," Fruma explained.

Authentic study is unique for every individual. There is a lovely expression: "The Torah that a person has studied is named after him." It means that the person has reached that Torah in his individual way, and his knowledge of it is not indifferent to who he is. It's not knowledge in a book. It's my knowledge. Why is it mine? Because my way of reaching it and the conclusions I draw from it are unique.

I asked if she came to Israel yearning to learn Torah. I half hoped she'd say she had studied Hebrew surreptitiously in Russia, in a hidden compartment, risking her life.

"*Tiri.* Look." Before she came to Jerusalem in the end of 1974, she had been a student of Russian and German literature in Kiev.

The truth is that in Russia I didn't really understand what Torah was. I simply did not know. I had a Pentateuch in German translation, but I didn't understand it. Not because I didn't understand the language, but because I just didn't understand. I opened it in the beginning and there was the Genesis story, followed by a list of generations and I didn't understand what it meant. I tried once more and then again, but I still didn't understand, so I closed the book.

Fluency in Hebrew, Fruma was now convinced, is crucial for the study of Torah. Torah needs to be encountered in the original. While translation is useful in a pinch, and certainly is better than nothing, it obscures meaning and aggravates one's alienation from the text. In the original Hebrew, Bible teaches itself. If you are sensitive to the repetition of Hebrew words, and the repetition and variations of root letters, the language guides you to discover meaning.

Upon arriving in Israel, Fruma did not know Hebrew. Not a word, not one letter. She learned Hebrew quickly in an ulpan, an intensive Hebrew class. Soon she was fluent enough to take regular classes at Hebrew University in comparative literature. She had heard that Professor Nehama Leibowitz was the best Bible teacher and she went to listen to her. The match was perfect. Nehama (everyone refers to her by her first name) was just what she was searching for. And though she had no inkling that she would one day be teaching Torah herself, or that she would still be studying with Nehama each week, she did know she wanted very much to study Torah.

Fruma originally approached sacred texts as a student of comparative literature, from a literary and linguistic point of view. Over the last thirteen years, as Nehama's student, she acquired the traditional bases for Bible study. That meant mastering the classical commentaries and learning Midrash and Jewish thought.

There was hardly anyone engaged in Bible study that I had met in Jerusalem, male or female, who had not studied with Nehama at some time or other. All told of being motivated by Nehama's love of Torah and love of her students. Some said she frequently appeared in their dreams. While she is renowned for her enormous learning of rabbinic commentators as evidenced in her books, she is most renowned—and beloved—as a teacher, the teacher par excellence of Bible.

She is the source, the real thing. To have studied with Nehama is to have been in analysis with Freud, to have been educated in nursery school by Maria Montessori, to have been inoculated against polio by Dr. Salk. In many communities Nehama's biblical interpretation has complete authority. And while all consider it an honor to have studied with her, being her student has never been a privilege limited to a scholarly elite. Anyone at all could study with her. Over the years from 1953 to 1971 her mimeographed self-instruction sheets on the weekly Torah portion, *Gilyonot Le-iyyun Befarashat Ha-shavua,* were distributed around the world. Her students, including young mothers, factory workers, street sweepers, nurses, farmers, soldiers, kibbutzniks, and teachers used the sheets to learn the Torah portions on their own. They answered the questions she posed and she offered corrections in red ink. For years she gave a weekly radio lesson. Her studies, placing Bible in the context of ancient and modern Jewish Bible commentary, have been edited into the best-selling and widely translated six-volume *Studies in the Weekly Sidra,* complete with questions for self-instruction to spur on further learning. For beginners and for rabbis preparing their weekly sermons, Nehama's books are a major source. No student exposed to Nehama's instruction would find the Bible dry, with her prodding to know the text more deeply and more exactly, her underlying humanitarianism and religious Zionism, her knowledge of the most current literary criticism.

Her English translator, Aryeh Newman, has written that one could not dip into Nehama's teachings "without realizing the truth of the Biblical evaluation (Deuteronomy 32:47): *'Ki lo davar rek hu mikem'*—'For it is no dry-as-dust thing for you.'" Discussing this verse, the rabbis made the illuminating comment about the nature of the reader: *"Im rek hu*—if it *is* dry as dust," then *"mikem*—that's your fault!"*

Rabbi Pinchas Peli once referred to Nehama, now in her eighties (although you wouldn't know it from her rigorous teaching schedule, which could wipe out a much younger person), as Israel's most outstanding living rabbi. This was long before the ordination of women. What was he suggesting about Nehama, an Orthodox woman? He was referring to the original meaning of the word rabbi. A rabbi is, above all, a teacher of Torah.

While veneration for Nehama is nearly universal, there remain some doors that are closed to her because she is a woman. In May of 1987, Rabbi Shlomo Riskin invited Nehama to lecture at the Joseph Strauss Rabbinical Seminary, a division of the Blechner College of Jewish Studies. He had asked Nehama, very simply, because she was the best person to teach Bible. The best in the world. Rabbi Eliezar Schach of the Shas Party condemned Rabbi Riskin for engaging a woman to teach. A more lenient response came from the former Sephardic chief rabbi, Ovadia Yosef, who suggested Nehama could lecture to the rabbis, but from behind a screen (the Maid of Ludomir model). Since in Israel all news is everyone's business, a kibbutznik named E. M. Solowey sent a solution in to the editor of the *Jerusalem Post:* "I have a better idea. Let Professor

*Jerusalem Post, April 10, 1970.

Leibowitz be treated with respect and consideration like all other lecturers in the programme. Rabbi Schach and all his ilk can attend wearing burlap bags over their heads so they will not be distressed or distracted by the sight of an educated woman."* According to Rabbi Riskin, "Not only did Nehama teach that class, but she is *still* going strong, teaching the rabbinical students without a screen."

No obstacle deters Nehama from her task. Even in the winter of 1948, on the day the printing presses of the *Palestine Post* were bombed by the British, Nehama, warned to watch out for stray bullets, proceeded to the radio studio of Kol Israel to teach her lesson from the Book of Jeremiah and proclaim the Jewish right to the State of Israel. For sixty years Nehama has been Israel's master teacher, carrying her heavy black briefcase, dressed in a modest dark suit and a brown beret tilted to the right covering most of her gray hair, as she shuttles from class to class in the cab assigned to her, posing right questions that will lead to right answers.

Everyone knows Nehama. Who can't quote a feisty remark, a Nehama joke ("A Jewish woman is sick and goes to the doctor. He tells her she ought to read the Bible. She says, 'What do you think, I'm Christian?' ")? Who hasn't seen her poring over a pile of volumes in Jerusalem's National Library? Yet she assiduously retains her privacy, avoiding interviews, insisting that her disciples not write about her while she is still alive and working.† The teaching is what counts, the rest is superfluous.

In the *Encyclopaedia Judaica*, the entry for Nehama Leibowitz, the world's greatest female Bible scholar, is a brief eleven lines. Moreover, it comes as a subheading under the entry (four times as long) for Nehama's older brother, Yeshayahu, the Israeli scientist, philosopher, and outspoken public figure. The entry for Nehama provides a few facts. She was born in Riga in 1905; she came with

---

*Jerusalem Post, May 26, 1987.
†Indeed, Nechama preferred that I write about neither her nor her work.

her husband to Palestine in 1930; it lists her teaching, her radio commentary, her professorship at the University of Tel Aviv, her Israel Prize for Education in 1957. I wonder if this sketchy entry, a disappointment to her devotees, was what Nehama preferred, all she would permit.

Fruma considered Nehama altogether remarkable. As a teacher, a scholar, and a personality. She could be profound and still be clear and understandable.

Nehama manages to teach you all you could ever wish to learn. She teaches you how to open a text you've never seen before. She teaches you how to read it, how to let the text uncover its meaning, and most important, how you can teach it to others. She teaches you how to approach new texts. You learn not only the one class she is teaching, but one hundred other classes she enables you to teach yourself.

From her own experience learning Torah with Nehama, Fruma knew that the traditional basis for Torah study was Rashi's commentary. A Russian translation of Rashi did not exist. Of course, seventy years ago in Russia, those who wanted to study Rashi didn't need a translation. Fruma thought translating Rashi into Russian wouldn't be particularly difficult, although over time she came to change her mind about that.

The more one learns Torah, the more one learns how difficult Rashi is. His commentaries are among the most complicated. Not because of the language, but because of the knowledge you must have before you approach Rashi. But here is something beautiful about Rashi. Even an ignorant person can find things he understands in Rashi's commentary. If he keeps going back to Rashi and working hard on it year after year, he will make progress and raise his level of understanding. This was the reason we thought we must translate Rashi, in particular. Today many Russian *olim* [immigrants to Israel] who began

studying Torah in Moscow and Leningrad and other places tell
us they started with our books. They began with them, and
through them began to learn Hebrew. You cannot imagine the
situation. Almost every important Jewish book is translated into
English. Not so in Russian. It is very hard to publish a Russian
Torah with Rashi. But such a book is necessary for Russian
Jews. The entrance into Judaism is not simple, and Rashi provides a nice entrance. It's a studying book. When you study
Rashi, you see what Judaism is. This is our method. Not to tell
about something, but to suggest it.

"Who do you mean when you say *our* books?"
"I did the actual work on the translation. But I worked with my
father on the conception, the idea for publication. He collected some
donations, got a little help from the Jewish Agency."
"Was it difficult to send the books to Russia?"
"Yes. Now it's less difficult. *Tiri,* look, books arrive there, people
study them. That's what matters. Many Russians whom I've never
met before come to Israel and say, 'We are your students.' "
"Do they ask you to be their spiritual guide? Do they say they're
interested in learning Torah, but not in becoming religious?"

I've never asked my students if they want to be observant or
not. They decide. Nobody needs to ask my permission to enter
my class. Whoever wants to can come study. No one asks me
what Jews are supposed to practice. For me, personally, it's all
the same—study and practice—but I wouldn't ask that from
someone else. They come to me and ask all kinds of questions.
They tell me their problems. But I'm not a rabbi. I don't come
to convince anybody. I would like everyone to decide to observe the commandments, but I can't demand that. People have
free choice. They must know first what they are choosing, and
then decide.

Cantorial music on television was swelling. Fruma's father stood. He was pointing authoritatively at his watch. I quickly asked what had by now become my pet question: "Do you think there's anything so special about women studying Torah together?"

Look. My class is entirely different. It's not a men's yeshiva, it's not a university, it's not a school for young girls. It's studying that is close to life, studying that has a relationship to daily life. It's very alive. The idea of women's Torah education is altogether very new. No one has a complete notion of how it should be done. You can't create an approach on paper and then realize it. More institutions like Bruria will be established, and we will learn if there is any approach that is more appropriate for women. There is something very nice about Torah study. When a person is determined to study Torah, it becomes easier to study it more profoundly.

Fruma's father shut off the television. It was eight on the dot. Time to wrap it up. Fruma threw on her coat and raced out the door. What was the emergency? A doctor's appointment? I followed. A male friend was waiting in the parking lot near Fruma's apartment. We were introduced. It turned out he taught biblical grammar privately to some of my Pardes classmates. They were off to a private class at Nehama's house. I hopped into the back seat.

"Can you imagine," Fruma told the grammarian, "she asked such hard questions, I didn't even have the answers. I, who have the answers, even without questions."

The grammarian was in awe of Fruma. All the way to the Central Bus Station, behind which Nehama lived, he was quoting Fruma's memorable sayings and praising her knack for languages. When we got to the station, I waved good-bye as they ran across the street, the grammarian escorting Fruma. Flying off to get to Nehama's, they seemed like kids on a date pressing to be the first into a Bruce Springsteen concert.

I wanted to go to one of Nehama's classes, too. I had been working up the courage for months now.

People told legends about their first day studying with Nehama. If your Hebrew wasn't good enough, she might make mincemeat out of you. Dr. Rachel Salmon, now lecturer in the Department of English at Bar-Ilan, recalled that when she first began to study with Nehama some twenty years ago, she was unable to pronounce the words of the Torah correctly when her turn came to read aloud:

> I was told to leave the room. I soon had a companion. Nehama informed us that we could not rejoin the class until we had read the entire Torah, verse after verse, aloud to each other, and that we were not to attend any other lessons either until we completed the task. Permission was granted—if Nehama said so, it must be done. When we finally finished, I returned to the class with trepidation. To my surprise, Nehama was warmly welcoming, encouraged me when I was near despair about ever being able to learn properly and—in these long years—has never asked me to read aloud again.*

I had met a thirty-one-year-old Jewish day school teacher from Chicago named Sara Lynn. She was spending the year studying as a Jerusalem Fellow. Among the many privileges extended to the Fellows was the chance to study Bible with Nehama twice a week in her home. Sara Lynn said she'd bring me along to a class, the one in pedagogic techniques. I met her early Tuesday morning in front of the Central Bus Station. Sara Lynn noticed how pale I was, a situation that only worsened when she told me that one of Nehama's favorite pedagogic techniques, calculated to make sure everyone in

*Kol Emuna, Spring–Summer 1987.

the class understood the lesson, was to ask a question and then insist that all students write the answer in their notebooks. Nehama would go around the room and check. I hoped that if Nehama had already shared this favorite technique with the Jerusalem Fellows, she would have no need to review it this morning. But in case she did, I was just a visitor, so there was no way she would expect me to write an answer in my notebook. I knew I would not recover from being made into mincemeat.

Outside Nehama's door, Sara Lynn asked me what my Hebrew name was so that she could introduce me properly to Nehama. I said I had a Hebrew name but never used it.

"We'll see how that goes over," she said, suggesting I was already in hot water.

We sat at a large table in Nehama's study, a room lined from floor to ceiling with shelves of folders containing Nehama's *gilyonot*. There were five of us altogether. Aryeh Davidson, a professor of Jewish education at the Jewish Theological Seminary spending the year as a Jerusalem Fellow, was fixing tea in Nehama's kitchen. I didn't take any tea. I was afraid I would spill it all over the table, piled with the Bibles that students had left behind over the years.

"Who are you?" Nehama asked me.

I paused to recall. "I'm Sara Lynn's friend?" Sara Lynn reminded Nehama she told her I'd be coming, and for now, that sufficed.

Nehama reminded me of a tiny old woman of a fairy tale. She wore a brown beret, brown dress, brown shoes, brown sweater. Even her glasses were brown on top, clear on the bottom. Only her collar was white. She walked slowly, not at all doddering, just carefully around the table, passing out lemon and chocolate wafers and a dish of Israeli-style M & M's. She passed the food dishes around several times. Each time I said, "No thanks."

The first time Nehama noted my refusal, she said, "You belong to the lesson." The next time the food went around, she said, "You're part of the class now." The third time she commanded, "Take something!" Afraid to say I couldn't imagine eating sweet things at 8:30 in the morning, afraid to say I was too nervous to breathe, let alone eat, I took three mock M & M's. When Nehama turned to climb up on a stepladder to get down some *gilyonot,* I brushed the mock M & M's into my book bag and pretended to chew.

An uncomfortable thought struck me. If I was part of the class for eating, that could mean I was part of the class for participating.

I was catching about 70 percent of Nehama's Hebrew. It was exhilarating to understand; frustrating to miss words here and there. I would learn Hebrew better immediately, I vowed. This was just what Raphael had told me at Pardes, that I would learn Hebrew when I was motivated. I wanted to be one of the thousands of students who knew Nehama's love, interest, approval. I would learn Hebrew for her! I would learn Bible for her! Was this a crush, was it idolatry? I felt as if I were nine years old and in the fourth grade. The entire drama of elementary school returned—afraid I'd say the wrong answer and be thought stupid; yearning to get it right, to be good, to win the teacher's favor.

Nehama handed out the *gilyonot.* Some of the students reached into their pockets for change. Every eleven sheets, they paid a shekel.

The morning flew. I took notes like a court stenographer. For each pedagogic point Nehama made, there was an example in the *gilyonot.* One issue concerned when it is appropriate to include stories from the Midrash in teaching children Torah. Children tend not to distinguish between legends and Torah and will simply assume all they have heard is Torah.

I smiled. Not only did I feel confident I understood this point, but, as an adult, I still read a narrative in Torah and wonder what happened to the juicier parts, that is, the parts that belong to the legends.

"Why are you smiling?" Nehama asked.

Why ever had I smiled? I mumbled, I sputtered, my experience speaking in public as a college teacher evaporated. Every rule of

Hebrew conjugation left me. "I know children who get confused." I meant to say, "I am like the children who still get confused."

Not only children got confused, Nehama said. A man who works in a textile factory might forget all he learned in Torah as a boy except that Abraham broke his father's idols, an episode not in the Written Torah. It was not the worst mistake in the world, certainly not a sin.

To illustrate a fresh pedagogic point, Nehama turned to *gilyonot* on Exodus, the very section I had been laboriously studying at Pardes. I could have danced on the table. By now, I knew the chapter by heart, I made sense of the words, I knew the commentaries, I could put it all in context. So this was the point of Pardes's snail's pace: How wise! While I was celebrating my competence, Nehama slipped in her point and I lost it. Fool! Keep on the ball! You are in the presence of a living legend!

The next text was from Genesis, an episode in the Joseph story in which Jacob sends his sons to Egypt to procure food. I knew the story in English, but not at all, I worried, in Hebrew. Nehama proposed we use the text to do an exercise that was appropriate for teaching sixth graders. We were to look at the paragraph and determine what was irregular. Then write down the answer.

Irregular! What was regular? How would I know? The phone rang. Nehama went into the hall to answer it, cheerfully announcing, "Nehama!"

I waited until the clever Jerusalem Fellows did their assignment. Aryeh was looking hard at his text. You could almost see a light go on when he got the answer. Sara Lynn, who must have been the star of her Hebrew school, was already scribbling down the answers in her notebook as confidently as I signed my name on checks.

Nehama returned with Fowler's *Dictionary of Modern English Usage* and was leafing through it. What was the literary error, she asked us, committed by writers who varied the way they referred to a subject each time it was mentioned? For example, first writing Shakespeare, then "the bard," then "the English genius."

I raised my hand like the Statue of Liberty. My years teaching college composition were all redeemed. "Elegant variation," I announced and, in simple Hebrew, summarized Fowler's six-column entry in a sentence: "To avoid being dubbed a second-rate writer, it was better to repeat a word when you needed it than to come up with fancy variations each time." Nehama approved. I beamed. I was as proud as a two year old who just learned to use a potty.

Here was the irregularity Nehama wanted us to notice. If an epithet is repeated in the Bible with a variation, Nehama taught, there must be a reason. For the Bible is not guilty of elegant variation. What did the varied epithets in the Genesis passage signify?

I wondered what gems the Jerusalem Fellows would come up with.

Nehama caught my eye. "You, too!"

"I'll try." Oh God. I looked hard at the Hebrew text.

When Jacob saw that there were food rations to be had in Egypt, he said to *his sons,* "Why do you keep looking at one another? . . . So *ten of Joseph's brothers* went down to get grain rations in Egypt. . . . Thus the *sons of Israel* were among those who came to procure rations. (Genesis 42:1–5)

Nehama had italicized the variations. *His sons. Ten of Joseph's brothers. The sons of Israel.* Each phrase a different epithet for the identical subject. Why? I had no idea why. Everyone was scribbling. Sara Lynn was already done. I knew that the passage, in general, referred to the grain-buying expedition and previewed the confrontation between Joseph and his brothers. What did the phrases *lama titrau* and *lishbor bar* mean? I kept staring at the passage, hoping some idea would well up. I was so ashamed. How could I, a Jewish adult, not have the most rudimentary level of Bible down pat? Sixth graders could do this exercise. If I had found the time to learn French, German, and Italian, why hadn't I made Hebrew a priority? Like children who know they're not supposed to pray to God for bicycles but do so anyway, I asked for a teensy miracle. Please, just the right answer to this question and some hints for spelling the words. I was tempted to make the kind of deal my mother makes with God. Help me now and I will make it my priority to read the Bible in Hebrew and translate it into English, phrase by phrase.

No help came. Or perhaps it did. I recalled the trick we all used in college for answering essay tests: The more vague your response, the less blatant your ignorance you will appear.

Sounding the words out in Hebrew, I wrote: "They are important because they show differences in relationship. Relationship gives protection." Beats me what that meant.

Nehama went around the room to look over our shoulders. The professor got it right. So did the American rabbi sitting next to him. Of course Sara Lynn was more right than anyone. Nehama asked if she could look at my answer. "I'm embarrassed to show you," I said. "I can't really spell in Hebrew."

Nehama dismissed my apology. How could a person who could quote from Fowler so nicely not know how to spell? I handed her my notebook.

"Nahon," she said. Correct. A miracle. *"Hatzi nahon,"* she added. Half correct. Still a full miracle.

Nehama explained the significance of the variations, an issue that Rashi takes up as he comments on the epithet "Joseph's brothers":

It is not written "the sons of Jacob," alluding to the fact that they repented of their stealing him and undertook to conduct themselves toward him as brothers.

The epithet "the sons of Israel" was used when the group went to Egypt to buy grain because in the eyes of the Egyptians, occupied with the feeding of many foreigners, this was the group from Israel. To the Egyptians, it is insignificant that they are Joseph's kinfolk. Nehama made this more concrete for us. She once had a student named Chana who said, "At home I'm Chana, at school I'm the girl

from Petach Tikva, and if I went abroad, I'd be the girl from Israel."
Nehama concluded the issue, just as she does in her book:

> As they stood before the Egyptian prince, who, as Providence
> would have it, was also their long-lost brother, the dramatic
> irony of the epithet, "Joseph's brethren," as they bow down to
> Joseph and thereby fulfill the dream, becomes apparent.*

Time ran out. Aryeh asked Nehama if she had a phone token he
could buy from her. She handed him a token but refused to let him
pay for it. Why did she permit her students to pay for *gilyonot*, he
asked teasingly, but not phone tokens? There was value behind
paying for some things, but not all. Nehama said she thought it
pitiful that machines were being installed to dispense phone tokens,
which were otherwise sold at post offices. Since people were always
in a rush to get phone tokens and didn't have the time to go to a post
office, they were happy to buy tokens from the poor old men who
sat on the ground for eight or ten hours in the Central Bus Station,
even though it meant paying a little extra. With the new token
machines, Nehama worried, these men would lose the little income
they had.

Nehama walked us downstairs so she could check her mail. The
rabbi asked if she would teach the Book of Jeremiah next year. "You
keep the angel of death from my door, and I'll teach you Jeremiah."

"She is the most remarkable woman," said the rabbi. "I'm in
love."

I walked with Sara Lynn and the rabbi through the Central Bus
Station. As if by reflex, they each bought a handful of tokens from
the first poor token peddler they saw. To learn Torah with Nehama
was to learn to be more human.

I continued to walk downtown, stopping for a croissant at my
favorite cafe in Zion Square. I needed no rituals of disengagement

---

*Studies in Genesis, trans. Aryeh Newman.

today, just some late breakfast now that I was calm enough to eat. I would need energy for all the Bible study I was going to embark on.

There was much I would have asked Nehama if not for her policy on privacy, which everyone respected. I didn't, I couldn't, ask. That's what her protégés told me. Speaking later to a professor of Jewish education in the Hebrew University School of Education, I told him what a mystery Nehama was to me. How frustrating not to know who or what had given her the confidence, the stamina to go on in Torah when the feat seemed so much more staggering for a woman. Had more doors been open to her because she taught Bible and not Talmud? She was the world's acknowledged role model for women in Torah learning. If women complain that Torah scholarship is closed to women, "Nehama!" is immediately thrown back into their faces. I wondered what price she had paid for her learning, if any. Were sacrifices for Torah like sacrifices for any form of professional excellence that a woman makes? If we took Nehama as our model and she had indeed paid a Torah surtax, was that a price we, too, would be willing to pay?

The professor suggested I look to Nehama's writing, not for answers, but for clues. In particular, he directed me to Nehama's study in Genesis of Rachel's relationship to her husband, Jacob.

In the narrative that Nehama comments on, Jacob the patriarch has fallen in love with shapely and beautiful Rachel. He worked seven years for Laban, her father, and expected that he would receive Rachel as his wife in return. At the wedding, Laban tricked Jacob and gave him Leah, his elder and less attractive daughter, a detail Jacob noticed only the next day, after he had slept with her. Though angered by Laban's deceit, Jacob served seven more years to claim Rachel. God, seeing Leah was the unloved wife, made her fertile. Leah considered her first three sons as consolation for being the less beloved and as a means of securing Jacob's affection.

Nehama Leibowitz considers the plight of Rachel, the barren wife:

When Rachel saw that she had borne Jacob no children, she became envious of her sister; and Rachel said to Jacob, "Give me children, or I shall die." Jacob was incensed at Rachel, and said, "Can I take the place of God, who had denied you fruit of the womb?" (Genesis 30:1–2)

Before reading Nehama's explication, and before consulting any commentaries, I knew I should try to consider the passage as best as I could on my own. I recalled how bizarre it was that Hava, the woman in Mea Shearim, had refused to look at a passage in Bible with her own eyes, respecting the taboo against wrestling alone with sacred texts. Yet I did the same thing, silencing my questions. While it is permissible to ask questions about the texts and notice inconsistencies, I know only the *right* questions get answered, and the *right* inconsistencies get rationalized. The rightness is dictated by the traditional guild of rabbis.

A memory came to mind. Once I joined my sister at her nontraditional Sabbath service in Washington, D.C. A successful professional couple in their mid-thirties, both wearing jeans and sharing a single tallit, came up to the Torah and recited a special blessing to commemorate having closed on a new town house the day before. "A town house? Narcissism! Disrespectful! An audacious, trite, and stupid gesture!" I whispered to my sister, as we watched the spectacle with snobbish disgust. Now I wanted to revise my original reaction. Why shouldn't the couple call on God in public? Maybe closing on that town house represented the boldest, most costly, and most dramatic event in their lives. Why shouldn't they sanctify that event as Jews, in the Jewish language and costume of celebration? It would be a Jewish town house, with a mezuzah hung on the doors, with Sabbaths and holidays celebrated in the dining room, and Jewish babies made in the master bedroom. How much penance must Jews pay for being in the modern world?

If I refused to ask what Bible meant to me out of respect for traditions of interpretation that often did not speak to me, then Bible would always mean nothing to me at all. It would remain an ancient and undecipherable document. That was clear to me. With trepidation, I sat down with the text, curious to see if the issues that concerned me would be very distant from those that are traditionally raised.

Two aspects of the biblical passage struck me. First, I wondered what Rachel was suggesting when she said "I shall die." Was she saying that if her barrenness continued, she would really commit suicide, or was her threat to die simply hyperbole, a reflection of her great suffering? I thought she meant suicide. How would I respond to childlessness? I had no idea. My own children were conceived in a snap. I had to rely upon the reactions of my infertile women friends to check the verisimilitude of Rachel's response. My friends had been overwhelmed with bitterness and rage. They suffered from periods of deep depression. Because they were denied the experience of bearing a child with a man they loved, because they were denied the opportunity to continue their line—yes, it was enough to make them feel suicidal, even though others tried to offer consolation: Well, at least you don't have cancer and you have a successful career and you're still in love with your husband. If they didn't commit suicide, they said it was only because they held a glimmer of hope that if they held on long enough, doctors might yet discover a miracle.

When Rachel's miracle of birth did come, it extracted an enormous price. She got her children, *and* she died giving birth to her second son, whom she would not have called Benjamin (son of the right hand or son of the south) as Jacob did, but rather Ben-oni (son of my suffering). From the name she chose, I wondered if Rachel ultimately believed that having children justified her death. If I thought having children meant my own death, I would find that price too great to pay. Wouldn't it have been preferable simply being Rachel and having Jacob's love?

Second, I wondered why Rachel commanded Jacob to give her children, as if he alone could end her infertility. I doubt she believed he was giving children to Leah and deliberately withholding them from her. It was possible though. Her jealousy of Leah was enormous. Rachel was probably still angry with Jacob for allowing Laban to make her wait fourteen years until she could marry and have children. Maybe she wanted Jacob to show his concern, his loyalty to her, and his remorse by praying harder for her child. Rachel knew, recalling the once barren matriarchs Sarah and Rebekah, that God answered the prayers of the patriarchs by providing the yearned-for child.

Having read the text in my own way, I then turned to Nehama's stunning lesson. As it turned out, the traditional commentaries she has assembled did not seem at all distant to me. She begins her lesson by telling us that the rabbinic sages were quick to draw attention to the failings of the patriarchs and the punishments they received. Later commentators, she teaches, were more apt to justify or understand patriarchal deviation. Nehama explains that Jacob's strange and unfeeling response to his beloved Rachel's misery was a source of puzzlement for all commentators; and she devotes her lesson, a conference call with major commentators, to understanding Jacob's anger.

Nehama first explicates Ramban, the acronym for the Spanish commentator Rabbi Moses ben Nahman (1194–1270). Ramban says that according to the sages, "Whoever is childless is accounted dead." The sages upbraid Jacob for having answered a troubled woman so callously. On the other hand, the sages say Jacob chastised Rachel for assuming God would answer his prayers. According to Nehama:

> Jacob's anger was not caused by her words or her adopting the pose of spoilt wives who threatened their husbands with suicide if they cannot have their will. He was concerned with the misleading approach to prayer evident in her words, her incomprehension of the real relation between man and God. Herein

surely lay the differences between superstition, idolatrous media of intercession and the pure undefiled prayer of man to his Maker!

Nehama next turns to Radak, Rabbi David Kimhi (1160–1236) of Provence. He, like Ramban, blames Rachel, who has sinned for "attributing powers to him [Jacob] rather than to God to whom alone is the power."

The third commentary Nehama turns to is that of Isaac Arama (fifteenth century) of Spain. Known as *Akedat Yitzhak*, it is most striking for addressing the primacy of a woman's intellectual and moral capacities.

The two names "woman" (*ishah* and "Eve") indicate two purposes. The first teaches that woman was taken from man *(ish)*, stressing that like him you may understand and advance in the intellectual and moral field just as did the matriarchs and many righteous women and prophetesses and as the literal meaning of Proverbs 31 about "the woman of worth" *(eshet hayil)* indicates. The second alludes to the power of childbearing and rearing children, as is indicated by the name Eve—the mother of all living. A woman deprived of the power of childbearing will be deprived of the secondary purpose and be left with the ability to do evil or good like the man who is barren.

In this new light, Nehama explains that Jacob became angry at Rachel because she had forgotten that the chief purpose of her existence was no different from a man's:

She in her yearnings for a child saw her whole world circumscribed by the second purpose of existence (according to the *Akedat Yitzhak*, 'the *secondary* purpose'!) to become a mother. Without it her life was not worth living. "Or else I die." This was a treasonable repudiation of her function, a flight from her destiny and purpose, a shirking from the duties imposed upon her, not in virtue of her being a woman, but in virtue of her being a human being.

The revelation of Nehama's text is fantastic. Within the tradition—the same tradition famed for grouping women with minors, slaves, and imbeciles—a voice says the Jewish woman is, above all, an intellectual, moral human being. Nehama seemed to be saying the Jewish woman who denies her intellectual and moral mission misses the point of her being. Is this what the professor thought I would conclude?

My original mystery still remained unresolved. What price did women pay when they scaled the heights of Torah scholarship?

Twelve

It was a great moment when the Torah scrolls were taken out from the ark.

In my grandparents' one-room synagogue, a Mr. Diamond (my uncles said that's what he was made of) first parted the thick blue velvet curtains covering the ark. The curtains were decorated with ferocious guardian lions of golden braid and sequins and the embroidered saying, *Da lifnei mi ata omed:* Know before whom you stand. Were there those who needed reminding? Even I, a child, knew without being told by my uncles that it was God inside the ark, God inside the Torah scrolls.

Each week, during those many years when both my grandparents were well enough to stroll to synagogue, my grandfather was given the honor of embracing one blue velvet *sefer torah* in his arms while the rabbi confirmed, "Hear O Israel, the Lord is our God, the Lord is One." To be so honored week after week, my grandfather, I thought, was royalty. So did my grandmother, who spent much of the Torah service dabbing the tears she shed out of pride on her white cotton hankie. Grandfather contrived to detour the Torah procession to where I, feeling I was too old to sit with the men, now stood with my grandmother in the front row of the women's section. I bided my time fiddling with the elastic band on the sailor's hat my mother had picked up for me at Best and Co.'s after-Easter sale. I thought if I pinged the elastic against my neck loudly enough, my grandfather would notice me. He stopped inches away from me, but on the wrong side of the *mehitzah*, that curious filmy curtain as tall as a grown-up that separated the women from all the action. He tilted his Torah over the *mehitzah* in my direction. For me, the Torah my grandfather held was as high up, as unreachable, as bright and desirable as a full moon. I kissed my fingertips, covered in a white kid glove, and stood on the tips of my Mary Janes. I could not get high enough to touch the Torah with my fingers. I could only get close enough to hear the small ringing of silver bells attached to the tops of the wooden rods on which the scroll was wound. My grandmother bent down and let me sling myself on the back of her shoulders like a koala and be hoisted up to the edge of the curtain. I touched my whole hand to the Torah, making an impression on the blue velvet, then brought my fingers back to my lips as my grandmother lowered me back to earth. That's how Jews kissed God, that's where God was. In the space between the Torah, my grandfather's cheek of day-old white whiskers and my grandmother's silver bun, secured with Alberto VO 5 and the circle of hairpins that I was permitted to help her tuck in on Sabbath mornings. God was in that space between love, velvet, and parchment.

I continued my Torah learning even when my enthusiasm waned. The work meant paying attention to details while ignoring any number of disturbing or offensive ideas. And while I could sometimes be touched by a numinous presence evoked in a stir of images, or energized for a spell by a class at Pardes, a lecture with Aviva, or studying Nehama Leibowitz's lessons on my own, the result of my plodding in the territory of still-alien texts was too frequently a kind of restlessness, boredom even. The fires lit under me lasted as long as the flames of birthday candles.

Yet as a practical matter, I would still stick to my regimen of Torah. If not now, when else? Where else? To give up was to give up for good. No American city I had ever lived in could offer the diverse opportunities for Torah study available in Jerusalem. Whatever your inclination, wherever you stood in dealing with your alienation from sacred texts, there was a pocket of learning in Jerusalem that could accommodate. Moreover, studying Torah was a commonplace in Jerusalem, as unremarkable as buying challah in the supermarket for the Sabbath. If I took time out at midday in the States to study the weekly Torah portion, I would be the first to consider myself a religious fanatic.

About one aspect of my study I had no ambivalence, and that was my enthusiasm for Esther's learned women. I would get to the bottom of Esther's list and it would begin anew: "Of course you must meet the sisters Gabi Lev and Ruth Wieder, actresses brought up in a religious home in Sydney, Australia, who perform innovative theater pieces based on their studies of Bruria and Queen Esther. And you must meet, you must if you haven't already, an American Talmud prodigy still in her twenties who teaches Talmud at Michlelet Bruria and the Pelech Religious Experimental High School for girls. She began studying Torah with her father at age eight, and now she is permitted by a leading Israeli Talmud scholar to sit at a table in the back of his advanced Talmud class for yeshiva men."

I had never met more remarkable women. I couldn't be in their presence long enough. To be with them was to sizzle with joy. Like rabbinic sages, they were so tightly identified with Torah that their words were Torah. For me, being with the learned women was as much an honor as carrying the Torah was for my grandfather. To be with these Women of the Book was to have a taste of royalty. They were certain before whom they stood; and the source of all their certainty, it seemed, was their learning. Learning was their food, their protection. Like men, they struggled to know Torah better, to serve God in their learning. They were not deterred by the fact that a strong sector in the religious establishment considered the bringing of women's concerns to Torah an abomination, an intrusion of ephemeral and meaningless secular values into sacred space. Unlike members of my women's circle, who, as adults, were preoccupied with licking the wounds of childhood (myself now included—I had readily gotten the hang of it), the learned women focused their energies on the present, honoring their parents and not blaming them, serving and praising God, striving to perfect themselves.

Esther's women stayed with the texts, embracing them tightly even when the texts were problematic for them as women. Holy sparks, however problematic, were holy. If I couldn't be like these women, I could at least be with them. I loved them with all their quirkiness, and that love roped me in. Stick around, urged the love. You may yet discover how you can maintain your private perceptions while still seeing reality through the prism of Torah.

I knew more Torah now than I had ever known before, yet all I could think about was my ignorance. Such humiliation is supposed to spur the learner on. What would my little Torah learning amount to? It was nothing in comparison with the learning of the Pardes students who studied full-time. Their learning was nothing compared with that of Batya Miller, who had been at Pardes for three years and was now studying Talmud at the university. Her learning would never equal the learning Aviva and Malke Bina ingested as children from their fathers. Their learning couldn't compare with the learning of young boys who start studying in yeshivot at four and continue into young manhood. And what is their learning compared with the Torah geniuses of this and earlier generations who never, never stopped learning Torah? Nevertheless, the sages say that each moment any person spends studying Torah has a redeeming value. Some see it as a cosmic redemption; for me, it was a private redemption, the chance to claim morsels of Torah for myself.

When Chana Safrai was recognized by the Israeli Ministry of Education for her work in women's education, an old friend, now a rabbi, said he recalled hearing Chana at age twelve or thirteen asking her brother as they walked home from school in Jerusalem: "Do you notice that Grandfather is now reluctant to teach me along with you? I'm not going to allow him to exclude me."

Chana Safrai has strong opinions and speaks her mind, even though that runs counter to views held in the Israeli Orthodox community. Her unpopular views have branded her as audacious. Since learning Torah is so important in Jewish life, she thinks that women must be part of it. She thinks that there must be some way of both keeping Jewish tradition and recognizing present realities, for a tradition that ignores reality will be the death of the Jewish people. She thinks we need tradition to sustain us, and reality, too. She thinks her role is to ask questions, even when male Talmud scholars chide her, saying that one doesn't ask such questions. To them Chana responds, "But I'm raising it. If it's an issue to me, then it needs to be addressed."

Chana is opinionated. That struck me right off. The more I listened, the more completely I trusted her. I was certain this was a woman with authority.

Nehama Leibowitz had been her mentor, a tremendous help in launching her career in Jewish scholarship. Nehama was a friend who enriched Chana's world, an adviser about all sorts of things, even boyfriends.

When I mentioned to Chana that I wished I could know more about Nehama, she said, "I'm different from Nehama. She doesn't want publicity. I'm willing to talk about myself, but it's not for my own sake. I know the importance of having role models in our world, people who push you."

Chana had been described to me by Esther as an Israeli in her forties, raised in Jerusalem, the director of the Judith Lieberman Institute, which offered programs in Torah study for Israeli women.

Chana, the daughter of Samuel Safrai, professor of Jewish history at the Hebrew University, was herself an accomplished Talmudist. I pursued her after finding an anonymous manuscript in my mail entitled "Lost at Sinai." The subject of the essay, which was being circulated around the university, was Chana Safrai. Intrigued, I tracked down the author of the essay—Dr. Molly Myerowitz, a professor of classics at Howard University who had previously taught at Bar-Ilan University in Israel. The essay was a sharp, accurate statement about contemporary women's Torah learning; it speaks of Chana as "wonderfully feminine and utterly different from the elitest male scholars whom she seeks to rival and subdue." I was not surprised when Myerowitz told me that every Jewish journal to which the essay had been submitted praised it highly and then found different reasons for rejecting it.* As far as I could tell, the essay told a grim truth about women's Torah learning that no one—not the progressives and not the conservatives—wanted to hear. As Myerowitz writes:

> In a small study off the main sanctuary of the local synagogue in the Bavli section of Tel Aviv, Chana Safrai teaches a handful of women. The subject tonight is "Women at Sinai." The question: "There or not there?" The methodology is a blend of traditional Jewish scholarly approaches and the critical canons of women's studies. The texts are exclusively Jewish: Torah and Midrash.
>
> The women in the room think that they were there at Sinai when the Torah was given. They believe that God spoke to them as He/She spoke to the men. But they are not entirely sure. Between Sinai and this room, generations of male scholars have seen fit to question the presence and participation of

---

*A version of the essay was finally accepted for publication by the *Radcliffe Quarterly* and was retitled "The Taste of Tiflut: Opening the Talmud to Women" (December 1989).

females at the revelation of the Ten Commandments. The question seemed legitimate, even appropriate.

. . . The group of women at the table is immediately remarkable for its utter plainness. All are as devoid of coquetry as is Chana herself . . . who seems to dismiss any affect of feminine allure. She wears a loose dress, unflattering hairdo, and little makeup, as do most of the women in the room. Her speaking style is direct and hearty, slightly impatient, and almost faintly mocking as it imitates the gruffness of the Sabra male.

. . . But Chana the teacher is generous and beautiful. When she begins to teach, her features grow as mobile as her mind . . .

Chana has a project. Her project is so enormously Utopian that even she would probably despair if she allowed herself to consider it within the frame of history and culture. Chana hopes to reverse several thousand years of Jewish tradition and yet to stay within that tradition. Chana hopes to educate Jewish women as males have been educated for centuries. Chana does her work with an inspiringly activist brand of feminism that refuses to discriminate on the masculine scale of intellectual elitism.

. . . She has driven down to the coast in her tiny blue car to teach Torah to middle-aged ladies who take copious notes. The gap between her and these women is obvious and painful. Still, she loves and respects them.*

I had met Chana briefly at a conference she helped organize on Jewish feminist theology held in the Bet Hillel building of the Hebrew University.

"How was the conference? Who was there?" Esther called to ask me, because she had been too sick or harried to go.

---

*From "Lost at Sinai," printed with permission from Molly Myerowitz.

"The truth? Hardly anyone knew what Jewish feminist theology was. Or if such a thing even existed. That didn't seem to bother anyone though. Most participants saw the conference as another chance to talk about all of women's problems in Judaism. Even though the conference was in Hebrew, most of the women who came were English-speaking immigrants. Few native-born Israelis seemed interested in coming. The tone of the conference was reminiscent of 1970s-style American Jewish women's consciousness raising. Who was there? A hodgepodge of women. Smart academic women of the caliber of Chana Safrai, who had the language and background to wrestle with Jewish feminist theology, and a bunch of funny ladies."

"We're all funny ladies," Esther reminded me, a fact that stayed with me and continued to simmer.

I telephoned Chana to hear her post-mortem on the conference. She said, "I'm waiting for the time when a day like this will give *me* something. I see this as part of a long-term campaign to make people aware. To create a crowd that can talk about these issues. To open the window a crack. There were good people there. Women from Haifa and Beersheva made the effort to come."

"Would you say people were speaking about theology, but in nontheological language? Throughout the conference, I kept thinking that this was like a conference in feminist biology in which one woman says: Oy, my womb hurts, and another says: Oy, my obstetrician doesn't treat me with respect. It is real pain they're talking about, it does concern women, and it is biology, but it's not quite addressing feminist biology."

"Most Jews," Chana explained, "not just women, do not know how to talk theology. Does a feminist Jewish theology exist or not? We have to decide from a position of knowledge and not total ignorance. It was a day of raising consciousness. There were eighty people there. So many were invited. I expected thirty people would come. I would have done it with three."

I spent a more leisurely time with Chana at her apartment in Talpiot, where she lives by herself. She was going to demonstrate her new computer software, which contained essentially all of rabbinic literature. From Chana's description, it sounded wonderful: "It democratizes Talmud study. It will do a lot for women." So far Chana was the only woman who had bought such a program. Soon she would get a spare to take with her to Amsterdam, where she taught seminars in Judaica. She approached her computer with a child's excitement. Was it appropriate, she had asked a rabbi, to recite the *Shehehianu* prayer for special times and new beginnings over the computer? He said he didn't think so. It was too big a step not to sanctify, Chana thought. She decided to recite the prayer.

And that is the point of Chana's computer prayer. Chana knows Jewish law. To read it deeply, to interpret from it, to apply it to life. With wisdom, with authority. Which is just what she does. The knowing gives her power and it gives her permission. If she creates a religious gesture, it is authentic.

Just as I was about to go out, Chana called to say she had been sick for days. "Don't come if you expect cookies. But if you bring your own cookies, I'd like a visitor."

I asked if she needed bread or milk.

"No. I'm my mother's daughter. My house is always ready for a siege."

Talpiot, in southeast Jerusalem, is only a ten-minute ride from downtown. But with its many shady trees, birds, and winding roads, it has a countrylike stillness. I strolled a bit before going in, just to enjoy how good it felt to be visiting a learned woman without needing to go in disguise. When Chana opened her door for me it was the genuine "me" there in my pink madras sundress, my hair uncovered and in a braid.

And Chana herself looked like the lovely ample goddess of some native tribe, in a black sleeveless Guatemalan caftan covered with an explosion of multicolored embroidery. The armholes were scooped low. "I can only wear this at home," said Chana. At the conference, Chana came across as headstrong in her thinking, but muted and matronly in her appearance, perhaps her notion of how an Orthodox female academic ought to appear in public. She asked if I minded her smoking her Montanas. I didn't. It was such a treat to see a leading woman Jewish scholar hanging out at home in offbeat clothes, eating cookies, smoking, talking with a girlfriend. Being so damn normal. Even the English she spoke was colloquial and spunky.

The apartment was a cozy place, a showcase for collections of knickknacks and home-decorating projects. There was an old-fashioned globe, a fancy abacus, potted plants scattered about, maybe a hundred green glass bottles grouped on shelves in the living room, markers and games to occupy her brother's children when they visit. Out on the closed porch were Chana's sewing supplies. A *heimish* place, the kind of place about which people once said: It shows a woman's touch. Afghans were tossed over chairs, and embroidery was everywhere.

"I'm not a scholar only," she said, showing me around. "While Nehama might disagree, I think there's more to the world than learning. I also do embroidery and I'm writing a book on embroidery." This was not said to boast. She sincerely meant that if she did not achieve the heights in Jewish scholarship because she took time to make lovely things, it was worth the sacrifice. "I went to Mexico to see the embroideries. I went berserk and brought back five kilos of junk."

I could picture Chana going berserk, stuffing cloths into a straw bag. How wonderful, how frivolous. Not berserk over Passover preparations, not berserk over preparing for Sabbath before sundown. A Talmudist berserk over a rainbow of satiny threads.

She took out an embroidery she had designed and executed on themes and characters from the Purim holiday. The chain stitches, satin stitches, and French knots were tight and tiny. The design was Persian, whimsical. This magnificent piece had been exhibited and had won an award. Chana unwrapped other pieces of work: an embroidered challah cover, a cornerpiece for her father's tallit.

To the left of the living room was Chana's study, a no-nonsense place, a place of the mind. It consisted of a desk with a silver-blue pack of Montanas, a red-and-white telephone, an open volume of Talmud. The computer sat on a red Formica table to the left of the desk, and there was a black bentwood rocker. Among the many volumes of books packed on her shelves was a set of Armenian dictionaries from a doctorate Chana started out doing in classics, a study of an Armenian translation of Pseudo-Philo. Books everywhere, enough for a library.

I asked Chana if she had read Molly Myerowitz's essay. She had. And she wanted to explain why she looked poorly the day Molly had described her. A young man she knew, like a son to her, had been in the hospital. The doctors had botched his operation. She had been consumed with worry. Under such circumstances, who could look well?

When I asked how she had become so learned, Chana told me that she had studied with her father as a child, a common denominator among most of the learned women I had been meeting.

So, too, in fiction. Yentl, in Isaac Bashevis Singer's story, studied with her bedridden father, Reb Todros. After telling Yentl to "lock the doors and drape the windows," they "pored over the Pentateuch, the Mishna, the Gemara and the Commentaries." When he died, she lost her teacher, her key to the gates of learning. With him, she did not have to disguise herself to learn. Without him, she would be consigned to the "noodle board and pudding dish." What choice did she have but to impersonate a man and enter a yeshiva? And ultimately, to disappear.

Not surprisingly, each learned woman I met credited her mother for love and encouragement, but the source of sacred knowledge was always the father. In the drama of learning Torah, the mothers hovered like benevolent shadows. When the women recalled their fathers' teachings, it was gratitude not so much for the material they taught as for the concrete expression of love.

I had met the very young woman who taught Talmud at Bruria and Pelech, and her memory of studying Talmud with her father reveals this. "When I was twelve or thirteen," she recalled,

I started learning Gemara with my father. I resented that. There were a few girls I knew who learned with their fathers, but no one else learned Gemara with her father. I didn't have too much appreciation for the Talmudic methodology at that age. It seemed rather trivial and pointless. We started with *Betzah*. I remember one line was incredibly funny. There is a *halakhah* about whether or not you're allowed to use an egg that was laid on a holiday. Food that you want to use on a holiday is supposed to have been prepared previously, in the sense of being in the world. So there's a whole give and take in the Gemara over the legal status of this egg. The Gemara quoted a source which dealt with using an egg for purposes other than eating. The example given was "to hold up the legs of the bed." I got up from the table and ran to my mother to tell her how funny it was. That was the end of learning that day because I was laughing too hard, picturing an egg holding up a bed. But that was also when I started my career learning Gemara. My father was relaxed. If there was something funny, I could laugh. My first experiences learning Gemara were in that pleasant environment. An appreciation was instilled in me.

Chana said the girls at the public religious school she had gone to in Jerusalem were trained to be wives.

I asked how that was done.

"By not teaching us anything, by not teaching us Mishnah and Gemara, by not awakening our curiosity." She recalled a rabbi addressing a group of seventy or eighty young women who had spent the day in intensive Torah study. "I have nothing to say to you because one is not allowed to teach women."

The young women asked, "At least tell us why."

"I can't tell you why," he said. "To tell you would be to teach you."

"As far as my father was concerned," said Chana, "my learning Torah as a woman was not an issue. Never! My father never differentiated between me and my brother Zeev, who is two years younger and is now a professor of the geographic history of Israel at Bar-Ilan University. We were the same in his eyes. He always made sure I had the opportunity to study. When I was thirteen, he almost canceled his sabbatical abroad because he feared he wouldn't find someone to teach me in his place. He went only because he found a teacher willing to teach both me and my brother.

Ever since I can remember, my father would tell us stories, sets of legends we'd request. He's a terrific storyteller. His teaching of Torah was integrated with stories, and this was always—when we traveled, when we were put to bed. Every *shabbat*, of course, we'd go through the *parashat hashavua*, and we'd learn two or three additional times each week. It wasn't always fun. Sometimes I liked it, sometimes I hated it. Sometimes we were nuisances and made trouble. Still, he'd sit with us and teach us Talmud. When we were very small and just starting school, my parents would want to sleep late on a Saturday morning. They'd promise us ten *grushim* (less than a dime) for learning a chapter of Bible by heart. We'd wake up at five o'clock and by eight we'd have the chapter in our heads. At ages eight and nine, we learned a chapter of Mishnah by heart. Today, I still have these chapters in my mind. By eleven years old, we'd study a whole page of Talmud during the week and by the end of the week, we'd know it by heart. At twelve, we learned the whole of tractate *Taanit* by heart, and then *Sanhedrin*. It was fun. It was like memorizing lines for a play. When we were done, we'd be so happy and burst into our parents' room and rattle off what we'd learned. After *shabbat,* we got the money. The money was no big factor. I don't even remember what I did with it. We would have learned for just a kiss.

Chana said that while her father was hot-blooded and easy to anger, he was always available to his children. His study—just like the studies Chana and Zeev have now—was always open. He wasn't bothered if the children came in and climbed behind him to see what he was doing.

To get my father out of a bad mood, we'd ask him a question and get him to study with us. Then we were immediately in his good book.

Our father's teaching didn't alienate us. It encouraged us. We have both followed in his footsteps. My brother publishes a great deal, as my father does, and I'm a very good lecturer, as he is. Now I lecture in many of the places he did. Slowly, I'm taking over all his extracurricular activities.

I asked if I had heard correctly, that Chana had completed the *daf yomi.* I wanted to know what it was.

It's an ongoing study of Talmud. You study one page a day, and within about seven years, you go through the entire Talmud. The nice part about it is that people all over the world are doing it; that is, there's a calendar of what page one does each day. When I began to get more deeply into learning, I thought this would be a good way to proceed. I would wake up early. At the beginning of my studies, it would take about three hours. If I missed a day, I'd get discouraged, then I'd need to catch up. At the end of the cycle, it would take me no more than twenty-five minutes. Now I can work through twenty pages in an hour. Of course, that's not deep learning. After a time, this kind of study loses its attraction because you can't take the time to go deeply. My father used to do this kind of study, too. The *daf yomi* gives you the initiative, the stamina to go on. It gives you a sense of security and a sense of belonging. You have material to talk about with others.

"With other women?" I asked.

"I know of one other woman who did this. The *daf yomi* is not meant for women. God forbid," she said, with mock horror.

I'd finish my learning and then call my father by breakfast time and we'd discuss it. I think this study of mine was what earned me the right to inherit my grandfather's Talmud. It's true, the boys got their own for their bar mitzvah. This, undertaking the *daf yomi,* was the "in" sign. I managed to convince them I was "in" on the game. Now, I'm studying it all again. I wasn't well enough acquainted with the lingo the first time.

For Chana, a woman who wanted to effect real change within Judaism had no choice but to begin by acquiring familiarity with Talmud and the processes by which laws evolved. "Those women who follow a fundamentalist approach, who limit their study to Bible and Midrash, do not initiate change. Their study leads nowhere new. Them ladies are cheating! Learning that is not connected to halakhah maintains precisely what I'd like to see changed. We're in for trouble if we're not opening up new possibilities that are based on women's study of law."

The very young Talmud teacher I had met appeared to agree with Chana's premises.

How much room is there to make changes in halakhah that take account of changes in society? People are reluctant to make change. They say: Old is better and We don't have to react to the society around us. I don't know how long people can function like that. Eventually they'll have to react. The laws practiced today were formulated in the time of the Talmud. Then, they may have been relevant and practical. Today they may cause friction with the way people want to live. But halakhah, like most legal systems, is very conservative. It's not that there isn't room for change, but change takes place over a long period of time. The system does provide that option of making change. People, for the most part, are just scared to use it because change causes problems in society, a blurring of issues. In terms of women's issues, the Orthodox community is afraid of the barriers between women's and men's roles falling down, for the structure of that society is built on clear distinctions between roles. Any change with regard to women's roles would create an upheaval, questioning the basis of the communal structure. People are scared of that and for good reason: no one wants his world to fall apart from underneath him.

But the issues have to be addressed. The more women are knowledgeable, the more they will know what changes are and aren't feasible. It's a slow process. I think it *should* be a slow process. Theoretically, I understand that a legal system that responded to every fad and wave in society wouldn't have stability. But on the emotional level, it's less easy for me. I and my students feel frustrated that we're not going to see the fruits of our learning during our lives. I personally enjoy learning Talmud tremendously. I would like to think I'm doing something new and contributing to a developing process. That makes me feel good. On the other hand, I wonder if this will end up in a dead end.

I wanted to know about Chana's work at the Judith Lieberman Institute, the utopian project mentioned in Myerowitz's essay.

The institute was named in honor of Judith Lieberman. The *Encyclopaedia Judaica* lists her under the entry for her husband, the famous Talmudic scholar, Saul Lieberman. The brief entry describes her as the wife of Lieberman and the daughter of Rabbi Meir Berlin (Bar-Ilan), a central figure in religious Zionism. In the forties, she was first the Hebrew principal and then dean of Hebrew studies of the first Jewish day school for girls in North America, the Shulamit School for Girls in New York. The brochure of the institute describes her as a "pioneer educator" who "influenced thousands of young women with her exemplary personality."

According to Myerowitz:

> At the Judith Lieberman Institute Chana trains her commandos of *Torah Shebe'al Peh* (oral lore consisting of Mishna, Gemara, Midrash, biblical exegisis, rabbinic responsa and scholarly literature which is the focus of normative Judaism and the focus of study at yeshivot). Several hundred women come into contact with the Institute each year through short seminars, courses, and correspondence courses. The Institute, which is housed in a small stone building at the educational center of Ramot Shapira in the pine-capped hills hills of Shoresh, physically consists of a single room, a clean rectangular space with seminar tables arranged in a U and walls lined with sacred texts. . . . The experience can do little more than to arouse debate, inspire discontent, reawaken old pain, new doubt; in short, to rouse the consciousness of women who live in a male-dominated religious tradition.
>
> The true core of Chana's efforts must be those thirty to forty women who each year attend twenty-two hours of weekly study in what the catalogue calls "Basic Sources." These are women who reach for the keys to the kingdom of the male monopoly of Jewish scholarship: the texts. . . . These are the women who are being taught first not to fear the text; then to master and criticize; to ask new questions, to seek new answers; . . . to reweave a new fabric, a cloak that women, too, might wear easily.

Chana told me she was not sure why she was the one chosen in 1981 to be the institute's first director. She accepted because she felt, using the Christian term, "a strong calling." There were already schools in Israel for English-speaking women who were not equipped with the proper skills for Torah study but who at least believed that Torah study was important for women. Michlelet Bruria, for example. By contrast, there were Israeli women who were native Hebrew speakers and had, just in the course of their public schooling, acquired a background in Bible and Mishnah. For them, the language of the Bible is the source of the language of every day. For them, when the Bible says "the land is good," it is the land under their feet. When the Bible refers to "the children of Israel," they can look around on the bus, and in the movie theater and still see the same crowd. In nursery schools, religious and secular, Israeli children learned the words not to "Jack and Jill" but to the lives of Adam and Eve, Abraham and Sarah. While Bible may come from another dimension, for Israelis, it has a local, personal, continuous flavor. Still, there was a powerful impediment to certain Israeli women learning Torah. Chana described these women, the crowd she wanted to awaken, as "numb to the notion of women in Torah learning. You can be well versed, but not awakened." This seemed to describe our Israeli baby-sitter, a high school girl who did her Rashi homework sprawled out on our living room rug while watching "Dynasty" or "Dallas."

An unawakened state can dwell even at the successful Pelech School in Jerusalem. There, the pages of the sacred texts have been open to Israeli high school girls and presented at a sophisticated level for eighteen years. (It did not surprise me, given the allocation of resources in Torah education, to see that this school, which offered serious and enlightened Torah education for women, was underfunded, housed in a run-down building in Bakka, and unable to accommodate the many young women who yearned to study there.) According to co-principal Aryeh Geiger, who directs the school along with Professor Alice Shalvi, "We have Pelech graduates who could take yeshiva students with their learning and fit them in their back pockets. Yet we don't have many who believe that. They've been indoctrinated."

Dafna, the daughter of my friend Shanit and a Pelech junior, expressed her tentativeness:

Many boys in B'nai Akiva [the religious youth group she belonged to] have told me: What! You're learning Gemara? It's forbidden for you to learn Gemara. I didn't know if it was really forbidden or not. At Pelech, we study the same material as the boys, and I've been able to explain difficult material in Talmud to *them*. I felt so proud of the depth of my understanding. I needed to know what to say to the boys about women studying. For myself I had to know. I was sure Pelech wouldn't do anything that is forbidden according to the halakhah, but Pelech is such an open school. Maybe learning wasn't exactly permitted for women. So, in school we studied those passages in older and more recent sources concerning women's learning. From what we read, I understood that women are allowed to study Gemara. The changes in the modern world caused a change in the conception of women. Today, a woman studies science, so the rabbis allow her to study Gemara as well. Being able to quote the sources relieved me.

The first goal of the Judith Lieberman Institute was for unawakened Israeli women to master the sources, to stand confidently on their own feet in Torah learning, not to be afraid. Chana believed it did *not* take a person ten years of total devotion in order to achieve proficiency in sacred texts, including Talmud.

I was stunned. What Chana said went against the widely held assumption that the sea of Talmudic material was too large ever to absorb. "What does it take, then?"

"I think it takes courage," she said.

The second goal of the institute was to consider the position of Jewish women in the sources and in modern times. The premise was that this would encourage women to study.

Chana was given a free hand in running the institute. Finding teachers was no problem. Nehama Leibowitz, happy to lend her presence to the fledgling institute, would teach Bible. Chana would teach Midrash and Mishnah. At the beginning, the rest of the teachers were men. Finding students was more difficult. There were three women from Kibbutz Sa'ad. Chana said she would have opened the institute with only one student. Driving there on the first day, she worried: What will we do if no one shows up? At first there was little enthusiasm. Now Chana has won prizes for the institute, and other, similar institutes for Israeli women have been created. Now a hundred students are enrolled in a correspondence course in Mishnah and women soldiers come to weekend seminars. Now Orthodox young women who have studied with Chana consider it legitimate to investigate the position of women in Judaism. If half the Jews are feeling pained by the tradition, then, following Chana's example, they acknowledge that the reality of those pains must be recognized.

Chana's phone kept ringing. It was Tova, her secretary at the institute, calling to arrange meetings and order books. "Go home," Chana told Tova. "Tomorrow is a new day."

There is so much groundwork to be done at the institute. "I'm doing base work," she sighs, "not flying."

How much difference will Chana's teaching make? In her essay, Myerowitz's prognosis holds out little optimism:

Perhaps one day, from one of these fellows of the Institute a true scholar or two will emerge, another Chana. But numbers and time have a real role to play. Not hundreds but thousands of students, not one generation but three. Not one woman alone against a male establishment gripped by almost paranoic dread, trapped in a doomed and self-defeating attempt to maintain power by a monopoly over Talmudic scholarship, but a massive educational program directed and (in its early stages) by that elite establishment itself. . . . Give me the front door of the yeshiva and kolel, give me the ultimate bastion of male

superiority and exclusiveness in traditional Judaism. Split ritual but make scholarship open to all and on equal terms. Until
then, there is no possibility of a female scholar to rival the males
on their own terms. The entrance of females through the back
doors of academia or of Conservative ordination can only
. . . enable the Talmudic elite to perpetuate their superiority by
regarding women scholars and rabbis with bemusement as
shams.

To open learning to women is always a battle. Fortunately, Chana
has the stomach for fights, big ones, subtle ones. She is not shocked
by the sound of her own raised voice or by the intensity of her anger.

There was the episode with the Talmudic software, for instance.
In order to inspect the software before she purchased it, she went
down to Benei Berak, a city near Tel Aviv where many of the
ultraobservant live. A male friend offered to accompany her, to act
as a buffer between Chana and the ultraobservant computer repre-
sentatives who might prefer not to communicate directly with a
woman. The salesmen spoke to Chana through her friend. "That's
the world I'm living in," she remarked to me. Soon enough, a computer representative was to come to her apartment to deliver and
install the software. This time the male friend was not there.

Chana dressed modestly for the visit. The man arrived, and she
showed him to her office. He cast his eye over the sacred books, the
bibliographical aids, the concordances, the massive files.

"This is a man's room," he said.

"No," said Chana, "this is my room."

"It was important for him to see this," Chana told me. "For him
to realize that the office is mine. I'm the one who uses these books."

Chana noticed that when the program had been installed, the
computer representative had typed in the name *"mishpahat* Safrai,"
the Safrai family, as the owner. Chana asked him why he did that.
She was not the Safrai family. She, the owner of the Talmudic

software, was a single Jewish woman named Chana. It was *her* name that should be the password that opened the program. *Chana Safrai.* That was the name to type in.

The man couldn't bring himself to change the name. "It will be for the family," he offered. "Your father will use it."

By now Chana is used to being the lone women among men. She had been the only woman student in Talmud classes at the university. Where else could she have studied? No woman's yeshiva offered Talmud study at her level. No men's yeshiva would have welcomed her. Today that is still the situation. An Orthodox woman who wants to study Talmud at the very highest level within a religious context (that is, not in a university) has no place to go. As Batya Gallant, the Michlelet Bruria teacher, had told me when I asked her why she was doing her Ph.D. in Jewish thought at a university, "I had no alternatives. I can teach at Bruria but not learn there. It is not for someone who learned Torah at age five years with a Lithuanian father. By contrast, a men's yeshiva is set up for men of all ages to study for life."

The only options for advanced study of Talmud were within the Conservative or Reform movements. Those were satisfactory options for Conservative and Reform women. But if an Orthodox woman studied in those institutions (as several have chosen to do), neither she nor her learning would be respected by her own community.

I stood behind Chana as she turned on the computer. Pick a name for a search, she said. I picked Rachel.

The computer cast its wide net. It scanned the Babylonian Talmud, then the Jerusalem Talmud, locating each occurrence of the name Rachel. Then the computer screen revealed the actual sources, then the sources in context. So much information, so easily gotten. If in preparing for a class or for her own scholarly purposes Chana wanted to find out, say, all the contexts for a certain phrase or each instance two particular rabbis disputed, such a search would have taken her days. With the computer, the search took minutes. Enough time, I imagined, to do a line of cross-stitching.

In the fall, Chana would be off to Amsterdam University in Holland for a longer period than usual. There, she would teach and continue her research project on women's religious activity during the Second Temple period. The project, supported generously by the university, would draw upon her scholarship in Jewish texts, classics, and women's studies. Chana looked forward to the fall. Amsterdam was a welcoming place. For four years now, she had been brought there to give seminars on the Jewish origins of Christianity. She was well liked; she was a good teacher and did not intimidate the students. And she was happy there. At the Catholic university, she could teach from the perspective of faith, something she felt she could not do when she had taught at the Hebrew University. She hoped she would get a lot of writing done in Amsterdam. There, it was almost possible to encase herself in a bubble, isolated from the daily social and political concerns that were so distracting in Israel. I wondered, did Chana recognize the greatest perquisite Amsterdam offered? There, she was just another professor of some arcane subject going about her business. The anomaly of being a Jewish woman teaching sacred texts went unnoticed. The pressure of being a maverick was off. If Chana were offered the chance to teach in Amsterdam permanently, I was willing to bet she would jump at it.

What price did a woman have to pay to climb to the top of Jewish scholarship? According to Molly Myerowitz, if that woman is Chana, the price is enormous:

Today Chana's brother is a grown man, a professor, a husband and father. Chana lives alone. There is no husband. The game on the coffee table . . . is for her nephew who visits. Chana's coffee is strong; her china is pretty and flowered. Her kitchen is neat, but not too neat. She can cook. She, like her brother, studied Talmud. Unlike her brother, she pays the daily price for her anomaly. Alone in her kitchen she has occasion, I imagine, to ponder the definition of Rabbi Eliezer's *tiflut*.

When I saw Chana the week before my return to Hamilton, she confided, "If you speak the truth and no one can bear to listen, that could make you crazy." What did she mean by that, I wondered, as I walked back to the bus that would bring me away from Talpiot. I felt exhilarated, as I always felt after spending time with Chana, but I felt sad, too. I think Chana was saying that she had proof, in the texts and in her bones, that the God of Israel had not intended to exclude women from the sacred texts. But try proving that every single day of your life to the people of Israel, to the men and women who refused to listen, who simply did not want to know.

Chana was a strong woman. She and her friends and family were devoted to each other, she had students galore, she traveled around the world, she had important work to do and was unimpeded in carrying it out. Wasn't that, by some definition, a good enough life?

The professor of Jewish education had told me, "It's no surprise learned women feel the religious world views them oddly. It's not by chance that Bruria went crazy at the end of her life."

Thirteen

On a morning in early summer, Esther and I spread a blanket on my lawn in Nayot, and she tried to interest her latest baby in *Pat the Bunny* so we could talk and say our good-byes. What was this baby called? Yosef Yohanan, Yohanan Yehiel? I wasn't sure. Esther called him *motek*, sweetie, which is what she called all her children. This baby *motek* was especially beautiful. His red curls appeared golden in the sun. And Esther continued to nurse him though he was no longer an infant.

It was unbearably hot. Not so bad for me, because I was wearing my sundress, but surely uncomfortable for Esther, dressed in a long black skirt, a long-sleeved pink satiny blouse splotched with baby stains, stockings, and that red wig of hers. Esther, now suffering from summer allergies, was not as sunken-cheeked as she had been last time I saw her. I didn't ask if the skin on her bones was a sign of well-being or another pregnancy. "I just hope you're taking better care of yourself," I said, meaning I hoped she was looking out for herself in concrete ways and no longer blaming her sicknesses on mystical imbalances.

I offered Esther fruits and lemonade. The level of my *kashrut* being suspect, she would accept only a paper cup of water for herself and ice cubes for the baby, which he sucked and rubbed against his body. "For goodness' sake," I said, "here's an unopened box of rice and seaweed crackers you can eat. Check the label. It's been blessed by renowned rabbis who themselves donned flippers and harvested the seaweed, flinging blessings to the deep." Esther examined the package, approved the pedigree of the rabbi who endorsed the crackers, and fed one to *motek*.

"If what I'm going to ask now bothers you, don't answer me," I said.

But I have to say this before I leave. I'm concerned about you, even if you're not. Ever since you finished your dissertation, you've left physics behind. Physics is the last thing on your mind; I wouldn't be surprised if you gave it up. The children come first, and Reuven's learning Torah, and your learning Torah, and the Sabbath coming tonight. Do you really have no need for a public life that defines you and builds up your self-esteem with a professional title, a job, a salary, and publications? I'm not saying that all my self-esteem comes from my profession, but I do need to see myself spread out some, beyond the limits of my mind, beyond the nest of my family. But for you, obedience to tradition comes before obedience to your own instincts, your own whims.

"Are you suggesting my sicknesses are connected to the way I live out Jewish observance?"

If her interpretation of Jewish observance meant she had relinquished all sense of herself, then yes, that's what I was suggesting. If her stake in this world was shadowed by her expected stake in the world to come, then yes. It was one thing for Reuven to practice self-abnegation by giving up his career in mathematics to study Torah around the clock. Esther had put physics on the back burner for fourteen hours a day of child care and a smidgen of Torah study. At least Reuven's spiritual regimen left him robust.

Though I ought to have been the last person to speak about providing for one's own good health. I had been well for a good many months by then, but I couldn't say with certainty why it was. Having children who now slept through the night, or a fluke, or the weakening powers of the evil eye. I was almost inclined to agree with my doctor who had called my sicknesses "a run of bad luck."

When Esther spoke this time, she did not look directly at me and through me as she always did, and I found the absence of her gaze disconcerting. Speaking of herself, Esther looked off beyond our fruit trees, her eyes focusing on nothing. Ideally, Esther said, she learned Torah and raised a Jewish family because those activities had intrinsic significance. If her ideals weren't coterminous with the ones around her, she didn't care, although she admitted that such an attitude, taken to an extreme, was risky.

Yet this was how she had been brought up. From a young age, she and her two sisters were taught to set inner priorities. It was in the tradition of her father's branch of the family to work on their authenticity, to move toward spiritual development by rooting out secondary, distracting considerations. This heritage of ethical fine-tuning of character stemmed from the Musar movement of Rabbi Israel Salanter, which began to take hold in mid-nineteenth-century Lithuania. "I grew up with certain values," Esther explained.

First, to get to the heart of all matters. Second, to be uninfluenced by external packaging, that is, to see things as they are. My father was always examining me for my motivations. It was a difficult process, I assure you. As I got older, I examined myself. It was an environment of continuous questioning. I learned to differentiate between what was essential and what was extraneous, what was trivial and what was absolute. That was the genius of his approach. It enabled him to maintain a spiritual life in the face of difficult and complicated day-to-day problems.

Unlike most learned women I had met, Esther traced the legacy of her connection to Torah through her mother as well as through her father.

My mother's father was a rabbi and judge in a rabbinical court in Hungary. Her formal Torah learning may have been more limited than mine, yet she had the experience of being in a room when people discussed the big Torah matters of the day. She identified with her father's authority, she absorbed what she heard. And consequently, she had a sense of herself as knowledgeable. Her broad awareness of Torah determined her sense of connection. And hence, my own.

For Esther, this was the bottom line: "Torah learning should be subordinate to *ahavat hashem,* love of God. Learning should be a devotional activity, done for its own sake. One doesn't look for superficial approval."

"You seem to have no ego needs," I continued. "With Torah, you soar. That is altogether foreign to me."

"Still?" she asked. "You're certain of that?"

"Certain."

"Surely you've read a great work of literature and been transported?" she asked.

"That kind of transportedness I know well."

"Describe it," she said.

"The first time I read Vladimir Nabokov or Doris Lessing. The author finds language for what you had thought was private or unnameable. There's an enormous joy, a sense of camaraderie even. But that couldn't be what it means to be transported by Torah."

"It's not as different as you think. Imagine the effect you've described in literature as not being transitory or haphazard or a small, cerebral pleasure. Then, if you could count on the effect as being continual, you would accommodate your life accordingly." The *motek* was screaming. Esther rushed to gather him up and pack him into his umbrella stroller. She was gone before she could satisfactorily untangle her words for me or pin them down concretely. My question had disturbed her. Not because it was hard for her to answer, I think. But because I had asked it at all, because after all my months of studying Torah, I couldn't answer the question myself.

I felt agitated for the rest of the day, disturbed with myself for having annoyed Esther after all her kindnesses to me. I had thought that by now our relationship could survive my being candid with her. But I should have kept quiet. If I couldn't effect the transformation she had hoped for, at least I should have shown more respect for her world. As I cleared students' papers and my notes off my desk, more to calm down than to prepare for the Sabbath, I played some tapes of Hasidic melodies that Esther had brought along for my family as presents. How easily music roused, how uncomplicated its effect.

I then went up to Palmach Street to buy a sweet challah at the bakery and Friday's *Jerusalem Post*. On my return, I found a phone message from Esther. Peter had scribbled it on the back of a Visa receipt from the Supersol. The message was marked *urgent*. If I truly wanted to understand the total way her life focused on Torah study, she said, then I should read Psalm 119 aloud, even in English. Then I would grasp the humility, the egolessness she felt in the presence of the sacred texts.

I waited until I had put the girls to sleep and Peter was occupied in the kitchen with the piles of Sabbath dishes. I closed the bedroom door and got into bed with an English Bible and a Hebrew Bible. Esther had already given me the gift of the learned women, a gift I had not received all that enthusiastically at first. And now, I believed, she was giving me this psalm as a second gift, a good-bye token. I grabbed it up. I trusted this psalm would do more than just clarify those aspects of Esther that still remained curious to me. It would open up something powerful within me. The words would shake me up. I would respond to sacred text in a way I had never before. This would be one of life's big moments, sweet moments. Everything was about to change. I gripped myself for full-scale revelation.

Right off, I winced. This was one long psalm, the very longest. It was an acrostic, eight verses for each of the twenty-two letters of the Hebrew alphabet. Already my hopes for the sudden rush of insight brought on by a few pointed words I might meditate upon were diminishing. I had a regular treatise here, one hundred and seventy-six verses. I read aloud, first in English:

> Happy are those whose way is blameless,
>   who follow the teachings of the Lord.
> Happy are those who observe His decrees,
>   who turn to him wholeheartedly.

That described Esther well enough: happy to learn, happy to observe the laws, capable of knowing God, and connecting herself to God through sacred learning and ritual. She, who sustained Torah by learning it, keeping it, and teaching it to others, would in turn be sustained by Torah. It would keep and protect her and her children. In this world, in the world to come.

But what could I, lacking a taste for a world to come, derive from this psalm—King David's rambling paean to learning God's word, to following the commandments ever more scrupulously, to calling those who mock the teachings wicked? The psalmist pressed home his point. Turning one's full attention to the Torah was potentially the source of all happiness, the end of desires. The poetic images of obedience, of eternal satisfaction aroused nothing in me, no blurted-out affirmations of "yes, I know."

Speak to me now, I asked of the text, swallow me now, reach out to me, include me in the life of the Jewish mind.

And at the same time, I dared the text to oblige my commitment.

I was losing my concentration, struggling to stay awake and focused. I escaped into sleep before I could finish the psalm. I tried reading it aloud again Saturday morning on my balcony when Peter was at synagogue with the girls. I tried again Saturday afternoon while everyone napped and now I was trying once more while Peter and two of his former students from Colgate, both recent converts to Judaism, sat down at our kitchen table to study *Ethics of the Fathers*. With each effort, my despair increased.

In Hebrew, in English, aloud, and silently, I read verse 130 of the psalm:

> The words You inscribed give light,
> and grant understanding to the simple.

Somewhere in my stomach I thought I could detect some churning that might be signaling some response. The churning turned into an insight, a product of my months of Torah learning. Perhaps I could find my way into the psalm if I studied it properly by working with a commentary. I turned to the Midrash on Psalms,* a collection of miniature rabbinic homilies compiled as early as the second century. What does it mean for words to give light, asked the rabbis of the Midrash. It is the words of Torah that give light. "The words of Torah lead into one another. The Torah is like gates and doors."

I heard my name being called from the kitchen door. Peter and the two guests invited me to join them. I could hear they were having a good time together inside. I was fond of the young men who had so often been part of our household on Sabbaths that Juliana and Dede thought of them as honorary uncles. I opened the door and went in. My solitary learning on the balcony was just not taking off. The Midrash on the psalm had asked, "What did the psalmist mean by saying 'I have more understanding from all my teachers'? He means that it is necessary for a man to have companions and

---

*Trans. William G. Braude (New Haven: Yale University Press, 1959), p. 282.

disciples in the study of Torah." Alone on my balcony, I stood outside the gates to the text. Alone, the text was impossible, which is what Esther, with her endless list of learned women, had been trying to show me all along.

They were very beautiful to me, these three lanky men learning Torah together, their heads bent down over Hebrew letters. For a time, I simply beheld them, an ancient tableau come to life. My daughters pinched and tickled the students, trying to get their attention back. One student had been a Jew for a whole year now. Already he was wearing a *kippah* full-time, a *tallit katan* under his shirt. For months he had been waking up at five o'clock every morning to study Talmud with his rabbi before he went to work. He, who had never lacked a girlfriend hanging on to his arm as an undergraduate, was now abstaining from physical contact with his fiancée until their marriage, still two years off. The other student—still "normal" in his collegiate costume and demeanor—had been circumcised as part of the conversion ritual just yesterday and was being ribbed by the others.

In some rituals, both the young men were still self-conscious. They held their Sabbath wine cups and prayer books with the heightened intentionality of actors holding props. But when learning Torah they seemed thoroughly at ease, as if they had grown up *lernen* with Lithuanian grandfathers. I glanced over their shoulders to see which text the men were about to read: "Do not converse excessively with a woman. They said this even about one's own wife; surely it applies to another's wife. Anyone who converses excessively with a woman brings harm to himself, for he neglects the study of Torah and will eventually inherit Gehinnom" (*Ethics of the Fathers* 1:5). I perched on my kitchen counter, offering them my own Midrash: "What if I told you this is what this verse meant? Since your wife is so learned in Torah, it would be sinful to distract her or her learned women friends with your conversation."

"This text, new as it is to you, is totally yours," I said to the young men. "Imagine what it feels like for me knowing I have to edit out or ignore chunks of sacred texts. Imagine if you read in *Ethics of the Fathers:* Don't chat with men, they're ninnies. Would either of you have chosen to ally yourself with a group that treated your sex with such disdain?" To the men, I described the seminar for women that had been held at the Laromme Hotel to mark the Lindenbaum family's donation that would turn ailing Michlelet Bruria into a flourishing Midreshet Lindenbaum. The goal, according to the PR material distributed, was to relocate Bruria to a "cluster of newly renovated stone buildings on grass-covered grounds" in Bakka. The donation would commemorate the memory of Nathan Nata Lindenbaum, Marcel Lindenbaum's father, who had died in a plane crash in 1946 after returning to New York from Europe, where he had been seeking out information about relatives who had been lost in World War II. Rabbis Riskin and Brovender addressed the hundreds of women who had gathered. Nearly every learned woman whom I had met in Jerusalem was present that day, either to teach or learn. In their lectures, the two rabbis presented the textual sources that indicated that women must become learned in sacred texts and can become spiritual leaders and religious judges. One had to admire these rabbis. Within the Orthodox community, where others had refused to give women access to sacred learning, these men had moved mountains to empower women with learning. According to Rabbi Riskin, "Anyone who does not teach his daughter Torah in depth is teaching her immorality. That's the guiding light of all our schools."

I should have been delighted to hear these prominent rabbis validating women's learning. But sitting in that audience, I shuddered. Why did we women need rabbis to give us the good news? They said the texts permitted us to study! The texts permitted us to be leaders! Why had we opened ourselves up to condescension for so long?

I imagined a learned Jewish woman addressing a group of men and telling them: It's OK, there's been some misunderstanding, but you can learn Torah now and be leaders. Would the men ask if they had heard right, if the texts truly sanctioned their learning and leadership, offering grateful thanks?

I believed men would say: You're telling us what we can learn and become? We define the world, we don't need you to decide what we can do. If men believed Judaism discriminated against them, they would demand immediate repairs.

At a luncheon for invited guests following the seminar, over a meal of melon fans, strips of goose breast that looked like bacon, and something called Laromme Delight, I sat next to Malke Bina and the women who studied with her in Rehavia. Rabbi Brovender passed by us saying, "It's the Bina team." Belda Lindenbaum had asked Malke to meet her the next morning, surely to invite Malke to return to the refreshed Michlelet Bruria. I gathered that Malke, by now committed to the Women's Institute for Torah Studies, would have to decline.

Malke was telling us a story of the time she had told a young woman, a former student of hers, that it was not only permissible for her to kindle the Hanukkah candles, but appropriate. The young woman maintained that a man must light the candles on a woman's behalf. Malke remembered the young woman seemed so confident in her stance, so sure it was God's will that prohibited her from lighting. (Indeed, the custom of men lighting candles arose when it became the practice for Hanukkah candles to be lit outdoors. According to the responsum of Rabbi Moshe Sofer of the nineteenth century, men kindled for the women since it was considered inappropriate for women to be outdoors at night. Even though candles are now lit indoors, the custom of a man lighting has still remained in some communities.) Malke told her husband that the young woman seemed so convinced of her rightness that she was forced to wonder "whether she might not be right after all."

Rabbi Bina responded to his wife, Malke, "You show me where in the texts it says so."

———

Why had I told all this to the students sitting at my kitchen table, now staring down at their laps, as quiet as if I had shamed myself in front of them? In part, I wanted to tell them, these fledglings I felt protective of, that if ever as new Jews they felt aspects of the tradition were cut off from them, then they were not alone. How many Jews, after all, felt fully aligned with all of tradition?

But this was not the only thing I wanted to convey and this is what must have aroused their discomfort. I couldn't resist raining on their parade of easy affiliation to Judaism. These young men, whose earliest memories of the Sabbath, holidays, and customs of Jewish family life could be traced to *my house* in Hamilton, to my burnt casseroles—they already held the sacred texts in their hands more comfortably than I ever would. Even the young man whose first twenty-four hours as a Jew had not even gone by. My jealousy was enormous. How dare they feel so instantly connected!

Before breakfast, Peter and I sat outside on our stoop in Hamilton, New York. It was very hot and had been for days, almost as bad as the heat wave we had known in Jerusalem. Both of us were dressed in shorts, T-shirts, and the sandals we had picked up in Israel that made our feet look like travel mementos. Mr. Livermore was already on his tractor mowing his lawn next door; Mrs. Wilcox was picking blackberries across the way, and Mr. Wilcox was tucking in his black-and-white striped shirt before driving off to umpire a baseball game in Utica. It was the Jewish Sabbath. We and the girls would hike down Payne Street to the farmers' market on the town green to greet friends we hadn't seen for many months and check out the zucchini, fresh basil, maple syrup, and litters of puppies being sold. To keep the Sabbath, we would buy nothing.

On our stoop, Peter presented me with an anniversary present he had bought in Jerusalem. I guessed the box held a ceramic platter I had once admired in a store window. From the box I pulled out the Talmudic tractate *Ketubbot* (wedding contracts) in Hebrew with

Rabbi Adin Steinsaltz's explanations. The same text the women in Rehavia had been studying with Malke Bina. My own Talmud. My first Talmud. "For Leah," Peter had inscribed in Hebrew, "from your Yaakov." Leah, Yaakov. They were like people in a dream, people I half knew.

"Want to learn a page of Talmud?" Peter asked.

"Sure." I wanted to see if I could make sense of Talmud with Steinsaltz's crutches, if they could render the Talmud sufficiently less abstruse. On the top outermost corner of each oversized page, Steinsaltz explained difficult or unusual terms and filled in words that by our sense of language seemed left out. On the bottom of the page, under the classical Talmudical commentaries, Steinsaltz expanded his explanations. That was written in teensy Hebrew script without vowel marks, so it was hardly a gold mine of information for me. Still, I had before me on my knees a page I could handle without needing to resort to dictionaries and translations.

"Why don't you start?" Peter said.

I read the passage from the Mishnah out loud and then translated from the Hebrew: "A virgin or a maiden is married on the fourth day of the week, and a widow on the fifth day, because courts were held in the cities twice a week: on the second day and the fifth day, so that if a husband had a claim as to his bride's virginity, he could go to court early."

The rabbis of the Talmud wanted to know why a maiden was married on the fourth day. "Said Rabbi Joseph: Lord of Abraham! He [Samuel] attaches a Mishnah that was taught to a Mishnah that was not taught. Which was taught and which was not taught? This was taught and this was taught! But: he attaches a Mishnah, the reason of which was explained, to a Mishnah, the reason of which was not explained . . ."

This what? That what? Which Mishnah? Samuel who? Peter was already cruising through the logical mysteries of the "this" and the "that" and was onto clauses that provided for the feeding of brides. The mysteries were not so obscure that with an ounce of diligence

I, too, could not have penetrated them. But already I had drifted off into speculation. How did the brides feel when their husbands went off to court to complain about having acquired damaged goods? How did the brides busy their hands on that dark fifth day of the week? Could they keep the wedding meal of the night before in their stomachs? Did they know feisty wrath, or did they wrap themselves in sheets and lean into the shadows of their rooms, hoping the day would swallow itself? If they proved their innocence, could they ever love their husbands again?

I drifted back to Jerusalem, to the day I had asked a rabbi who staffs a men's yeshiva if he would ever hire a teacher like Aviva Zornberg to teach his students. It was OK with him. Personally, he was familiar with Aviva's teaching and admired it. She had a thing or two to teach the men. But he would be shunned by his community if he hired a woman. It was a gesture for which they were unprepared. However, if she wrote a book, then people would know such a phenomenon as Aviva existed. He joked, "Then people could put a brown cover on her book and read it surreptitiously."

I didn't laugh. I couldn't tolerate the analogy, even in jest, between Aviva's teaching and the smut people read on subways. What if Aviva's reading of the Torah somehow revealed the cure for cancer? Would prohibitions of modesty would fly away like the last leaves of late fall after a puff of wind?

I couldn't obscure my lapse of interest in the passage of *Ketubbot* from Peter. Maybe if I ate some breakfast, he thought, I could better sustain my attention. He went in to get his prayer book and tallit. I watched him begin his Sabbath morning prayers standing in the shade of the high maples in our backyard, our Labrador's paws arched over his feet. I was still on the stoop, grouching about the new, beautiful, aggravating Talmud belonging to Leah which was both mine and never easily to be mine at all.

In the course of this day, I would have no occasion to continue what had become my habit in Jerusalem: pointing out the learned women to Juliana and Dede as we saw them buying a bouquet of carnations on the street or strolling up to the botanical gardens with their families on the Sabbath. *"She* is a Torah scholar," I would say, emphasizing that the feminine pronoun, a linking verb, and the words "a Torah scholar" made a credible sentence, one that referred to something concrete in the world.

In the course of a day in Jerusalem, I would often walk past a religious school for girls near my neighborhood. From window to window, the size of the girls would increase according to their grade, yet they were otherwise identical, sitting at their desks, facing their wigged teachers, reciting from sacred or secular books, all learning. Watching these girls learn, I thought: Isn't this the greatest of all things a human can do, to be able to learn more each day, to know that the Egyptians built pyramids, that multiplication undoes division, that blood clots, that God forged a covenant with Israel? So many little Eves, gobbling at the knowledge served up, some plotting to know what remained untaught. To learn was a sacred activity. To pass on one's knowledge was sacred work. All along it had eluded me, how learning Torah could be worship. Studying Torah didn't feel like worship. It felt like school, alternating between interesting and boring, compelling and trite, clear and tangled. But here it was. Learning was a holy thing; and sacred learning, holier yet.

I was a poor Torah teacher for my daughters. However, in Hamilton, New York, I was the only woman my girls would see that day—that year—with a Talmud on her knees. I could not teach them Torah as Aviva had taught me, but I could at least demonstrate that the Torah was potentially mine and theirs. That we could have the Torah in the women's camp. They didn't have to be hoisted over a curtain to kiss it. I dug back into the Talmud. I dug back for Juliana's sake, for Dede's. I dug back for myself. To what did the "this" refer? To what the "that"? What rights were accorded brides and grooms of the Talmudic period, and how did the whole business sit with me? How would it sit with Esther, Aviva, Yehudis, Nechoma, Malke, Fruma, Nehama? How would it sit with my teachers at Pardes, Jonny and Aryeh? How would I have talked it through with Raphael, my study partner at Pardes? How would we have found a way for the text to speak to us? They had all unlocked doors for me, they had pushed me toward sources of wisdom I was reluctant to touch. In other texts, I turned to verses in *Sifre Deuteronomy*, the oldest rabbinic commentary on Deuteronomy. The rabbis ask what it means to hold fast to God. How can a human ascend and cling to God, a consuming fire? How does one go about loving God? The rabbis provide God's counsel: If you desire to know God, "attach yourself to the sages and their students and I will consider it as if you had ascended on high." To be a student, to connect oneself to Torah through a teacher—that was the route to God. Not through candles lit or holiday foods prepared, but mediated through the intellect and hearts of my teachers.

I had loved my teachers. Through their eyes, through their lives, I had glimpsed at the Torah they loved. The rabbis said that was like glimpsing God.

My daughters, eating Cheerios out of the box, leaned up against me as I learned. I leaned up against my teachers, straining to glimpse with them. The rabbis say that when a parent teaches a child Talmud, it is appropriate for the parent to don a friendly face. I flipped to the back of my Talmud to find passages that would make my face friendly: A woman, we are told, who eats mustard in pregnancy will give birth to an intemperate child; a woman who eats briny fish will give birth to children who blink excessively. Was it true, the girls wanted to know, that what a mother ate affected her child? "Not precisely as the rabbis said, but in other ways, yes." The girls wanted to know what I ate when I carried them. "What do you think?" I asked, and they inspected each other for outward signs of my influence.

Thus, we sanctified the day.

Afterword

Friends in Jerusalem said they hoped I would let women know that Torah is open to them. I remain unsure if Torah and Torah learning communities *are* altogether open to women. I did not write this book to convince anyone that they were. Nonetheless, I do believe that women must open Torah wide and seize it for themselves, though they know full well that the consequences may even be dangerous. This has been discovered dramatically by a group of women in Jerusalem whose attempts, since December of 1988, to read from the Torah or simply pray together at the Western Wall are shattered each month by the ultraobservant men who have assaulted them.

Yet there are grounds for some optimism. In the weeks after I left Jerusalem, the Women's Institute for Torah Studies opened in Bakka with Malke Bina as its educational director. Twelve young women scholars are studying Talmud and other sacred texts full-time, and over a hundred part-time students are enrolled. At the same time at Pardes, a new semester began with four women on the faculty, among them, Dr. Aviva Zornberg.

Shortly before I left, an article appeared in the *Jerusalem Post* about the progressive school my friends Naamah Kelman and Elan Ezrachi were helping to create in Jerusalem for the Israeli Reform movement. Illustrating the article was a photograph of two children captioned, "Leora and Benjamin share the honor of leading morning prayers." Leora Kelman-Ezrachi and her schoolmate Benjamin stood shoulder to shoulder, both wearing white *kippot* and child-sized prayer shawls. Commenting on the photograph of her daughter, Naamah said, "That's an image we never had growing up."

In these pages I have skimmed the surface of women and Torah learning, limiting my explorations to just a few circles of learned women, predominantly college-educated and English-speaking. This is by no means a comprehensive portrait of the variety of women's Torah learning in all Jewish communities. I hope other women learned in Torah will chronicle the stories of their education. Without those stories, younger women will not feel the solidity under their feet of the tradition of Torah scholarship by women. I hope, as well, that students of religious education will engage in scholarly projects that describe the established and new institutions around the world where women can learn Torah.

This book is based on my own experience and upon the lives so generously shared with me. When the text has departed from literal truth from time to time and chronology has been adjusted, it was either to meet the exigencies of my narrative or to obscure the identities of informants who preferred privacy.

I am grateful to numerous old and new friends in Jerusalem; Hamilton, New York; New Haven, Connecticut; and now, Morristown, New Jersey. They offered assistance, clarification, and encouragement along the way. My special thanks go to those I mention in the book by name or pseudonym. In particular, I am indebted to the friend I have called "Esther" here, for it was she who opened up the first and subsequent doors to my learning. I thank as well Debbey Altman-Diament, Allan Arkush, Marilyn Arthur, Vincent Curcio, Steven Englund, Guita Epstein, Elan Ezrachi, Steven Fraade, Ricki Gross, Michal Held, Katherine Hellerstein, Deborah Hertz, Naamah Kelman, Vicky McMillan, Alice Nakhimovsky, Nessa Rapoport, Reena Ribalow, Beth Sandweiss, and Shoshana Zonderman. To Daphne Merkin, Claire Wachtel, Elizabeth Harper, and Ilene Cohen goes my appreciation. Finally, to Molly Friedrich and Susan Schnur, *todah rabbah.*